Russian Warfare and Influence

T0322471

Russian Warfare and Influence

States in the Intersection Between
East and West

Edited by
Niklas Nilsson and Mikael Weissmann

BLOOMSBURY ACADEMIC
LONDON • NEW YORK • OXFORD • NEW DELHI • SYDNEY

BLOOMSBURY ACADEMIC
Bloomsbury Publishing Plc
50 Bedford Square, London, WC1B 3DP, UK
1385 Broadway, New York, NY 10018, USA
29 Earlsfort Terrace, Dublin 2, Ireland

BLOOMSBURY, BLOOMSBURY ACADEMIC and the Diana logo are trademarks of
Bloomsbury Publishing Plc

First published in Great Britain 2024

Copyright © Niklas Nilsson and Mikael Weissmann, 2024

Niklas Nilsson and Mikael Weissmann have asserted their right under the Copyright,
Designs and Patents Act, 1988, to be identified as Editors of this work.

Cover image © Adobe Stock

All rights reserved. No part of this publication may be reproduced or transmitted
in any form or by any means, electronic or mechanical, including photocopying,
recording, or any information storage or retrieval system, without prior
permission in writing from the publishers.

Bloomsbury Publishing Plc does not have any control over, or responsibility for, any
third-party websites referred to or in this book. All internet addresses given in this
book were correct at the time of going to press. The author and publisher regret any
inconvenience caused if addresses have changed or sites have ceased to exist,
but can accept no responsibility for any such changes.

A catalogue record for this book is available from the British Library.

A catalog record for this book is available from the Library of Congress.

ISBN: HB: 978-1-3503-3522-6
PB: 978-1-3503-3521-9
ePDF: 978-1-3503-3524-0
eBook: 978-1-3503-3523-3

Typeset by Newgen KnowledgeWorks Pvt. Ltd., Chennai, India
Printed and bound in Great Britain

To find out more about our authors and books visit www.bloomsbury.com
and sign up for our newsletters.

Contents

Contributors

Dorthe Bach Nyemann, Associate Professor, Institute for Strategy and War Studies, Royal Danish Defence College.

Jānis Bērziņš, Senior Researcher, Center for Security and Strategic Research, National Defence Academy of Latvia, and docent at the BA School of Business and Finance.

Johan Engvall, Stockholm Centre for Eastern European Studies, the Swedish Institute of International Affairs (UI).

Grigory Ioffe, Professor at Radford University and the Jamestown Foundation.

Shota Kakabadze, Policy Analyst, Georgian Institute of Politics.

Kornely Kakachia, Professor of Political Science and Jean Monnet Chair at Ivane Javakhishvili Tbilisi State University, Georgia and Director of the Tbilisi-based think tank Georgian Institute of Politics.

Niklas Nilsson, Associate Professor, Department of War Studies and Centre for Societal Security, Swedish Defence University. Co-convenor of the Hybrid Threats Research Group (HTRG) and the Land Warfare Research Group (LWRG).

Hanna Shelest, Director of Security Programmes at Foreign Policy Council 'Ukrainian Prism' and Editor-in-Chief at U.A.: Ukraine Analytica, Ukraine.

Vuk Vuksanovic, Senior Researcher at the Belgrade Centre for Security Policy (BCSP) and an associate at LSE IDEAS, a foreign policy think tank within the London School of Economics and Political Science (LSE).

Mikael Weissmann, Associate Professor, Deputy Director, Land Operations Division, Swedish Defence University. Co-convenor of the Hybrid Threats Research Group (HTRG) and the Land Warfare Research Group (LWRG).

Russian warfare and influence:
States in the proximity of Russia

Mikael Weissmann and Niklas Nilsson

Introduction

The turmoil descending on Europe with Russia's full-scale invasion of Ukraine in 2022 has altered many of the pre-existing conceptions of Russia as an actor in European security. Russia's first invasion of Ukraine and the annexation of Crimea in 2014 served to reintroduce Russia as a main focus of security debates across Europe. Crucial insights that could have aided in anticipation were not deduced after the 2008 invasion of Georgia, that is that Russia was no stranger to the use of force in pursuit of its national security objectives. Nevertheless, in the perceptions of the threat posed by Russia, military options were understood to be reserved for states that the Russian regime claimed were within its legitimate sphere of interest. Other, non-kinetic and hybrid means of power and influence were thought to be the main cause for concern to the rest of the Western world. Russian interference in the 2016 US and 2017 French elections, as well as funding of right-wing populist parties across Europe; concerted activity in the cyber arena; and a range of influence operations seemed to vindicate the nature of the new security environment. Russia's decision to launch the full-scale invasion on 24 February 2022, followed by the unified Western response in the form of sustained military and economic support for Ukraine, comprehensive sanctions against Russia and decisions by Sweden and Finland to join NATO, has fundamentally altered the map of potential threats that the West needs to confront.

The war in Ukraine has demonstrated that Russia is both prepared to go further in retaining its influence and domination in its 'near abroad', and to accept larger risks in this regard, than previously anticipated. Moreover, the preparations, planning and conduct of the Russian operation have revealed surprising degrees of incompetence and strategic miscalculation, and therefore of recklessness, which has served to alter the conceptions of deterrence previously applied. Previous instances of post-1991 Russian warfare abroad, in Georgia, Syria and Ukraine, were all delimited in scope, utilizing a controlled amount of force in operations designed to avoid triggering third-party involvement and unwanted escalation. Yet as an effect of its failure to subdue Ukraine, and the significance of Western military support in this regard, the Russian regime now claims to be at war with NATO. And while the Russian regime likely understands that this is not really the case and what a war with NATO would actually imply, escalation beyond Ukraine is a scenario that remains unlikely but whose consequences would be too serious to ignore.

However, while its engagement in Ukraine makes Russian military adventurism elsewhere unlikely at present, there is an extensive catalogue of other measures that Russia can employ in its conflict with the West. These capabilities have not receded to the same extent as Russia's military capability and the risk of more brazen actions against states other than Ukraine grows in tow with the Russian regime's desperation and the increasing threat to the longevity of the regime. A recent example is the apparent attempt to stage a coup in Moldova, disclosed in February 2023. Many of these are well known and have frequently been discussed in terms of a strategy of hybrid warfare or hybrid threats emanating from Russia (along with a whole range of similar but not synonymous terms).[1]

While the conflict with Russia warrants extensive rethinking and funding of defensive capabilities, military and civilian, across the West, nowhere is this conflict felt more acutely than in the states geographically located at the intersection between Russia and the West. Moreover, these states have considerably longer experience in managing the implications of 'living close to' Russia than their counterparts located further away from Russia. In this context, the states emerging after the break-up of the USSR have followed radically different trajectories in their foreign and domestic policies, and they have developed diverse relations with Russia along with the former imperial power's increasingly assertive external policies.

---

[1] For the purpose of this volume, no distinction will be made between hybrid warfare and hybrid threats unless explicitly stated by the chapter author. For a discussion of the scholarship on hybrid warfare, hybrid threats and the Russia factor, see N. Nilsson, M. Weissmann, B. Palmertz, P. Thunholm and H. Häggström, 'Security Challenges in the Grey Zone: Hybrid Threats and Hybrid Warfare', in *Hybrid Warfare: Security and Asymmetric Conflict in International Relations*, ed. M. Weissmann, N. Nilsson, B. Palmertz and P. Thunholm (London: I.B. Tauris, 2021), 1–20; 2–5.

This volume seeks to draw on the experiences of states at the geographic intersection between Russia and the West, posing the question of how Russian warfare and influence has manifested itself in different national contexts along Russia's western borders. Yet it also recognizes that the outcomes of Russian attempts to dominate its 'near abroad' are not unidirectional; the states concerned have all developed domestic and foreign strategies of their own, both in pursuit of their own national interests and in response to Russian attempts to define these for them. Their varying room for manoeuvre has given rise to a diverse picture of defensive capabilities and societal resilience in the face of Russian strategies for influence from which much can be learned. Thus, while focusing on Russian influence and interference, this volume makes a point of studying these paramount concerns for the rule-based security order from the perspective of the states most immediately subjected to them and how they have devised coping strategies in response.

In order to provide a diverse yet comprehensive picture of Russian strategies for influence as well as the corresponding strategies developed by states in its surroundings, this volume provides a number of case studies of states in Russia's proximity: the Baltic states, Ukraine, Belarus, Serbia, Kosovo and Georgia, as well as a chapter dedicated to Russia's role in and utilization of the unresolved conflicts over Transnistria, Abkhazia, South Ossetia, Nagorno-Karabakh and Ukraine's Donbass.

The volume takes its conceptual point of departure in an inclusive perspective on warfare and influence in order to address the full range of tactics and hybrid means pursued by Russia against states in its proximity. Taking a holistic and interactive approach and studying Russian warfare and strategies for influence from the perspective of these states, the volume addresses their societal vulnerabilities, Russian attempts to exploit them and policies crafted in response to this security predicament.

The intention is to provide a more nuanced understanding of vulnerabilities in different contexts. This is an important contribution since much of what is written on this topic focuses exclusively on Russian patterns of behaviour and tends to treat countries subjected to these as passive recipients, thus providing an exceedingly unidirectional picture of this relationship. This book instead treats these states as actors in their own right, assessing their potential to address and counter the specific security problems arising from their geographic and political position.

More specifically, the volume has three overarching aims. First, it provides an extensive inventory of the components of Russian strategies for domination, in different empirical contexts. Second, it takes a perspective focusing on these states as actors and stakeholders, rather than on the competition among major powers. Finally, it combines an academic and practitioner-oriented approach, providing analysis and conclusions that cater to the interests of a broad audience. To fulfil these aims, leading international researchers and experts, including authors from the countries in question, have been invited to contribute chapters.

Russian warfare and influence

As set out in the introduction, this book is about Russian warfare and influence. There is an abundance of writing on Russian warfare and influence, with a large number of concepts and terms circulating in these writings, such as political warfare, information war, net-centric war, new generation war (NGW), new-type war (NTW), fifth-generation warfare and *Gibridnaya Voyna*, to mention a few.[2] Sufficient to say, there is a limited need to once again give an overview of the development in the field. Instead, for a good overview of the developments, including an excellent timeline of their developments in Russia and the West, read Offer Friedman's book *Russian Hybrid Warfare* or Mark Galeotti's 2019 book

---

[2] See, for example, Timothy Thomas, 'The Evolution of Russian Military Thought: Integrating Hybrid, New-Generation, and New-Type Thinking', *Journal of Slavic Military Studies* 29, no. 4 (2016): 554–75; Tony Balasevicius, 'Looking for Little Green Men: Understanding Russia's Employment of Hybrid Warfare', *Canadian Military Journal* 17, no. 3 (2017): 17–28; Ofer Friedman, *Russian 'Hybrid Warfare': Resurgence and Politicisation* (London: Hurst, 2018); Mark Galeotti, *Hybrid War or Gibridnaya Voina? Getting Russia's Non-Linear Military Challenge Right* (Prague: Mayak Intelligence, 2016); Mark Galeotti, *Russian Political War: Moving beyond the Hybrid* (Abingdon, Oxfordshire: Routledge, Taylor & Francis Group, 2019); Markus Göransson, 'Understanding Russian Thinking on Gibridnaya Voyna', in *Hybrid Warfare: Security and Asymmetric Conflict in International Relations*, ed. Weissmann et al. (London: I.B. Tauris, 2021); David Kilcullen, *The Dragons and the Snakes: How the Rest Learned to Fight the West* (London: Hurst, 2020); Michael Kofman and Matthew Rojansky, 'A Closer Look at Russia's "Hybrid War"', *Kennan Cable No. 7* (Wilson Center: Kennan Institute, 2015); Andrew Radin, *Hybrid Warfare in the Baltics: Threats and Potential Responses*, Rand project air force (Santa Monica, CA: Rand Corporation, 2017); Raphael S. Cohen and Andrew Radin, *Russia's Hostile Measures in Europe: Understanding the Threat* (Santa Monica, CA: RAND Corporation, 2019); Timothy Thomas, 'Russia's Military Strategy and Ukraine: Indirect, Asymmetric – and Putin-Led', *Journal of Slavic Military Studies* 28, no. 3 (2015): 445–61; Rod Thornton, 'The Russian Military's New "Main Emphasis"', *RUSI Journal* 162, no. 4 (2017): 18–28; United States Army, Asymmetric Warfare Group, *Russian New Generation Warfare Handbook* (2016), https://info.publicintelligence.net/AWG-RussianNewWarfareHandbook.pdf; Mikael Weissmann, 'Hybrid Warfare and Hybrid Threats Today and Tomorrow: Towards an Analytical Framework', *Journal on Baltic Security* 5, no. 1 (2019): 17–26; Mikael Weissmann, 'Conceptualizing and Countering Hybrid Threats and Hybrid Warfare', in *Hybrid Warfare*, ed. Weissmann et al.,; Mikael Weissmann et al., eds, *Hybrid Warfare: Security and Asymmetric Conflict in International Relations* (London: I.B. Tauris, 2021); Mark Galeotti, *Russian Political War: Moving beyond the Hybrid*, First edition (London: Routledge Taylor & Francis Group, 2019); Ofer Fridman, *Russian 'Hybrid Warfare': Resurgence and Politicisation* (Oxford: Oxford University Press, 2018).

Russian Political War.[3] Another two recommendations are Timothy Thomas's article 'The Evolution of Russian Military Thought: Integrating Hybrid, New-Generation, and New-Type Thinking', Rod Thornton's 'The Russian Military's New "Main Emphasis"' or Markus Göransson's book chapter 'Understanding Russian thinking on *gibridnaya voyna*'.[4]

Despite extensive writing, the use of terminology is being contested and the existing scholarship lacks common definitions of concepts such as hybrid threats.[5] The term 'hybrid' itself is associated with 'a blend of conventional and nonconventional warfare where a hostile actor is exploiting the blurred area between peace and war'.[6] But when moving away from this basic understanding, there is a lack of consensus about the definition as well as how terms are used. There is also a problem with the tendency to use hybrid warfare or hybrid threats as a catch-all phrase.

To be able to capture the full spectrum of Russian warfare and influence, this volume draws on the view of hybrid threats outlined by the European Centre of Excellence for Countering Hybrid Threats (Hybrid CoE).[7] Hybrid CoE defines hybrid threats as coordinated and deliberately targeted actions 'conducted by state or non-state actors, whose goal is to undermine or harm a target by influencing its decision-making at the local, regional, state or institutional level'.[8] These forms of activities can occur in different domains including the political, economic, military, civil and information domains.

Regardless of the definition problems, the hybrid dimension adds an important contribution to the debate on Russian warfare and influence as Russia's establishment and utilization of different pressure points against countries in its neighbourhood need to be analysed as an integrated whole – only by doing so can we properly assess the vulnerability of countries in this region to Russian pressure

---

[3] Galeotti, *Russian Political War*; Fridman, *Russian 'Hybrid Warfare'*.
[4] Thornton, 'The Russian Military's New "Main Emphasis"'; Thomas, 'The Evolution of Russian Military Thought'; Göransson, 'Understanding Russian Thinking on gibridnaya voyna'.
[5] Weissmann, 'Conceptualizing and Countering Hybrid Threats and Hybrid Warfare', 63–9; Weissmann, 'Hybrid Warfare and Hybrid Threats Today and Tomorrow', 18–19; Nilsson et al., *Security challenges in the grey zone*.
[6] The Norwegian Institute of International Affairs, "Multinational Capability Development Campaign 2015-18 (Countering Hybrid Warfare)", *Nupi*, www.nupi.no/en/About-NUPI/Projects-centres-and-programmes/Multinational-Capability-Development-Campaign-2015-18-Countering-Hybrid-Warfare.
[7] Hybrid CoE – The European Centre of Excellence for Countering Hybrid Threats, 'Hybrid Threats as a Concept – Hybrid CoE – the European Centre of Excellence for Countering Hybrid Threats', Hybrid CoE, https://www.hybridcoe.fi/hybrid-threats-as-a-phenomenon/.
[8] While the Hybrid CoE definition is focusing on actions targeting democratic states and institutions, for the purpose of this volume actions are seen as hybrid threats regardless of whether the target is democratic or not.

and influence, relative to the lure of European and Transatlantic integration.[9] Such pressure can be found in at least seven dimensions frequently utilized when analysing hybrid threats and influence: (1) Diplomatic, (2) Economic, (3) Cyber (technological), (4) Information and influence operations, (5) Unconventional methods, (6) Civil (non-military) means and (7) Military means.[10]

Russia's outlook since the collapse of the Soviet Union

At the end of the Cold War, it was not only the then US president George H. W. Bush who envisioned 'a new world order' characterized by collaboration and peaceful resolution of differences seeking 'to achieve the universal aspirations of mankind – peace and security, freedom, and the rule of law'.[11] The general feeling in the West and Russia was at the time optimistic and the future looked bright, with a unipolar world order led by the United States where the Soviet Union/Russia was to be integrated into the Western security, political and economic system.[12] As we all know, this was not how things turned out, with relations between Russia and the United States and Europe deteriorating and Russia using an extensive range of hybrid methods to counter Western policies and intervening with kinetic and non-kinetic military means in different parts of its post-Soviet territories including in the areas in focus in this volume.

The 1995–2000 period was, as has been outlined by Andrei P. Tsygankov,[13] characterized by a policy of containing NATO. After the initial post-Cold War honeymoon period, opposition to the pro-Western foreign policy rose due to severe hardship as a result of the 'shock therapy' at home and criticism about Boris Yeltsin and Foreign Minister Andrei Kozyrev's security policy abroad. The criticism intensified after NATO launched air strikes against the Bosnian Serbs in 1994 and NATO's decision to accept new members from the former Soviet Bloc. The then director of Russia's Foreign Intelligence Service, Yevgeny

---

[9] Niklas Nilsson, *Russian Hybrid Tactics in Georgia* (Washington, DC: Central Asia-Caucasus Institute & Silk Road Studies Program, 2018), 17.

[10] Weissmann, 'Conceptualizing and Countering Hybrid Threats and Hybrid Warfare'.

[11] George Bush, 'Address before a Joint Session of the Congress on the State of the Union', https://web.archive.org/web/20180312161706/http://www.presidency.ucsb.edu/ws/?pid=19253.

[12] Roger E. Kanet, 'Introduction: The Russian Challenge to the Security Environment in Europe', in *The Russian Challenge to the European Security Environment*, ed. Roger E. Kanet (Cham: Palgrave Macmillan, 2017), 1.

[13] Andrei P. Tsygankov, *Russia and the West from Alexander to Putin: Honor in International Relations* (Cambridge: Cambridge University Press, 2012).

Primakov, came forward with sharp criticism of NATO's enlargement, warning that it could lead to increased Russian isolation.

After Yeltsin's critics did well in the 1993 and 1995 elections, Yeltsin altered his pro-Western agenda including sacking his Foreign Minister Andrej Kozyrev and instead appointing the director of Russia's Foreign Intelligence Service Yevgeny Primakov, who was a sharp critic to NATO expansion as new foreign minister from January 1996.[14]

From the perspective of the United States and NATO, the enlargement of NATO was never about the containment of Russia (although the new members saw it as directed at Russia for their security). At the time NATO was looking for new tasks, and in this case, the motive was to offer the former Soviet states a mechanism to integrate into the European security order. In fact, it was only after 2014 that NATO began to seriously reconsider its role as a defence alliance in which Russia was a potential adversary. For example, there were no military plans to defend the Baltics when they became members, which says a lot about how Russia has – probably deliberately – misinterpreted and misunderstood NATO. In fact, at least initially this was more a matter of Russian domestic politics to create an external threat than any real threat from NATO. The fact that the NATO enlargement today can be perceived as foremost directed at Russia is arguably a self-inflicted consequence of Russia's own aggression.

With Putin's arrival, Russia turned against the West.[15] Since the early 2000s focus of Russian policy has been to maintain and regain its influence as well as strengthen its efforts to increase its territory in the former Soviet Union republics.[16] The Western response was slow, as outlined by Starr and Cornell,

> only gradually did Putin's single-minded focus on restoring what he defined as the geographical integrity and honor of the Russian state become evident. And it took yet more time for the world at large to understand how far he was willing to go in pursuit of that end. The inability or reluctance of western and other policymakers, intelligence services, and independent foreign affairs experts to grasp this dedication on Putin's part ranks as an analytic failure of the first rank. Meanwhile, Putin seized the initiative in his military attack on Georgia in 2008,

---

[14] Tsygankov, *Russia and the West from Alexander to Putin*, 172–3.

[15] It should be noted that the reason behind and who is responsible for Russia's turning against the West and the Russian hybrid war on the West is a hotly debated topic among scholars and pundits alike, see, for example, Mitchell A. Orenstein, *The Lands in between: Russia vs. the West and the New Politics of Hybrid War* (New York: Oxford University Press, 2019), 11–14.

[16] Agnia Grigas, *Beyond Crimea: The New Russian Empire* (New Haven, CT: Yale University Press, 2016).

in his multi-dimensional but non-military assault on Kyrgyzstan in 2010, and then in his invasion of Ukraine and seizure of Crimea and other territories in 2014.[17]

A major problem with the Western response was its choice to deal with the events individually rather than as part of a unified strategy. Indeed, those who actually insisted on 'connecting the dots' were seen as being suffering a Cold War hangover and 'yearning for a return to the bi-polar politics of yore'.[18]

At the same time, the 'Colour Revolutions' took place, being a series of political non-violent protests in various post-Soviet states aiming to overthrow autocratic regimes, primarily in Ukraine (the Orange Revolution, 2004), Georgia (the Rose Revolution, 2003) and Kyrgyzstan (the Tulip Revolution, 2005).[19] These 'revolutions' were in Russia seen as a new US and European form of warfare that threatened Russia's interests in its 'sphere of influence' by destabilizing other states to pursue their own security interests vis-à-vis Russia at low costs and risk. The 'colour revolutions', have been seen as, citing Foreign Minister Sergei Lavrov, 'regime change operations in sovereign states ... provoked by external forces', where 'attempts to impose homemade recipes for internal changes on other nations, without taking into account their own traditions and national characteristics, to engage in the "export of democracy", have a destructive impact on international relations and result in an increase of the number of hot spots on the world map'.[20]

The developments between the invasion of Georgia in 2008 and the seizure of Ukrainian territory in 2014 forced policymakers and international affairs specialists alike to acknowledge that Russia under Putin had in fact 'reorganized its entire foreign and domestic policy in order to pursue a single objective, namely, the establishment of a new kind of union comprised of former Soviet republics and headed by Russia itself'.[21] Now discussions on Russia's new course focused on his declared intention to rectify the outfall of the collapse of the

---

[17] S. F. Starr and Svante E. Cornell, 'Introduction', in *Putin's Grand Strategy: The Eurasian Union and Its Discontents*, ed. S. F. Starr and Svante E. Cornell (Stockholm: Institute for Security and Development Policy (ISDP), 2014), 5–6.

[18] Starr and Cornell, p. 5.

[19] Donnacha Ó Beacháin and Abel Polese, eds., *The Colour Revolutions in the Former Soviet Republics: Successes and Failures* (London: Routledge, 2012). Besides chapters on Georgia, Ukraine and Kyrgyzstan, the volume includes chapters on Moldova, Armenia, Azerbaijan, Belarus, Russia, Uzbekistan, Tajikistan, Kazakhstan and Turkmenistan.

[20] Sputnik International, '"Color Revolutions" Cause Apparent Damage to International Stability – Lavrov', https://sputniknews.com/20140523/Color-Revolutions-Cause-Apparent-Damage-to-International-190067813.html.

[21] Starr and Cornell, 'Introduction', 6.

Soviet Union in 1991, which he, in 2005, in an address to the Russian Parliament called 'the major geopolitical disaster of the century'.[22]

The 2014 annexation of Ukraine and its aftermath was a rude awakening. While many Russia experts expected an active Russian economic policy against its neighbouring states and a struggle for supremacy over Ukraine, few foresaw an all-out Cold War-style military conflict.[23] To cite Agnia Grigas,

> In fact, before Russia's annexation of Crimea, a consistent threat to the post-Soviet space seemed implausible. After Crimea, Donetsk, Luhansk, and Mariupol, however, Russia's ability to redraw Europe's map and incite wars is evident. Following upon the pro-Russian separatism and conflict in South Ossetia, Abkhazia, and Transnistria in the 1990s and 2000s, the Ukrainian conflict suggests a continuing and worrying trajectory. Revanchist and resurgent, Russia appears ready to challenge the current post–Cold War order.[24]

Consequently, by 2015, most scholars, analysts and Western leaders alike all agreed that Russia was a challenge to Europe and the United States, not a partner.[25] Needless to say, at the time of writing this chapter this direction has both remained and been proven correct.

Structure of volume

The volume starts with an introduction, outlining the purpose of the volume and providing a conceptual starting point for analysing how the countries selected as case studies respond to Russian influence and warfare. Thereafter the book covers eight case studies from the Greater Baltic region, Eastern Europe, the Balkans and South Caucasus. The case selection is intended to provide broad coverage of states neighbouring Russia or located in its immediate proximity, albeit with a wide variety in their domestic political context, strategic outlook and availability of resources, as well as their perceived vulnerability vis-à-vis Russia. To ensure broad geographic coverage, the case studies include examples from the greater Baltic Region, Eastern Europe, the Balkans and South Caucasus. Finally, the findings of the eight case chapters are wrapped up and synthesized in the concluding chapter.

---

[22] Starr and Cornell, 'Introduction', 6.
[23] Grigas, *Beyond Crimea*, 1.
[24] Grigas, *Beyond Crimea*, p. 1.
[25] Grigas, *Beyond Crimea*, p. 1.

The empirical chapters are guided by a shared framework that covers key thematic areas for understanding Russia's warfare and influence towards small states on its western flank and their ability to respond and resist. This includes an understanding of the state's relationship with Russia and how Russian hybrid methods and influence are executed in their respective national context, including the possible existence of specific vulnerabilities and unique approaches and methods. The framework also covers the state's self-perception as a stakeholder and its room for manoeuvre in the context of Russia's warfare and influence as well as identifying means devised by the state in question to protect against and counter unwanted foreign influence.

The first two empirical chapters focus on Ukraine and Belarus. with a chapter on Ukraine by Dr Hanna Shelest, director of Security Programmes at Foreign Policy Council 'Ukrainian Prism' and editor-in-chief at UA: Ukraine Analytica and one on Belarus by Professor Grigory Ioffe of Radford University and Jamestown Foundation. Next follows the chapter on the Baltic states by Dr Jānis Bērziņš of the National Defence Academy of Latvia. Thereafter follow two chapters on the Balkans, with a chapter on Serbia by Dr Vuk Vuksanovic of the Belgrade Centre for Security Policy and one on Kosovo by Dr Dorthe Bach Nyemann of the Royal Danish Defence College. Next follows a chapter on Georgia by Professor Kornely Kakachia, Director of the Georgian Institute of Politics, and Shota Kakabadze, Policy Analyst at the Georgian Institute of Politics. The final empirical chapter by the editors and Dr Johan Engvall of the Swedish Institute of International Affairs (UI) addresses Russia's utilization of the five key unresolved conflicts in Nagorno-Karabakh, Abkhazia, South Ossetia, Transnistria and Ukraine's Donbass.

Overview of chapters

Chapter 2, 'Is It Still Hybrid? Russian Aggression against Ukraine', is written by Dr Hanna Shelest, the director of Security Programmes at Foreign Policy Council 'Ukrainian Prism' and editor-in-chief at UA: Ukraine Analytica. The chapter focuses on Ukraine's relationship with Russia with a particular focus on the period since the start of the Russian aggression in 2014. It asks whether we can still, after 24 February 2022, talk about hybrid warfare as open aggression, at first sight, clearly prioritized a military approach to influence Ukraine, but on the other hand, it proved that the non-military actions in support of the army's activities had not lost their relevance. The chapter addresses malign influence methods in the political, diplomatic, information, religious, subversive, economic and energy, and cyber dimensions.

Next follows a chapter by Prof Grigory Ioffe of Radford University and Jamestown Foundation titled 'Does Russia Need a Hybrid Belarus Policy?' The chapter argues that Russia is hardly in need of a hybrid Belarus policy in view of Belarus's crucial vulnerabilities with respect to Russia. All Russia needs to keep Belarus on a short leash is to exploit these vulnerabilities and perhaps additionally ingratiate itself to a critical mass of Belarusians by making financial concessions to its junior ally.

In Chapter 4, 'Russia's Influence Operations in the Baltic States', Dr Jānis Bērziņš, Senior Researcher at the Center for Security and Strategic Research, National Defence Academy of Latvia, discusses the main features of Russia's influence operations in the Baltic states in the following areas: politics, economic and social issues, diplomacy and information, and energy. This chapter mostly uses Latvia as its main case study because of the similarity of the Russian influence operations in the Baltic states.

After these case studies, the volume moves on to the Balkans and South Caucasus with chapters on Serbia, Kosovo and Georgia. First out is Serbia, with a chapter by Dr Vuk Vuksanovic of the Belgrade Centre for Security Policy, titled 'The Vulnerable Little Brother: Opportunistic Partnership and Serbia's Exposure to Russia's Spoiler Tactics'. This chapter outlines Serbia and Russia's opportunistic partnership, where Russia uses Serbia to gain leverage and a bargaining chip with the West at the same time as the Serbian leadership uses Russia to leverage the West on issues like Kosovo and deter the West from criticizing illiberal trends in Serbian politics. It is argued that Serbia's main economic and security partnerships continue to revolve around the West, leaving Russian influence in Serbia reduced to three specific instruments: energy, the unresolved Kosovo dispute and Russia's popularity among parts of the population. These instruments can also be the source of Serbian vulnerability that Russia can use if Belgrade makes a full tilt towards the West.

Chapter 6 on Kosovo, by Dr Dorthe Bach Nyemann from the Institute for Strategy and War at the Royal Danish Defence College, focuses on the narrative 'Kosovo is Serbia' that takes centre stage in every influence campaign in Kosovo and Serbia. The image of Kosovo belonging to and being Serbia is enhanced by the Serbian government's policies and actions and promoted by different NGOs, local Serbian groups within Kosovo, in the media and the Serbian Orthodox Church. The role of Russia in this campaign is not that easy to pinpoint. However, this chapter aims to show how and why Russia shapes and promotes the Serbian agenda denying Kosovo the benefits and recognition of statehood. The chapter argues that Russia plays a two-level game to ensure its interests. One is the overt game of influencing the Serbian government and the international community on which policies to pursue regarding Kosovo. The other is more subtle. Russia also works to influence groups inside and outside Kosovo to keep the narrative of 'Kosovo is Serbia' vibrant and relevant. This happens regardless of the interests of the Serbian government.

Next, our focus moves to Georgia, with a chapter titled 'Russian Hybrid Methods and Influence: Case of Georgia' by Professor Kornely Kakachia, professor of Political Science and Jean Monnet Chair at Ivane Javakhishvili Tbilisi State University, and the director of the Tbilisi-based think tank Georgian Institute of Politics and Dr Shota Kakabadze at the Georgian Institute of Politics. The chapter examines the case of Russian Warfare against Georgia, which started already in July of 2008 when coordinated massive cyberattacks were later accompanied by military aggression. It engages with the analysis of Russian hybrid activities in Georgia that take place in several domains: ideological and informational, cyber, and through proxy forces in South Ossetia and Abkhazia. The second part of the chapter examines specific vulnerabilities that Georgian society is facing and what are the state's capacities to mitigate these challenges. It also offers lessons that can be drawn from the case of Georgia and its wider applicability. This chapter argues that partnership with NATO and the European Union must be a fundamental pillar for Georgia's resilience to hybrid threats and Russian subversive activities. It will also very much depend on Georgia's proactive policies in seeking security guarantees as well as on close cooperation between the private, non-state and state stakeholders, to avoid becoming Russia's next target after the failed blitzkrieg in Ukraine.

Chapter 8, 'Russia's Utilization of Unresolved Conflicts and Proxy Regimes', by Dr Niklas Nilsson, associate professor in War Studies at the Land Operations Division & the Centre for Societal Security, Swedish Defence University, Dr Johan Engvall of the Stockholm Centre for Eastern European Studies at the Swedish Institute of International Affairs (UI) and Dr Mikael Weissmann, associate professor in War Studies and the deputy director of the Land Warfare Division at the Swedish Defence University, focuses on five conflicts in post-Soviet territories, Transnistria, South Ossetia and Abkhazia, Nagorno-Karabakh and Donbass. The chapter outlines the five unresolved conflicts and analyses how they have provided Russia with means for influencing the politics and societies across the affected states and how the influence has been wielded across political and military dimensions. It also discusses how the impact of Russia's full-scale invasion of Ukraine in February 2022 has stood many of the prevailing assumptions regarding Russian strategy and influence in its neighbourhood on their head and how it has led to a substantial re-evaluation of Russia's priorities, propensity for risk and capabilities.

Finally, in the concluding chapter 'A Diverse Picture of Russian Warfare and Influence', Dr Niklas Nilsson and Dr Mikael Weissmann of the Swedish Defence University summarize the chapters and the findings of the book.

Bibliography

Balasevicius, T. (2017), 'Looking for Little Green Men: Understanding Russia's Employment of Hybrid Warfare', *Canadian Military Journal*, 17 (3): 17–28.

Bush, G. (1991), 'Address before a Joint Session of the Congress on the State of the Union', 29 January. Available online: https://web.archive.org/web/20180312161 706/http:/www.presidency.ucsb.edu/ws/?pid=19253, updated on 23 March 2023 (accessed 23 March 2023).

Cohen, R. S., and A. Radin (2019), *Russia's Hostile Measures in Europe: Understanding the Threat*, Santa Monica, CA: RAND Corporation.

Fridman, O. (2018), *Russian 'Hybrid Warfare': Resurgence and Politicisation*, Oxford: Oxford University Press.

Galeotti, M. (2016), *Hybrid War or Gibridnaya Voina? Getting Russia's Non-linear Military Challenge Right*, Prague: Mayak Intelligence.

Galeotti, M. (2019), *Russian Political War: Moving beyond the Hybrid*, London: Routledge.

Grigas, A. (2016), *Beyond Crimea: The New Russian Empire*, New Haven, CT: Yale University Press.

Göransson, M. (2021), 'Understanding Russian Thinking on gibridnaya voyna', in M. Weissmann, N. Nilsson, P. Thunholm, B. Palmertz (eds), *Hybrid Warfare: Security and Asymmetric Conflict in International Relations*, 83–94, London: I.B. Tauris.

Hybrid CoE – The European Centre of Excellence for Countering Hybrid Threats (2023), 'Hybrid Threats as a Concept'. Available online: https://www.hybridcoe.fi/hyb rid-threats-as-a-phenomenon/ (accessed 3 February 2023).

Kanet, R. E. (2017), 'Introduction: The Russian Challenge to the Security Environment in Europe', in R. E. Kanet (ed.), *The Russian Challenge to the European Security Environment*, 1–9, Cham: Palgrave Macmillan.

Kilcullen, D. (2020), *The Dragons and the Snakes: How the Rest Learned to Fight the West*, London: Hurst.

Kofman, M., and M. Rojansky (2015), 'A Closer Look at Russia's "Hybrid War"', *Wilson Center: Kennan Institute* (Kennan Cable No. 7). Available online: https://www.files.ethz.ch/isn/190090/5-KENNAN%20CABLE-ROJANSKY%20KOFMAN.pdf (accessed 16 November 2023).

Nilsson, N. (2018), *Russian Hybrid Tactics in Georgia*, Washington, DC: Central Asia-Caucasus Institute & Silk Road Studies Program.

Nilsson, N., M. Weissmann, Mikael; B. Palmertz, P. Thunholm and H. Häggström (2021), 'Security Challenges in the Grey Zone: Hybrid Threats and Hybrid Warfare', in M. Weissmann, N. Nilsson, P. Thunholm and B. Palmertz (eds), *Hybrid Warfare: Security and Asymmetric Conflict in International Relations*, 1–18, London: I.B. Tauris.

Nupi (2020), 'Multinational Capability Development Campaign 2015–18 (Countering Hybrid Warfare)', *Nupi*. Available online: www.nupi.no/en/About-NUPI/Proje cts-centres-and-programmes/Multinational-Capability-Development-Campa ign-2015-18-Countering-Hybrid-Warfare (accessed 17 March 2020).

Ó Beacháin, D., and A. Polese, eds (2012), *The Colour Revolutions in the Former Soviet Republics: Successes and Failures*, London: Routledge.

Orenstein, M. A. (2019), *The Lands in between: Russia vs. the West and the New Politics of Hybrid War*, New York: Oxford University Press.

Radin, A. (2017), *Hybrid Warfare in the Baltics: Threats and Potential Responses*, Santa Monica, CA: RAND Corporation.

Sputnik International (2014), ' "Color Revolutions" Cause Apparent Damage to International Stability – Lavrov'. Available online: https://sputniknews.com/20140 523/Color-Revolutions-Cause-Apparent-Damage-to-International-190067813.html, updated on 23 May 2014 (accessed 6 February 2023).

Starr, S. F., and S. E. Cornell (2014), 'Introduction', in S. F. Starr and S. E. Cornell (eds), *Putin's Grand Strategy: The Eurasian Union and Its Discontents*, Stockholm: Institute for Security and Development Policy.

Thomas, T. (2015), 'Russia's Military Strategy and Ukraine: Indirect, Asymmetric – and Putin-Led', *Journal of Slavic Military Studies*, 28 (3): 445–61.

Thomas, T. (2016), 'The Evolution of Russian Military Thought: Integrating Hybrid, New-Generation, and New-Type Thinking', *Journal of Slavic Military Studies* 29 (4): 554–75.

Thornton, R. (2017), 'The Russian Military's New "Main Emphasis"', *RUSI Journal*, 162 (4): 18–28.

Tsygankov, A. P. (2012), *Russia and the West from Alexander to Putin: Honor in International Relations*, Cambridge: Cambridge University Press.

United States Army, Asymmetric Warfare Group (2016), *Russian New Generation Warfare Handbook*, https://info.publicintelligence.net/AWG-RussianNewWarfareH andbook.pdf (accessed 15 January 2024).

Weissmann, M. (2019), 'Hybrid Warfare and Hybrid Threats Today and
   Tomorrow: Towards an Analytical Framework', *Journal on Baltic Security*, 5
   (1): 17–26.
Weissmann, M. (2021), 'Conceptualizing and Countering Hybrid Threats and Hybrid
   Warfare', in Mikael Weissmann et al. (eds), *Hybrid Warfare: Security and Asymmetric
   Conflict in International Relations*, 61–82, London: I.B. Tauris.

2

Is it still hybrid? Russian aggression against Ukraine

Hanna Shelest

Ukraine's relationship with Russia

The date of 24 February 2022 became a watershed moment in Russia-Ukraine relations. Even if the initial act of aggression and occupation had happened nine years before this in 2014, it was the year 2022 that led to the end of all sentiments, attempts to accommodate Moscow's position and the break of diplomatic relations. The full-fledged war became the ultimate essence of the centuries of malign Russian influence over Ukraine.

From church autonomy assimilation to language prohibition, from the eradication of the intelligentsia and national movements to the Holodomor and Soviet repression, these pages of the bilateral relations have always been undermined and covered by the Russian Empire and later the Soviet Union. While much of the malign influence of those centuries could be described as a classical colonial policy, the Russian Federation never ended this policy towards Ukraine even after the collapse of the Soviet Union, gaining independence and establishing the so-called democratic governance in Russia.

The thirty years since the USSR collapse shaped Russian methods. The malign influence had constantly been present, even if often not acknowledged by the country's leadership. It had created ties and channels, the basis for the future hybrid warfare that easily could be utilized when the crisis came. It became obvious in 2014 when the Russian Federation started its aggression against Ukraine. The next nine years have been symbolized by all different manifestations of the hybrid warfare – energy, cyber, information, religious, political proxies and media, backed by the military presence in the east of Ukraine and Crimea.

Attack on the 24 February 2022 and the full-fledged war raised a question on whether we still can talk about hybrid warfare as open aggression, at first sight, clearly prioritized a military approach to influence Ukraine, but on the other hand, it proved that the non-military actions in support of the army's activities had not lost their relevance.

Overview of Russian hybrid methods and influence

Studying the Ukrainian case is important as practice showed that it is often a testing ground for tools and methods the Russian Federation's actors later use in different countries around the globe. The prioritization of the methods Russia used has been changing over the years, depending on the loyalty of the Ukrainian political actors, the domestic situation in Russia and the goals that were necessary to achieve. Political and information influence has steadily remained in focus, with subversive operations being active but less public.

The Russian Federation used all malign influence methods that comprised its hybrid warfare against Ukraine. They can be grouped as following.

Political

The utilization of proxy opinion-makers and politicians was among the top priorities over the years. Sponsoring the pro-Russian politicians both at the national and regional levels, as well as demonstrating their close ties with the Kremlin, thus influence, and backing their political and business interests, helped the Russian meddling in the domestic Ukrainian political process. Such proxies have been actively used for political discourse and media presence setting, gaining access to restricted information and as a possibility to influence decision-making. Party of the Regions, which later transformed into the Opposition Platform – for Life was the brightest example. Since 2014 they have been actively promoting the Russian narratives and securing Russian business and political interests, especially in the energy sphere. Most of their Members of Parliament escaped Ukraine a few days before the full-fledged invasion[1] but were ready to take power as soon as Kyiv was occupied.[2]

[1] Aleksandra Klitina, 'Lawmakers from Opposition Platform – For Life Have Fled or Regrouped', *Kyiv Post*, 25 April 2022, https://www.kyivpost.com/post/6910.
[2] Igor Burdyga, 'These Are the Men Russia Wanted to Put in Charge of Ukraine', *Open Democracy*, 4 March 2023, https://www.opendemocracy.net/en/odr/ukraine-russia-opposition-platform-for-life-medvedchuk-boiko/.

More dangerous were small groups operating at the local level; they could be present as the NGOs, initiatives and charity foundations that never or very seldom reported their financing sources. Some were affiliated with above-mentioned pro-Russian politicians, others received direct financing from Russia. Their task was to organize protests against the governmental authorities and NATO (e.g. military exercises[3]), hold different public discussions or spread anti-Western, anti-Ukrainian sentiments. Often, they have been initiators of the anti-Ukrainian language or anti-LGBT rights manifestations, and the like. Ex-Communist Party activists or those affiliated with radical religious groups are often involved.

Intervention into the political discourse. The Russian Federation often amplifies the existing weaknesses inside of the targeted country or manipulates existing political debate. In the Ukrainian case, three issues took their particular interest: Soviet nostalgia, the use of the Russian language and the so-called federalization.

Russia actively promoted and supported Soviet nostalgic narratives that influenced political discourse and perception of Moscow. Despite a decrease in numbers from 48 per cent in 2013 to 33 per cent in 2020, the number of people who feel sorry that the USSR has collapsed has still been high in Ukraine.[4] While it has generational flavour, many aspects of this nostalgia were instrumentalized for the younger generation as well. 'The USSR as a great power respected by all', 'strong leadership that brings stability', 'great economy of Soviet republics when they were together' and 'stability and predicted future' – these are just a few narratives actively promoted for this purpose. All these were de facto instrumentalized to demonstrate Moscow's superiority and necessity to stay under its control as well as questioning the necessity of Ukrainian independence and nationhood.

Last but not least is Russian calls for a federalization of Ukraine, what is done both via separatist entities and directly within peace negotiation formats. However, this narrative has deeper roots than 2014 demands, as it had been actively promoted with the idea of the uniqueness of eastern and southern territories, facilitating their individual ties and cooperation with Russian regions, and also promoting special 'free economic zones'. However, the real

---

[3] 'Акция протеста против учений Си Бриз в Одессе' [Protests against Sea Breeze in Odessa], *UNIAN*, 10 July 2007, https://www.unian.net/politics/53230-aktsiya-protesta-protiv-ucheniy-si-briz-v-odesse-10-foto.html.

[4] 'Оцінка радянського минулого: травень 2020 року' [Perception of the Soviet past, May 2020], *KIIS*, 22 June 2020, https://www.kiis.com.ua/?lang=ukr&cat=reports&id=950&page=1&t=3.

'federalization' issue started with the Donbas occupation and Minsk agreements, when the special status, often called by Russia a federalization of Ukraine, started to be promoted both by Moscow and its proxies in the occupied territories.

In January 2016, the most blatant attempt was made when the representatives of the so-called Donetsk People's Republic, after yet another round of negotiations, submitted the proposals for constitutional reform in Ukraine, which went far beyond the Minsk Agreements and standards of international law and practice on decentralization. For example, in addition to the request to have a quota for their members in the Parliament of Ukraine, to use Russian as an official language and to have close economic ties with Russia, they insisted on the right to approve all Ukrainian laws as well as the right to veto foreign policy decisions. They also demanded the right to form their own police, security services, judiciary, prosecution, border guard service and other agencies without the approval of the authorities in Kyiv.[5]

Those demands faced two crucial difficulties. One was the possibility that if conceded, the separatists could paralyze any state activity, rendering the country completely dysfunctional. Bearing in mind the opposing visions of the foreign policy orientation between the conflicting parties (pro-Russian vs. pro-European), reforms, trade agreements, political arrangements and foreign policy activity could be completely blocked. If we add to this police and security services beyond the control of the central government, that is de facto loss of the monopoly on the use of force, such a dangerous accumulation of power will be far from preventing conflict, but provoking it. The proposition of the separatist regions envisaged special powers only for these two territories of Ukraine, while legally, the country would continue to be made of twenty-five equal regions.[6] So this could lead to further separatism promotion, conflicts between the regions and constant social distrust.

Diplomatic

Hybrid warfare against Ukraine is exterritorial. It started not in 2022 but had been so originally, as Russia needed not only to gain their goals inside of Ukraine, but to decrease support from the partners, to build a case for the international community, and to discredit Ukraine. Thus, Moscow not only used a classical

---

[5] '"DPR" Offers Special View of Amendments to Ukrainian Constitution'. *Censor*, 27 January 2016, http://en.censor.net.ua/n371293.
[6] Hanna Shelest, 'Imposed State-Building', *Southeastern Europe* 42, no. 3 (2018): 327–49. doi: https://doi.org/10.1163/18763332-04203003.

technique of building alliances but actively undermined trust and support both political and public towards Ukraine. Russia has been actively working against Ukraine in the diplomatic domain. Here it is possible to divide it into several main dimensions:

Working with third countries to minimize isolation caused initially by the attempted annexation of Crimea. These efforts were aimed predominantly not only at big players like Germany, France, the United States and Turkey but also at countries like India, China and South Africa, which struggled for regional leadership. Big players were targeted with the idea of the necessity to deal with grand issues – terrorism, arms control, ISIS, Syria, Libya, nuclear security and the like – thus proposing 'to ignore' Russia attempting any mischief against Ukraine.

Since 2022, the focus was changed to the so-called Global South – predominantly Africa, the Middle East and Asia – where anti-American sentiments could be cultivated; thus, the US support towards Ukraine has been streamed against Ukraine. Here Russia presented itself through the lens of the Soviet opposition to 'Western imperialism', support of those in need and so on. A Grain Deal (signed in July 2022) and possible food crisis were instrumentalized for this purpose. Smaller states are predominantly targeted, aiming to reject the support of anti-Russian sanctions and anti-Russian resolutions in international organizations.

Disruptive work within international organizations is another element. There are several instruments used here: blocking or sabotaging pro-Ukrainian resolutions and decisions, preventing anti-Russian monitoring and sanctions, presenting Ukraine as a country that violates the law, active work through the Russian staff within the secretariats and jeopardizing agenda to manipulate the issue.

Information

There are two directions of the Russian information malign influence – domestic (aimed at the Ukrainian audience) and international (aimed at creating an image of Ukraine and events in Ukraine for the international audience). Since 2014, direct Russian propaganda in Ukraine has decreased, while indirect or covert influence has been enhanced. The most dangerous way of influence was promoting Russian narratives through Ukrainian opinion-makers, media and political parties. However, since 2022 information operations have taken the lead, especially in social networks.

International media. Several elements should be emphasized here. Russian media, such as Sputnik and RT, have actively promoted the Russian agenda for years. While in the EU states they have been gradually closed, their Spanish and Arabic versions, as well as their presence in the Balkans and Africa, just increased. This allowed the promotion of the Russian vision of the war and a decrease in support towards Ukraine. The second element is the journalists themselves, especially at the beginning of the war. As most of the international media had their correspondents covering Ukraine in Moscow, so they appeared under the significant influence of their Russian contacts and information bulb. Third, Russia started to promote (sponsor) articles against Ukraine in international media or leak the misinformation to the media. Often there were no Russian authors, but some foreign experts who spread either pro-Russian narratives or blamed Ukraine for misbehaving, therefore undermining support (e.g. allegations that Ukraine sells Western weapons to the black market[7]).

Ownership of the local media. Even though Ukraine has blocked Russian television channels to stop them from spreading war propaganda after 2014, there was a certain number of pro-Russian TV channels, stand-alone websites and journalists who continued the subtle dissemination of pro-Russian messages in Ukrainian media.[8] Even if legally they belonged to Ukrainian citizens (due to the law on the necessity to show the final beneficiary), some of them have been sponsored by Russia. The most famous cases are definitely associated with the notorious figure of Viktor Medvedchuk, a Ukrainian politician who was considered a personal friend of Russian president Putin.

Intervention in social networks. Trolls and bots' factories are the most well-known and widespread instruments. It creates visibility to the necessary news and provokes disputes, conflicts or manipulation of public opinion if necessary. If originally the Russian side predominantly was writing such comments in Russian language, later, to build greater trust when undermining governmental

---

[7] E.g. 'Ukraine Sells Weapons on Black Market Due to Limited Ability to Use', *Almayadeen*, 7 July 2022, https://english.almayadeen.net/news/politics/ukraine-sells-weapons-on-black-market-due-to-limited-ability.

[8] David Stulík, *Russian Economic Interference in Europe: Case Studies of Germany, Ukraine, Poland, Austria and the Czech Republic*, European Values Center for Security Policy, 2020, p. 16, https://eur opeanvalues.cz/en/russian-   economic-interference-in-europe-case-studies-of-germany-ukraine-poland-austria-and-the-czech-republic/.

authorities, they started posting in Ukrainian,[9] in most cases Google-translated versions, that led to numerous anecdotal situations.

Also, for this purpose, Russia creates fake accounts of the Ukrainian military, both individuals and units, where it promotes panic and distrust in command, sometimes posting news that can present the Ukrainian military in a negative sense. Also, the practice of anonymous Telegram channels has been widespread for years, many of which are sponsored by Moscow.[10]

Information operations. Fake or unchecked news still poses a serious danger. A huge number of websites presenting themselves as news ones, but being just a reposting website creates an information bulb. Appearing on such websites, information is widely shared by other similar websites and social media networks while also being at the end published by some real media or reported on TV as real news.

Control over the media in the occupied territories. The problem remains with broadcasting Ukrainian TV and radio channels to the occupied territories. Both in Donbas and Crimea, the signal has been jammed since 2014, so to limit access to Ukrainian news. This is multiplied by blocking Ukrainian websites and creating local propagandist media. The same tactic was chosen for the newly occupied territories, where the first thing done was destroying or taking TV towers under full control, blocking radio signals and immediate introduction of the Russian media at the Ukrainian frequencies,[11] as well as introducing Russian internet providers that allowed control over the content access and surveillance.

Religious

Using the Russian Orthodox Church (ROC) in Ukraine has been a key tactic of the malign Russian influence over the years. This involved influencing the public discourse, political influence, interference in the local governance issues

[9] Tom Bateman, 'Ukraine War: Meta Takes Down Russia-Based Disinformation Network Targeting Ukrainian Social Media', *Euronews*, 28 February 2022, https://www.euronews.com/next/2022/02/28/ukraine-war-meta-takes-down-russia-based-disinformation-network-targeting-ukrainian-social.

[10] Sofiia Telishevska, 'The Security Service of Ukraine Has Published a List of 100 Pseudo-Ukrainian Telegram Channels, Which Controlled by Russia', *Babel*, 15 July 2022, https://babel.ua/en/news/81511-the-security-service-of-ukraine-has-published-a-list-of-100-pseudo-ukrainian-telegram-channels-which-controlled-by-russia.

[11] 'Russia Says It's Now Broadcasting Throughout Ukraine's Kherson Region', *Radio Free*, 21 June 2022, https://www.rferl.org/a/russia-broadcasting-ukraine-kherson/31907822.html.

by being elected to the local councils, prevention of Ukrainian church autonomy and even priest as assets of Russian intelligence and security services.

There are several ways by which malign Russian influence is projected through the church: promotion of the 'Russian World' project and its attributes of pressing 'traditional values' and anti-Western sentiments; competition for power and the undermining of the authority of the Constantinople Patriarchate; intervention in the religious affairs; ROC activities in international organizations and others. In 2014, especially in the regions of Eastern Ukraine, pro-Russian priests have been actively involved in hiding the Russian military and their equipment,[12] allowing them to use the territory of churches for fighters' preparation or artillery deployment.[13] The connection between the Russian security agencies and the ROC has been widely reported by the media.[14]

As the ROC has always been deeply involved in Ukrainian politics, with priests being members of local councils, having moral authority and close connections with politicians, the dispute about the establishment of the Ukrainian autocephaly became political. Provocations and fighting near churches in villages were organized as well.

Over the years, the ROC has been smoothly integrated into the state political system. Its institutionalization is achieved via joint working groups with the ministries and state agencies, joint subject matter expert commissions and other similar formats. In Ukraine, the ROC Synodal Committee for interaction with Cossacks[15] actively cooperates with paramilitary groups. In 2014, the above-mentioned paramilitary groups were integrated into the Russian Orthodox Army (ROA).[16] In 2023, a number of priests were arrested for espionage or treason, and a few have already been convicted.[17]

---

[12] 'У нещодавно окупованому Лимані родина священика УПЦ МП вітала хлібом-сіллю окупантів' [In recently occupied Liman, a family of the priest welcomed the occupants], *RISU*, 1 June 2022, https://risu.ua/u-neshchodavno-okupovanomu-limani-rodina-svyashchenika-upc-mp-vitala-hlibom-sillyu-okupantiv_n129759.

[13] '«Церква поза політикою»: як єпископи РПЦ в Україні співпрацюють з бойовиками Донбасу та окупаційною владою Криму' [Church is out of politics, how bishops cooperate with fighters in Donbas], *Slidstvo Info*, 28 July 2020, https://www.slidstvo.info/articles/tserkva-poza-polityk oyu-yak-yepyskopy-rpts-v-ukrayini-spivpratsyuyut-z-bojovykamy-donbasu-ta-okupatsijnoyu-vladoyu-krymu/.

[14] Irina Borogan and Andrei Soldatov, 'Putin's Security Forces Find God', *CEPA*, 9 February 2023, https://cepa.org/article/putins-security-forces-find-god/.

[15] 'Synodal Committee for Interaction with Cossacks', https://www.skvk.org.

[16] 'Meet the Russian Orthodox Army, Ukrainian Separatists' Shock Troops', *NBC*, 16 May 2014, https://www.nbcnews.com/storyline/ukraine-crisis/meet-russian-orthodox-army-ukrainian-separati sts-shock-troops-n107426.

[17] Martin Fornusek, 'Priest of Moscow-Linked Church Sentenced to 15 Years for Spying for Russia', *The Kyiv Independent*, 25 October 2023, https://kyivindependent.com/priest-of-moscow-linked-church-sentenced-to-15-years-for-spying-for-russia/.

Subversive

The classical subversive operations and work of the spies and agents within the Ukrainian institutions have been remaining active throughout the years. Russian covert agents inside the Ukrainian military and security agencies were the main problem back in 2013 and 2014; as they comprised a significant percentage and openly sabotaged, transferred secret information and the like. While the scope of the problem decreased, it has remained a top issue for counterintelligence and internal security bodies. As 2022 proved, the recruiting process never stopped, while some remained sleepy agents before 2022 and thus securing their positions within the governmental hierarchy.[18]

Economy and energy

Energy and economy were always the most actively used mechanisms of Russian influence in Ukraine. The idea of Ukrainian dependency on Russian energy sources and trade links with the Russian market has been promoted for decades. Despite a decrease in economic interaction since 2014 and attempts to gain full independence from Russian energy resources, the Kremlin managed to secure this issue in their propaganda activities aimed not only at Ukraine but also at Ukraine's partners. Before 2014, the Ukrainian economy has been heavily dependent on Russian energy sources. Many spheres of the economy developed only because of the cheap energy prices and have not been modernized. All attempts to diversify sources were unsuccessful due to the Russian opposition or pre-buying of the Central Asian gas, thus limiting options. The so-called energy wars of winters 2005–6, 2008–9 and 2013–14 were the apotheosis of such influence. In parallel, the pro-Russian politicians have been actively working in this domain, organizing their own 'negotiations' to decrease prices for Russian gas to Ukraine (even though they do not have any official powers to do so). These trips and 'agreements' were actively used to promote the image of the pro-Russian parties during the 2019 parliamentary elections.[19]

The energy aspect received its exterritorial element with the Russian attempts to promote the Nord Stream and gas relations with different EU member states,

[18] 'Ukraine Detains Senior Public Figures Suspected of Spying for Russia', *Reuters,* 21 June 2022, https://www.reuters.com/world/europe/ukraine-detains-senior-public-figures-suspected-spying-russia-2022-06-21/.

[19] 'Putin Confirms Agreements Reached by Medvedchuk and Boyko in Moscow', *112 International*, 29 April 2019, https://112.international/russia/putin-confirms-agreements-reached-by-medvedchuk-and-boyko-in-moscow-39297.html.

thus persuading and blackmailing them that support for Ukraine would harm their own economic well-being.

Russian control over some strategic enterprises for years was an issue of economic security. Certain limitations introduced after 2014 had only limited effect as many Russian companies have been investing through offshore companies, so it was not always possible to stop such involvement legally.

Cyber

Cyberattacks became a trademark of the Russian actions against Ukraine. In the past ten years, cyber domain threats have steadily moved from the soft security issues the IT companies and private users care about to the hard security risks recognized by the states as sometimes equal to military threats by their impact. The cyber domain of the malign influence is important due to its significant interconnection with other spheres. The digitalization of state services, financial sphere, military equipment, communication systems and critical infrastructure is an open door for cyber operations. Cybersecurity is also closely connected with information security, as social networks and information gained through hacking are actively used in information warfare.

Attribution itself is a complex question to unpack in cybersecurity. There has long been a view that it is impossible in cyber operations, though that belief has started to fade.[20] While Russia is not a single malign influence actor in the cyber domain, it is the biggest and most active actor that widely use cyber instruments as a part of hybrid warfare. Three main reasons make attribution difficult: work through proxy groups (e.g. anonymous hackers); fake coverage under the name of other groups and often technical obstacles for identification.

In most cases, Russian cyber actions have been an addition to the already developing conflict situation rather than a separate attack. For example, in April–May 2021, when the Russian Federation military build-up was observed in the Black Sea and around the Ukrainian borders, which raised strong concern within NATO and the EU, the Ukrainian Security Services reported a significant increase in cyberattacks against critical infrastructure and state authorities of the country.[21]

---

[20] Ben Buchanan and Michael Sulmeyer, 'Russia and Cyber Operations: Challenges and Opportunities for the Next U.S. Administration', The Carnegie Endowment for International Peace, 16 December 2016, https://carnegieendowment.org/2016/12/13/russia-and-cyber-operations-challenges-and-opportunities-for-next-u.s.-administration-pub-66433.

[21] 'Russia Increases Number of Cyber-Attacks against Ukraine, Illya Vityuk, Security Services of Ukraine', Security Services of Ukraine, 13 May 2021, https://ssu.gov.ua/en/novyny/na-foni-kontsen tratsii-viisk-bilia-kordoniv-rf- zbilshyla-kilkist-kiberatak-na-ukrainu-illia-vitiuk

Yet one pattern that can be noticed that cyberattacks have been becoming an answer, a punishment, after the new sanctions' introduction, a strong statement or military purchase. For example, at the end of March 2021, when the sanctions against pro-Russian proxies and President Putin's friend Viktor Medvedchuk had been introduced – the National Security and Defence Council reported a rapid splash in both DDoS attacks and malware use against the Ukrainian web resources that had been well-coordinated in time and scope, with patterns associated to the Russian security forces.[22]

Governmental bodies and the military are the primary targets for the Russian attacks. For example, in June 2021 alone, the Situation Centre for Cyber Security at the Security Services of Ukraine reported seventy-six prevented cyberattacks against governmental institutions, including C&C Server, Brute Force Attack, Web App Attack, malicious scan, malware and the like.[23] Around one thousand such incidents were reported in the first half of 2021.[24]

Different methods are used by the Russian Federation security services (mainly GRU and FSB) and affiliated with them hacking groups, among which the most popular are the following:

- The creation of fake websites which mimic the original government websites and can spread both fake information and malware.[25]
- An online network of agitators[26] and propaganda spreaders.[27] Predominantly present in social networks and used during elections or difficult political-social periods, thus multiplying the problems that existed in society. They often are connected with IT troll and bot farms. While this method is often considered part of information warfare, it also may have a significant cyber effect. Trolls and bots are not only used for information sharing but also

---

[22] 'В СНБО рассказали о кибератаках России из-за санкций' [In National Security Council they told about the cyberattacks because of sanctions], *Hvylya*, 16 March 2021, https://hvylya.net/news/227026-v-snbo-rasskazali-o-kiberatakah-rossii-iz-za-sankciy.

[23] 'SBU: 76 Cyber-Attacks Hit Ukrainian Authorities in June, Security Services of Ukraine', Security Services of Ukraine, 9 July 2021, https://ssu.gov.ua/en/novyny/u-chervni-sbu-zablokuvala-ponad-70-kiberatak-na-ukrainski-orhany-vlady.

[24] 'SBU: 1,000 Cyber-Attacks Thwarted in Six Months', Security Services of Ukraine', Security Services of Ukraine, 21 July 2021, https://ssu.gov.ua/en/novyny/za-piv-roku-sbu-neitralizuvala-ponad-1-tys-kiberatak-na-derzhavni-resursy.

[25] 'Зафіксовано атаку на державні органи України з використанням веб-сайту, що імітує Офіційне інтернет- представництво Президента України' [An attack on the Ukraine's governmental website was identified], CERT-UA, 13 July 2021, https://cert.gov.ua/article/13156.

[26] 'SBU Neutralizes New Group of Online Agents Coordinated from Russia', Security Services of Ukraine, 30 July 2021, https://ssu.gov.ua/en/novyny/sbu-neitralizuvala-novu-hrupu-internetahentiv-yakykh-koordynuvaly-z-rf.

[27] 'SBU Opposes Hostile Information Operations', Security Services of Ukraine, 30 April 2021, https://ssu.gov.ua/en/novyny/sbu-protydiie-vorozhym-informatsiinym-operatsiiam-vykryto-merezhu-internetahitatoriv-na-poshyrenni-antykonstytutsiinykh-zaklykiv-naperedodni-travnevykh-sviat.

used for attacking certain social networks profiles of politicians, activists and organizations (including disinformation fighters and cybersecurity), resulting in their temporary or permanent blocking or deleting of certain content.[28] They also can be employed for a massive spontaneous spam attack.

- Unauthorized interference in communication systems and location determination systems of the military and security organizations. Here examples range from unauthorized radio frequency interference (as in the Ukrainian Joint Forces Operation networks stationed in the Luhansk region in April 2019[29]) to suspicious cases of the navy ships' navigation system's signal change – spoofing operation (as in the case of the HMS Defender in June 2021)[30].

- Spyware or cyber espionage. This set of activities ranges from getting kompromat to receiving access to the necessary networks and computers that can be used later, for example, during elections.

- DDoS attacks. Occurred regularly against governmental institutions, and banking systems, media websites.

- Leaking of personally identifiable information. As for now had limited success in the Ukrainian case but has already been tested against the partner states.[31]

- Critical infrastructure attacks. The most well-known case is probably a December 2015 attack on the electrical power grid of Ukraine. As the digital intruders manipulated almost sixty circuit breakers and substations throughout the system, electricity was cut off from homes and businesses of more than 230,000 people.[32]

- Disruption of networks by blocking them and undermining trust in governmental or banking systems. Such attacks often can be camouflaged by

---

[28] Ed Parsons and Michael Raff, 'Understanding the Cyber Threat from Russia', *F-Secure*, March 2019, https://www.f-secure.com/en/consulting/our-thinking/understanding-the-cyber-threat-from-russia.

[29] 'Donbas: SBU Blocks Unauthorized Russia's Interference in Joint Forces Operation Units', Security Services of Ukraine, 19 April 2021, https://ssu.gov.ua/en/novyny/sbu-zablokuvala-nesanktsionov ane-vtruchannia-v- radiochastoty-pidrozdiliv-oos-na-donbasi

[30] Tom Bateman, 'HMS Defender: AIS Spoofing Is Opening Up a New Front in the War on Reality', *Euronews*, 28 June 2021, https://www.euronews.com/next/2021/06/28/hms-defender-ais-spoof ing-is-opening-up-a-new-front-in-the-war-on-reality.

[31] Adam Meyers, 'Cyber Skirmish: Russia v. Turkey', *Crowdstrike*, 13 April 2016, https://www.crow dstrike.com/blog/cyber-skirmish-russia-v-turkey/; 'Millions of Bulgarians' Personal Data Hacked; Russian Link Suspected', *Fox News*, 16 July 2019, https://www.foxnews.com/world/millions-of-bul garians-hacked-russian-tie-suspected.

[32] Ben Buchanan and Michael Sulmeyer, 'Russia and Cyber Operations: Challenges and Opportunities for the Next U.S. Administration', The Carnegie Endowment for International Peace, 16 December 2016, https://carnegieendowment.org/2016/12/13/russia-and-cyber-operations-challenges-and-opportunities-for-next-u.s.-administration-pub-66433.

ransom malware or similar software. Petya/NotPetya, malware/ransomware case is a well-known example. What looked like ransom malware that affected Ukrainian banks, energy companies, governmental institutions and businesses associated with the Ukrainian government was wiping the master boot record of victim machines and planting fake, irreversible ransomware.[33] By targeting organizations rather than states, taking care to avoid positive attribution, and calibrating the impact to fall short of war, they can pursue their foreign policy goals while denying their opponents the ability to respond effectively.[34] The latest case is a hacker's attack against the biggest mobile operator Kyivstar that led to significant business loss, public trust lost and social disturbance within a week, as loss of the communication and personal data during the war is a significant risk.[35]

- Interference in the election process occurred regularly but was not successful as Ukraine actively cooperated with NATO and other partners to prevent it.[36]
- Possible interference in military equipment, first of all, 'blinding' radar systems, sending wrong GPS coordinates and so on.

Quasi-military

In addition to the traditional threat by exercises on the border, the Russian Federation has developed a set of instruments in the maritime domain that were actively used in 2014–22 against Ukraine. We call them quasi-military as they involved the military of the Russian Federation, but their main goal at that time was political or hybrid rather than classical military.

Provocations against ships in neutral waters and dangerous manoeuvres of both ships and aeroplanes became frequent in the Black Sea after 2014 and intensified especially after 2018. Such tactics were used both for power demonstration and bluff, as many actions were reported as so dangerous that they could lead to the incidents.[37]

---

[33] Andy Greenberg, 'Petya Ransomware Epidemic May Be Spillover From Cyberwar', *Wired*, 28 June 2017, https://www.wired.com/story/petya-ransomware-ukraine/.

[34] Parsons and Raff, 'Understanding the Cyber Threat From Russia'.

[35] Kateryna Tyshchenko, 'Russian Hackers Infiltrated Kyivstar System in May 2023 or Earlier – Security Service of Ukraine', *Ukrainska Pravda*, 04 January 2024, https://www.pravda.com.ua/eng/news/2024/01/4/7435792/.

[36] 'Уроки гібридного десятиліття: що треба знати для успішного руху вперед' [Lesson of Hybrid Decade], ed. Hanna Shelest, Cabinet of Ministers of Ukraine, 22 February 2019, https://www.kmu.gov.ua/ua/news/opublikovane-doslidzhennya-za-rezultatami-mizhnarodnoyi-konferenciyi-uroki-gibridnogo-desyatilittya-shcho-treba-znati-dlya-uspishnogo-ruhu-vpered.

[37] E.g.: 'US Accuses Russia of Unsafe Aerial Intercept over Black Sea', *Voice of America*, 7 September 2016, https://www.voanews.com/a/us-accuses-rusia-aerial-intercept-black-sea/3497831.html.

The so-called War of exercises comprised several elements. Regular close of the different sea areas for real or 'fake' exercises has been happening regularly. In 2019–20, there were times when 25 per cent of the Black Sea was closed by Russian notifications at the same time.[38] While not violating international law, it violated a sea practice, as often, those areas were closed for several months. The second element was overlapping zones of exercises, so disturbing Ukrainian or international activities. For example, in 2019, the Sea Breeze organizers needed to change the exercises scenario due to such intentional overlap.[39] Third was deploying excessive forces to the Black Sea under the pretext of exercises. This happened in April 2021,[40] when ten additional ships arrived but were not withdrawn after the respective announcement.

Blockade of the navigation routes happened regularly and continues to be a problem. This included a blockade of the commercial navigation routes under the pretext of exercises[41] or attempts to monopolize the Sea of Azov, by regular inspections of the ships going to the Ukrainian ports, preventing them from passing the Kerch Strait,[42] and definitely a blockade of the Ukrainian Black Sea ports since February 2022, that involved not only a military component as the Grain Deal negotiations demonstrated.

Identification of specific vulnerabilities

The past ten years significantly changed the vulnerabilities presented by the Ukrainian state and society to be under the malign Russian influence. Traditionally the Russian influence has concentrated on the existing social and economic weaknesses and dependencies of Ukraine, as well as democratic pluralism that was manipulated. Soviet nostalgia, old political connections

---

[38] Andrii Klymenko, 'The "War of Exercises" in the Black Sea: A New Very Dangerous Stage That Cannot Be Ignored', *Black Sea News*, 30 August 2020, https://www.blackseanews.net/en/read/167556.

[39] 'Navy Commander Says Scenario of Sea Breeze 2019 Changed Due to Russia's Actions', *KyivPost*, 2 July 2019, https://www.kyivpost.com/ukraine-politics/ukrainian-navy-commander-says-scenario-of-sea-breeze-2019-drills-changed-due-to-russias-actions.html.

[40] 'Росія сконцентрувала велику групу кораблів і літаків в Криму' [Russian concentrated a big group of ships and airplanes in Crimea], *BBC Ukraine*, 20 April 2021, https://www.bbc.com/ukrain ian/features-56820657.

[41] 'Держгідрографія проклала новий маршрут до портів в умовах російських навчань' [State Hydrography made a new routes to the ports due to the Russian exercises], *Militarnyy*, 15 February 2022, https://mil.in.ua/uk/news/derzhgidrografiya-proklala-novyj-marshrut-do-portiv-v-umovah-rosijskyh-navchan/.

[42] 'The Duration of Artificial Delays of Vessels in the Kerch Strait. The Monitoring for January-April 2021', *Black Sea News*, 15 May 2021, https://www.blackseanews.net/en/read/176324.

of elites and military, use of the Russian language, post-Soviet economic ties, energy dependency, oligarchic and political control over media – all these were utilized.

A specific vulnerability that Russia continue to utilize in the hybrid warfare against Ukraine are the issues of language and ethnic minorities' right, nostalgia for the Soviet-time connections, anti-Western sentiments, religious influence and promotion of the so-called traditional values. Economic ties and interests also remain among the weak spots. The information sphere, despite all restrictions and efforts, still is a risky zone because, during the war, most of the communications moved to social networks, which allowed the easier and less controlled spread of information, as well as a certain level of anonymity.

Playing on the ground of the third states and international organizations, especially where Ukraine lacks its diplomatic representation or political contacts, is gaining its priority for Moscow.

The state's capacity for agency and its room for manoeuvre in the context of Russia's hybrid strategy

Since 2014, when the Russian threat was finally acknowledged at the governmental level, all strategic documents, starting from the National Security Strategy to particular documents like Cyber Security Strategy, encompass the elements of preventing hybrid threats. In many cases, this strategic recognition led to the plans' elaboration and implementation of certain decisions to minimize such effects. At the same time, it was clear that it is impossible to be absolutely ready for any new threat, so the main focus was shifted to building a national resilience system. Still, in some spheres, particular decisions were made.

Since 2014, Ukraine has been aiming for full energy independence from Russia, primarily in the gas sphere. Since 2016 Ukraine has stopped buying Russian gas, diversified its suppliers and prioritized EU companies.[43] De-monopolization of the Ukrainian market, as well as unbundling of the domestic market, facilitated the process.

The biggest steps were made in the information sphere. First was a prohibition of the information products from the aggressor state. It started with the mass media, most of the programs and stations were prohibited on

---

[43] 'П'ять років енергетичної незалежності України' [Five years of Ukraine energy independence], *Cencor*, 2020, https://projects.censor.net/energyfreedom/.

the basis of the 'violation of territorial integrity of Ukraine' norm, meaning that they stated Crimea as a Russian Federation territory or due to the promotion of the state-aggressor Russia. Gradually it covered many Russian movies and entertainment programs, due to the same reasons, among others. Second was a legislation which made all media demonstrate their final beneficiary, so transparency in ownership. Last but not least, in February 2021, the National Security and Defence Council of Ukraine adopted a decision by which the three most popular pro-Russian TV channels appeared under the sanctions and were closed, including their YouTube versions. Other channels were sanctioned in 2022.

The significant facilitation in fighting hybrid warfare in the information sphere had non-governmental organizations and experts' community. The biggest anti-propaganda and anti-fake news projects/organizations are StopFake,[44] Internews (UkraineWorld),[45] and Hybrid Warfare Analytical Group.[46] In 2021 the government created a Centre for Countering Disinformation[47] under the National Security Council and the Centre of Strategic Communications and Information Security[48] under the Ministry of Culture and Information Policy which became especially instrumental since the beginning of the full-fledged war in 2022 with their daily debunking of Russian propaganda.

The third particular sphere for governmental efforts became a cyber domain. Ukraine adopted its first Cybersecurity Strategy in 2016,[49] as a result of the acknowledged threats in the cyber domain, after long experts' discussions about whether it should be a single document covering information and cyberspace or two different ones. As a result, two separate documents have been elaborated. For the first time, it was stated that 'cyberspace is transforming in a separate, in line with "Land", "Air", "Sea" and "Space", a sphere of the combat actions, where more and more actively the respectful units of the military forces of leading states are operating'. Moreover, it was stated that the 'economic, scientific, information, public services sphere, military and transport complexes, the infrastructure of electronic communications, security sector of Ukraine are becoming increasingly vulnerable for the intelligence and subversive activities of foreign intelligence services in cyberspace'.

---

[44] StopFake, https://www.stopfake.org/en/main/.
[45] UkraineWorld, https://ukraineworld.org/articles/infowatch.
[46] Hybrid Warfare Analytical Group, https://uacrisis.org/en/hwag.
[47] Center for Countering Disinformation, https://cpd.gov.ua/.
[48] Center of Strategic Communications and Information Security, https://spravdi.gov.ua/en/.
[49] Cyber Security Strategy of Ukraine, Order of the President of Ukraine, 15 March 2016, https://zakon.rada.gov.ua/laws/show/96/2016#Text.

In May 2021, a new version of the Cybersecurity Strategy[50] was adopted. Over there, the authors declare, 'Cyberspace, together with other physical spaces, is considered as one of the important theatres of military actions, so the capability of the state to protect national interests within it are considered as an important part of the cybersecurity'. Moreover, the strategy emphasizes that 'the Russian Federation actively implements a concept of the information combat, which is based on the symbiosis of combat actions in the cyberspace and information operations, mechanisms of which are actively used in hybrid warfare against Ukraine. … Such a destructive activity creates a real threat of cyber terrorism acts and cyber-sabotage against national information infrastructure.' De facto, Ukraine is defining its priorities for cybersecurity as developing capacities for deterrence and defence in cyberspace, resilience building and cooperation, including an international one.

Strong cooperation with NATO through the NATO Trust Fund on Cybersecurity and with the individual member states allowed the creation of a system of early warning and rapid reaction to cyber threats to improve responsible staff skills and physical networks.

Lessons learned from Ukraine

While the 'soft' component of the Russian hybrid warfare against Ukraine has decreased since military actions started in February 2022, as all attention switched to military warfare, many of the hybrid instruments remained relevant. The main lessons from Ukraine can be learned both at tactical and strategic levels.

In addition to military action to gain physical control over the territory, Russia's malign influence (hybrid) tactics have included undermining Ukrainian sovereignty, damaging the international coalition against Russian aggression, frustrating peace efforts (before 2014) and interfering in domestic affairs. Traditional energy and cybersecurity threats always have been accompanied by strong information campaigns.

At the strategic level, building a national resilience system can help with preventing information and economic effect, as well as limiting energy

---

[50] Cyber Security Strategy of Ukraine (2021–5), National Security and Defence Council, 14 May 2021, https://www.rnbo.gov.ua/files/2021/STRATEGIYA%20KYBERBEZPEKI/proekt%20strategii_k yberbezpeki_Ukr.pdf.

dependency and increasing cybersecurity. A clear understanding of possible threats, despite the level of their probability, is important, as neglect can lead to the weaknesses that Russia prefers to amplify or utilize. Understanding the weaknesses, including those perceived as democratic process strengths, should become an important step in preparation for possible hybrid attacks.

Significant attention to media ownership, investments in strategic industries and sponsorship of political parties and groups should become a priority of the security services. In many spheres, the Kremlin plays the long game, thus building the basis that can be used when the momentum comes.

Ukraine became a unique case of hybrid warfare as it encompasses all known methods of malign influence at once. Moreover, it is a clear example of the hybridity of influence when, in different periods, military and non-military methods took the lead, but both constantly remained on the agenda. The threat of the forces' use and the creation of the image of Russia as a great military and nuclear power was an important element in pushing other narratives or making the Ukrainian side to take certain decisions. This military threat, or the 'threat of escalation' remains one of the tops in the Russian arsenal against further support from international partners.

Bibliography

Al mayadeen (2022), 'Ukraine Sells Weapons on Black Market Due to Limited Ability to Use', *Al mayadeen,* 7 July, https://english.almayadeen.net/news/politics/ukraine-sells-weapons-on-black-market-due-to-limited-ability (accessed 16 November 2023).

Bateman, T. (2021), 'HMS Defender: AIS Spoofing Is Opening Up a New Front in the War on Reality', *Euronews*, 28 June. Available online: https://www.euronews.com/next/2021/06/28/hms-defender-ais-spoofing-is-opening-up-a-new-front-in-the-war-on-reality (accessed 16 November 2023).

Bateman, T. (2022), 'Ukraine War: Meta Takes Down Russia-Based Disinformation Network Targeting Ukrainian Social Media', *Euronews*, 28 February. Available online: https://www.euronews.com/next/2022/02/28/ukraine-war-meta-takes-down-russia-based-disinformation-network-targeting-ukrainian-social (accessed 16 November 2023).

BBC Ukraine (2021), 'Росія сконцентрувала велику групу кораблів і літаків в Криму'. [Russian concentrated a big group of ships and airplanes in Crimea], *BBC Ukraine*, 20 April. Available online: https://www.bbc.com/ukrainian/features-56820657 (accessed 16 November 2023).

Black Sea News (2021), 'The Duration of Artificial Delays of Vessels in the Kerch Strait. The Monitoring for January-April 2021', *Black Sea News*, 15 May.

Available online: https://www.blackseanews.net/en/read/176324 (accessed 16 November 2023).

Borogan, I., and A. Soldatov (2023), 'Putin's Security Forces Find God', *CEPA*, 9 February. Available online: https://cepa.org/article/putins-security-forces-find-god/ (accessed 16 November 2023).

Buchanan B., and M. Sulmeyer (2016), 'Russia and Cyber Operations: Challenges and Opportunities for the Next U.S. Administration', *Carnegie Endowment for International Peace*, 16 December. Available online: https://carnegieendowm ent.org/2016/12/13/russia-and-cyber-operations-challenges-and-opportunit ies-for-next-u.s.-administration-pub-66433 (accessed 16 November 2023).

Burdyga, I. (2023), 'These Are the Men Russia Wanted to Put in Charge of Ukraine', *Open Democracy*, 4 March. Available online: https://www.opendemocracy.net/en/ odr/ukraine-russia-opposition-platform-for-life-medvedchuk-boiko/ (accessed 16 November 2023).

Censor (2016), ' "DPR" Offers Special View of Amendments to Ukrainian Constitution', *Censor*, 27 January. Available at http://en.censor.net.ua/n371293 (accessed 16 November 2023).

Censor (2020), 'П'ять років енергетичної незалежності України' [Five years of Ukraine energy independence], *Censor*, 2020. Available online: https://projects.cen sor.net/energyfreedom/ (accessed 16 November 2023).

Center for Countering Disinformation. Available online: https://cpd.gov.ua/ (accessed 16 November 2023).

Center of Strategic Communications and Information Security. Available online: https://spravdi.gov.ua/en/ (accessed 16 November 2023).

CERT-UA (2021), 'Зафіксовано атаку на державні органи України з використанням веб-сайту, що імітує Офіційне інтернет-представництво Президента України' [An attack on the Ukraine's govermental website was identified], *CERT-UA*, 13 July. Available online: https://cert.gov.ua/article/13156 (accessed 16 November 2023).

Fornusek, M. (2023), 'Priest of Moscow-Linked Church Sentenced to 15 Years for Spying for Russia', *The Kyiv Independent*, 25 October. Available online: https://kyiv independent.com/priest-of-moscow-linked-church-sentenced-to-15-years-for-spy ing-for-russia/ (accessed 16 December 2023).

Fox News (2019), 'Millions of Bulgarians' Personal Data Backed; Russian Link Suspected', *Fox News*, 16 July. Available online: https://www.foxnews.com/world/ millions-of-bulgarians-hacked-russian-tie-suspected (accessed 16 November 2023).

Greenberg, A. (2017), 'Petya Ransomware Epidemic May Be Spillover from Cyberwar', *Wired*, 28 June. Available online: https://www.wired.com/story/petya-ransomware-ukraine/ (accessed 16 November 2023).

Hvylya (2021), 'В СНБО рассказали о кибератаках России из-за санкций' [In National Security Council they told about the cyberattacks because of sanctions],

Hvylya, 16 March. Available online: https://hvylya.net/news/227026-v-snbo-rasskaz ali-o-kiberatakah-rossii-iz-za-sankciy (accessed 30 December 2023).

Hybrid Warfare Analytical Group. Available online: https://uacrisis.org/en/hwag (accessed 16 November 2023).

112 International (2019), 'Putin Confirms Agreements Reached by Medvedchuk and Boyko in Moscow', *112 International*, 29 April. Available online: https://112.intern ational/russia/putin-confirms-agreements-reached-by-medvedchuk-and-boyko-in-moscow-39297.html.

KIIS (2020), 'Оцінка радянського минулого: травень 2020 року' [Perception of the Soviet past, May 2020], *KIIS*, 22 June. Available online: https://www.kiis.com. ua/?lang=ukr&cat=reports&id=950&page=1&t=3 (accessed 16 November 2023).

Klitina, A. (2022), 'Lawmakers from Opposition Platform: For Life Have Fled or Regrouped', *Kyiv Post*, 25 April. Available online: https://www.kyivpost.com/ post/6910 (accessed 16 November 2023).

Klymenko, A. (2020), 'The "War of Exercises" in the Black Sea: A New Very Dangerous Stage That Cannot Be Ignored', *Black Sea News*, 30 August. Available online: https:// www.blackseanews.net/en/read/167556 (accessed 16 November 2023).

Kyiv Post (2019), 'Navy Commander Says Scenario of Sea Breeze 2019 Changed Due to Russia's Actions', *Kyiv Post*, 2 July. Available online: https://www.kyivpost.com/ukra ine-politics/ukrainian-navy-commander-says-scenario-of-sea-breeze-2019-drills-changed-due-to-russias-actions.html (accessed 16 November 2023).

Meyers, A. (2016), 'Cyber Skirmish: Russia v. Turkey', *Crowdstrike*, 13 April. Available online: https://www.crowdstrike.com/blog/cyber-skirmish-russia-v-turkey/ (accessed 16 November 2023).

Militarnyy (2022), 'Держгідрографія проклала новий маршрут до портів в умовах російських навчань' [State Hydrography made a new routes to the ports due to the Russian exercises], *Militarnyy*, 15 February. Available online: https://mil.in.ua/uk/ news/derzhgidrografiya-proklala-novyj-marshrut-do-portiv-v-umovah-rosijskyh-navchan/ (accessed 16 November 2023).

National Security and Defence Council (2021), Cyber Security Strategy of Ukraine (2021–2025), *National Security and Defence Council*, 14 May. Available online: https://www.rnbo.gov.ua/files/2021/STRATEGIYA%20KYBERBEZPEKI/pro ekt%20strategii_kyberbezpeki_Ukr.pdf (accessed 16 November 2023).

Parsons, E., and M. Raff (2019), 'Understanding the Cyber Threat from Russia', *F-Secure*, March. Available online: https://www.f-secure.com/en/consulting/our-thinking/ understanding-the-cyber-threat-from-russia (accessed 16 November 2023).

Radio Free (2022), 'Russia Says It's Now Broadcasting throughout Ukraine's Kherson Region', *Radio Free*, 21 June. Available online: https://www.rferl.org/a/russia-broad casting-ukraine-kherson/31907822.html (accessed 16 November 2023).

Reuters (2022), 'Ukraine Detains Senior Public Figures Suspected of Spying for Russia', *Reuters*, 21 June. Available online: https://www.reuters.com/world/europe/ukra

ine-detains-senior-public-figures-suspected-spying-russia-2022-06-21/ (accessed 16 November 2023).

RISU (2022), 'У нещодавно окупованому Лимані родина священика УПЦ МП вітала хлібом-сіллю окупантів' [In recently occupied Liman, a family of the priest welcomed the occupants], *RISU*, 1 June. Available online: https://risu.ua/u-neshc hodavno-okupovanomu-limani-rodina-svyashchenika-upc-mp-vitala-hlibom-sil lyu-okupantiv_n129759 (accessed 16 November 2023).

Security Services of Ukraine (2021), 'Donbas: SBU Blocks Unauthorized Russia's Interference in Joint Forces Operation Units', *Security Services of Ukraine*, 19 April 2021. Available online: https://ssu.gov.ua/en/novyny/sbu-zablokuvala-nesanktsi onovane-vtruchannia-v-radiochastoty-pidrozdiliv-oos-na-donbasi (accessed 16 November 2023).

Security Services of Ukraine (2021), 'Russia Increases Number of Cyber-Attacks against Ukraine, Illya Vityuk, Security Services of Ukraine', *Security Services of Ukraine*, 13 May. Available online: https://ssu.gov.ua/en/novyny/na-foni-kontsen tratsii-viisk-bilia-kordoniv-rf-zbilshyla-kilkist-kiberatak-na-ukrainu-illia-vitiuk (accessed 16 November 2023).

Security Services of Ukraine (2021), 'SBU Neutralizes New Group of Online Agents Coordinated from Russia', *Security Services of Ukraine*, 30 July. Available online: https://ssu.gov.ua/en/novyny/sbu-neitralizuvala-novu-hrupu-internetahen tiv-yakykh-koordynuvaly-z-rf (accessed 16 November 2023).

Security Services of Ukraine (2021), 'SBU Opposes Hostile Information Operations', *Security Services of Ukraine*, 30 April. Available online: https://ssu.gov.ua/en/nov yny/sbu-protydiie-vorozhym-informatsiinym-operatsiiam-vykryto-merezhu-int ernetahitatoriv-na-poshyrenni-antykonstytutsiinykh-zaklykiv-naperedodni-travnev ykh-sviat (accessed 16 November 2023).

Security Services of Ukraine (2021), 'SBU: 76 Cyber-Attacks Hit Ukrainian Authorities in June, Security Services of Ukraine', *Security Services of Ukraine*, 9 July. Available online: https://ssu.gov.ua/en/novyny/u-chervni-sbu-zablokuvala-ponad-70-kibera tak-na-ukrainski-orhany-vlady (accessed 16 November 2023).

Security Services of Ukraine (2021), 'SBU: 1,000 Cyber-Attacks Thwarted in Six Months, Security Services of Ukraine', *Security Services of Ukraine*, 21 July. Available online: https://ssu.gov.ua/en/novyny/za-piv-roku-sbu-neitralizuvala-ponad-1-tys-kiberatak-na-derzhavni-resursy (accessed 16 November 2023).

Shelest, H. (2018), 'Imposed State-Building', *Southeastern Europe*, 42 (3): 327–49.

Shelest, H. (2019), 'Уроки гібридного десятиліття: що треба знати для успішного руху вперед' [Lesson of Hybrid Decade], ed. Hanna Shelest, Cabinet of Ministers of Ukraine, 22 February. Available online: https://www.kmu.gov.ua/ua/news/opubl ikovane-doslidzhennya-za-rezultatami-mizhnarodnoyi-konferenciyi-uroki-gibridn ogo-desyatilittya-shcho-treba-znati-dlya-uspishnogo-ruhu-vpered (accessed 16 November 2023).

Slidstvo Info (2020), 'Церква поза політикою»: як єпископи РПЦ в Україні співпрацюють з бойовиками Донбасу та окупаційною владою Криму' [Church is out of politics, how bishops cooperate with fighters in Donbas], *Slidstvo Info*, 28 July, https://www.slidstvo.info/articles/tserkva-poza-politykoyu-yak-yepysk opy-rpts-v-ukrayini-spivpratsyuyut-z-bojovykamy-donbasu-ta-okupatsijnoyu-vlad oyu-krymu/ (accessed 16 November 2023).

StopFake. Available online: https://www.stopfake.org/en/main/ (accessed 16 November 2023).

Stulík, D. (2020), 'Russian Economic Interference in Europe: Case Studies of Germany, Ukraine, Poland, Austria and the Czech Republic', European Values Center for Security Policy. Available online: https://europeanvalues.cz/en/russian-econo mic-interference-in-europe-case-studies-of-germany-ukraine-poland-aust ria-and-the-czech-republic/ (accessed 16 November 2023).

Synodal Committee for Interaction with Cossacks (2023). Available online: https:// www.skvk.org (accessed 16 November 2023).

Telishevska, S. (2022), 'The Security Service of Ukraine Has Published a List of 100 Pseudo-Ukrainian Telegram Channels, Which Controlled by Russia', *Babel,* 15 July. Available online: https://babel.ua/en/news/81511-the-security-service-of-ukra ine-has-published-a-list-of-100-pseudo-ukrainian-telegram-channels-which-control led-by-russia (accessed 16 November 2023).

Tyshchenko, K. (2024), 'Russian Hackers Infiltrated Kyivstar System in May 2023 or Earlier – Security Service of Ukraine', *Ukrainska Pravda*, 04 January. Available online: https://www.pravda.com.ua/eng/news/2024/01/4/7435792/ (accessed 15 January 2024).

UkraineWorld (n.d.). Available online: https://ukraineworld.org/articles/infowatch (accessed 16 November 2023).

UNIAN (2007), 'Акция протеста против учений Си Бриз в Одессе' [Protests against Sea Breeze in Odessa], *UNIAN*, 10 July. Available online: https://www.unian.net/ politics/53230-aktsiya-protesta-protiv-ucheniy-si-briz-v-odesse-10-foto.html (accessed 16 November 2023).

Verkhovna Rada of Ukraine (2016), Cyber Security Strategy of Ukraine, Order of the President of Ukraine, 15 March. Available online: https://zakon.rada.gov.ua/laws/ show/96/2016#Text (accessed 16 November 2023).

Voice of America (2016), 'US Accuses Russia of Unsafe Aerial Intercept over Black Sea', *Voice of America*, 7 September. Available online: https://www.voanews. com/a/us-accuses-rusia-aerial-intercept-black-sea/3497831.html (accessed 16 November 2023).

3

Does Russia need a hybrid Belarus policy?

Grigory Ioffe

Belarus is markedly different from other successor states of the Soviet Union. By expressing doubt regarding relevancy of hybrid policy framework to Russia's Belarus policy this chapter explores one aspect of that difference. The doubt rests on two foundations, one of which is Belarus's major vulnerability vis-à-vis Russia, the meaning and implications of which are discussed below. The second foundation is the West's own Belarus policy that drives the already strong dependency on Russia to the level that has no precedent in post-Soviet history.

I see 'hybrid' as an imprecise synonym of 'composite'; more exactly, composed of heterogeneous elements. So, if hybrid is an adjective describing policy, then some sort of elements that might add up to a policy must predate hybridization. I see policy as a course of action adopted and pursued by a government or a set of actions and procedures conforming to or considered with reference to prudence or expediency. These definitions allow me to suggest that up until 2019, Russia did not have a Belarus policy. What took its place? A general expression of friendliness with a tinge of condescension; no perception of being abroad when visiting Belarus from Russia; a belief that Belarus will always stay in Russia's orbit; a very close cooperation in the military and security areas and fairly close cooperation in manufacturing – just because the existing production chains, military infrastructure of Belarus, and its institutions of higher learning constitute the legacy of the Soviet Union's last three decades. Also available were an aggressive stance of Russian oligarchs salivating at the prospect of obtaining Belarusian assets; willingness to penalize Belarus as an intractable friend by suspending its food exports to the benefit of Russian competitors and at times even terminating natural gas supply to make Minsk pay its debts. However, these and other phenomena hardly come together as a policy. And neither does absolute dominance of the Russian language in Belarus or the fact that many high-level Belarusian officials work for Russian companies after their tenure in Minsk gets terminated. Multiple examples include at least two former prime ministers, two former ministers of foreign affairs, one chairman of the KGB and many others.

If there is a central element in all of the above, it is probably a lasting and unassailable belief that Belarus will always be at one with Russia. This belief has been dominant among Russia's ruling elite and in Russian society. However, this and other phenomena do not constitute a policy as they have little, if anything, to do with any integrated decision-making body that the above-mentioned understanding of policy presumes. Rather, they derive from lasting coexistence in the same polities: first, in the Russian Empire and then in the Soviet Union. Moreover, in order to succeed, most attempts to strengthen Minsk–Moscow ties or to receive financial aid have always required face-to-face communication at the highest level, that is, between two presidents. Without their nod, such attempts used to fail. For example, the two countries have not been able to get rid of roaming charges in mobile telecommunication for about ten years. And that is despite a commitment to do so first expressed in 2013 and endorsed by the chairperson of Russia's Parliament's upper chamber in 2017. They have finally succeeded only on 1 June 2022.

A course of actions and procedures most closely resembling a policy began to materialize only in 2019, when Belarus and Russia negotiated twenty-eight Union State programmes. Minsk resisted the endorsement of these programmes but had to comply in November 2021, four months before the start of Russia's war against Ukraine. Because of Western sectoral sanctions, Minsk lost a room for manoeuvre it used to have and could not resist signing those programmes any longer.

Why is it then that Minsk and Moscow have maintained close ties after the Soviet Union's break-up and up until recently even in the absence of Belarus policy on Russia's part?

Sheer inertia is unlikely because political and economic systems in both countries, especially in Belarus, entail substantial contribution of manual steering. One cannot possibly explain this by Russia's imperialist aspirations either, however tempting this line of reasoning may be. Because on several occasions, Moscow effectively pushed Minsk away in no uncertain terms. It did so back in 1999, when Russia's then deputy prime minister Anatoly Chubais thwarted the attempt to crown the union state with a joint administration. Moscow repelled Minsk yet again in 2002 when Russia's new president Vladimir Putin suggested that for Belarus to enjoy Russia's domestic oil and gas prices, Belarus's oblasts (civil divisions) should just join the Russian Federation one by one. The flow of Russia's natural gas into Belarus was first terminated in November 2002, then in February 2004; and in December 2006, Moscow threatened to do the same. Acrimonious episodes continued with bewildering regularity and culminated in the summer of 2020, when many Russian mercenaries (the members of the so-called Wagner group) were apprehended in Minsk on suspicion of preparing a Moscow-engineered coup in the Belarusian capital.

Belarus's major vulnerability vis-à-vis Russia

But if all of these outbursts of Belarus's rejection by Russia have not resulted in permanent detachment of the former from the latter, then, logically speaking, we must take a close look at some of Belarus's own vulnerabilities vis-à-vis its powerful eastern neighbour. What are they?

First, one may recall that prior to 2002–3, a solid majority of Belarusians opted for unification with Russia,[1] In June 1999, 60 per cent did.[2] Later on, Belarusians got used to statehood and began to appreciate it. Still, the April 2020 survey conducted by the Belarusian Analytic Workroom headed by the opposition-minded sociologist Andrei Vardomatsky exposed a critical facet of Belarus's vulnerability. When asked whether they were ready 'to preserve the sovereignty of Belarus even at the cost of lowering the living standards of citizens', only 24.9 per cent of respondents answered positively. However, maintaining the standard of living even at the cost of giving up sovereignty was supported by 51.6 per cent.[3] It appeared that only a quarter of Belarusians considered sovereignty an unconditional value worthy of defending. Obtained just four months before the post-election protests in Minsk, this result echoes those drawn from surveys in 2010 and 2013[4] and flies in the face of claims by the 2020 protest movement sympathizers that they represented the entire Belarusian society or much of it.

During my many trips to Minsk, I saw that Russian TV channels were watched more frequently in Belarusian homes than local channels. In some

[1] Grigory Ioffe, *Understanding Belarus and How Western Foreign Policy Misses the Mark* (Lanham, MD: Rowman and Littlefield, 2008), pp. 79, 235.
[2] 'Khotiat li belorusy v Rossiyu', *Novosti NISEPI*, #3 (13), September 1999; http://www.iiseps. org/?p=3125.
[3] Grigory Ioffe, 'Belarus: Elections and Sovereignty', *Eurasia Daily Monitor* 17, no. 111, https://jamest own.org/program/belarus-elections-and-sovereignty/.
[4] Denis Melyantsov and Elena Artiomenko, 'Geopoliticheskiye Predpochteniya Belorusov', *BISS*, Minsk, 19 April 2013, http://www.baltic-course.com/rus/_analytics/?doc=73630.

cases, satellite dishes that bundled together Russian and some European channels were available without Belarusian TV channels at all available in those bundles. When I asked why this is the case – after all, you live here, the responses ranged from 'Belarusian channels are parochial' to 'those channels' producers are unprofessional' and the like.

Last but not least, Russian is absolutely dominant as the language of mutual communication, including in the northwestern part of Belarus, which in terms of non-linguistic elements of culture, is most distant from Russia because of abundance of Roman Catholics. *Trasianka*, a peculiar mixture of Russian and Belarusian, is available too, but first, it is receding and second, the today's *trasianka* is overwhelmingly Russian with perhaps a dozen or so words from the Belarusian vocabulary and with a solid contribution of Belarusian phonetics. For quite some time Vladimir Putin has been more popular in Belarus than Lukashenka.[5] All in all, it does not seem like quite a few Belarusians cut the umbilical cord connecting them to Mother Russia. That some did is a valid observation, too, but they are by no means a majority.

More in-depth analysis shows Belarusians suffer from what may be called a split identity disorder. There are indeed two historical narratives or two versions of national memory, the Russia-centric (or neo-Soviet) version and the Westernizing one. Their crucial differences boil down to the interpretations of the Second World War and of the antecedents of Belarus as a national community. For the Westernizers, the Grand Duchy of Lithuania and the Belarusian People's Republic proclaimed in 1918 under German military occupation are the major hallmarks of the Belarusian political history. For the Russia-centric version, the Belarusian Soviet Socialist Republic is the first-ever Belarusian polity, and the partisan movement during the Second World War is seen as the expression of the formative collective effort and feat of ethnic Belarusians en masse. By most accounts, the Russo-centric version holds sway over most Belarusians while three efforts of Belarusian Westernizers to undermine its dominance (in 1924–9; 1943–4; and in 1992–5) have failed.[6]

Even when the war between Russia and Ukraine started, with the overwhelming majority of Belarusians unwilling to take part in it, a near-equilibrium was recorded between supporters of Russia and supporters of Ukraine. On 7 October 2022, the head of the Belarusian Analytical Workroom,

---

[5] Denis Lavnikevich, 'Belorusy Vybirayut Putina', *Gazeta.ru*, 21 May 2013, https://www.gazeta.ru/polit ics/2017/05/21_a_10684145.shtml.
[6] Grigory Ioffe, 'Split Identity and a Tug-of-War for Belarus's Memory', *Jamestown Foundation*, 20 December 2019, https://jamestown.org/program/84916/.

Andrei Vardamatsky, Belarus's most seasoned active sociologist, now in exile in Poland, shared the results of his September 2022 telephone survey. According to Vardamatsky, in May 2022, 50.3 per cent of Belarusian respondents sympathized with Ukraine, whereas in September 2022 just 33.9 per cent did. Also in May, 21.1 per cent of respondents sympathized with Russia, whereas in September, 32 per cent did. 'This data bleakly speaks for itself', concluded the researcher.[7]

In-person polling in Belarus by opposition-minded sociologists has been taboo since at least early 2020. At the beginning of July 2022, the results of two national surveys, both using indirect polling techniques, were publicized: an online survey conducted in June 2022 by the Chatham House and a mid-May 2022 telephone survey conducted by Belarusian Analytical Workroom.[8] Despite different polling techniques, the results have a lot in common. Thus, in both cases, most respondents (85 per cent and 85.1 per cent) would *not* like the Belarusian army to join Russia's military operation in Ukraine.

Additionally, on the issue of geopolitical preferences – that is the choice between the European Union and Russia – the advantage goes to Russia, according to both surveys. Moreover, according to Chatham House, the pull of both Russia and the European Bloc has increased (i.e. Belarusians became even more geopolitically polarized), but willingness to integrate with the Kremlin increased slightly more. Thus, in June 2022, 37 per cent of those polled by Chatham House preferred Belarus's union with Russia, whereas in September 2020, only 27 per cent did; the numbers for EU support are 9 per cent in 2020 and 18 per cent in 2022.[9]

Rygor Astapenia explained a seeming contradiction typical for many Belarusians who oppose Russia's war, on the one hand, but endorse union with Russia, on the other: 'For many Belarusians, Russia is part of their identity and their culture. It is therefore difficult to reject them even under the influence of strong shocks' caused by the unwelcome war. Yury Drakakhrust of Radio Free Europe/Radio Liberty shares Astapenia's view: 'In our everyday life, we may often condemn the act or behavior of a person close to us, be that a relative or friend. But does this undermine closeness, do we necessarily break off relations with such a person? Not necessarily. The same is true in relations between peoples.'[10]

[7] 'Ranei Nam Raseya Byla Siabrem, a Taper Tam Putin', *Svaboda*, 7 October 2022, https://www.svaboda.org/a/32068637.html.

[8] 'Chto Dumayut Belorusy o Voine', *YouTube*, 6 July 2022, https://www.youtube.com/watch?v=ralXfuzx7eE.

[9] Yury Drakakhrust, 'Tyya Nemnogiya, Khto Vystupaye Za Belarus ...', *Svaboda*, 7 July 2022, https://www.svaboda.org/a/31930149.html.

[10] 'Kak Belorusy i Ukraintsy Proshchayut Vinovatykh', *Zerkalo*, 7 July 2022, https://news.zerkalo.io/economics/17448.html?c.

So, the fact that Belarusian identity is half-baked, split and is not by any means detached from Russian identity is the major Belarus's vulnerability, which in that capacity, arguably outweighs just economic dependency on Russia. If and when you happen to acknowledge this vulnerability in presence of the activists of the Westernizing group, they would get offended and affix to you a label of a Russian-world sympathizer. But that is because those feeling offended genuinely believe they have the exclusive right to speak on behalf of Belarusians at large, whereas people not sharing their views are either intellectually immature or harbour treasonous ideas or both. That assurance, however, belies the fact that Westernizers have never ever commanded the majority in Belarus.

Belarus's economic dependency on Russia

Belarus' industrial spurt began with post-war reconstruction. The newly obtained cordon sanitaire of satellite states along the western border of the Soviet Union changed Moscow's perception of Belarus' location. It was no longer vulnerable. Belarus was now the locus of the major transit routes linking Russia with East-Central Europe. Later on, the significance of these routes increased even more, as the Soviet Union began to sell its oil and gas to the West, receiving consumer goods and food in return. From the late 1950s on, Belarus emerged as one of the major Soviet manufacturing regions, emphasizing tractors, heavy trucks, oil processing, metal-cutting lathes, synthetic fibres, TV sets, semiconductors and microchips. Much of Belarus' high-tech industry was military oriented.

Ten manufacturing giants and dozens of their smaller subsidiaries form the industrial core of Belarus. These enterprises fall into four branches: mechanical engineering, petrochemical, radio-electronic, and ferrous metallurgy. The petrochemical industry is based on two refineries: NAFTAN, based in Novopolotsk, Vitebsk region, and Mozyr NPZ in Mozyr, Gomel region. NAFTAN is the largest refinery in Europe, with a processing capacity of twenty million tons of crude oil a year, while Mozyr NPZ can process up to twelve million tons a year. The refineries are located on two different pipelines from Russia. The products of NAFTAN used to be further transported through pipelines from Novopolotsk to Ventspils suited forgasoline and diesel fuel. So, the Latvian port of Ventspils appears to be the major transshipment site for NAFTAN. The Mozyr NPZ receives crude oil from the pipeline Drouzhba; gasoline and other products are then delivered to Central Europe by tank-trucks and rail. The combined capacity of the two Belarus refineries exceeds domestic demand by a factor of three, and so export has been the major function of those refineries from the outset. Several chemical plants connected to the major refineries by local pipelines operate in Novopolotsk, Polotsk, Mozyr, Mogilev and Grodno.

Belarus was frequently called the assembly line of Soviet industry. If 'Soviet' were replaced by 'Russian', the label would not lose accuracy because it has been largely from Russia that Belarus has been receiving raw materials and semi-finished products.

Only three production cycles are Belarusian in their entirety. Those pertain to food processing, forestry and, most importantly, production of potassium fertilizers. The latter is based in Soligorsk District in the Minsk region where potassium is mined.

Prior to the latest reimposition of Western sanctions on Belarus in the wake of the crackdown on the August–September 2020 post-election protests and subsequently also as a result of Belarus's participation in Russia's war against Ukraine, the share of Russia in Belarusian exports was 45 per cent, and in imports 50 per cent. Russia also consumed 80 per cent of total Belarusian agricultural exports amounting to $6 billion, a no small feat for a country with submarginal quality of soil. The European Union occupied the second (after Russia) niche. More than 18 per cent of Belarusian exports used to be to the EU and approximately one-fifth of imports used to be received from the EU.[11]

Because of the never-ending price haggling on Russian hydrocarbons and Russia-imposed temporary bans on Belarus's dairy and meat supplies, Minsk declared that its goal was to diversify international trade, with one-third of exchange accruing to each of the following three – Russia, the EU, and all the other countries combined. This goal was never achieved, but one-time purchases of crude oil in Venezuela, Azerbaijan and even in the United States were indeed undertaken. Even so, Minsk never summoned the political will to try and diminish the dependency on Russian market – in contrast to, say, Latvia, whose economic profile during the Soviet years resembled that of Belarus. Latvia as well as Estonia succeeded in reorienting their economic ties largely through massive deindustrialization, the path that Belarus has never taken, and Minsk routinely expresses pride in that it has not.

---

[11] Myfin, Vneshnayia Torgovlya Respubliki Belarus, 7 April 2021, https://myfin.by/wiki/term/vneshny aya-torgovlya-respubliki-belarus.

The Lukashenka phenomenon

It is a truism to say that Lukashenka is an authoritarian leader. Perhaps less of a truism is the notion that as a phenomenon of political culture authoritarianism is typical for societies with a deficit of horizontal social ties and of self-organization. 'If a people is not a community of citizens but a collection of inhabitants, only an authoritarian figure can accomplish something with this people.'[12] One can, of course, argue that it is the authoritarian regime itself that brings about the atomization of society. To some extent this may be true. Still, when it comes to Belarus, attributing a deficit of self-organization and trust at a grassroots level entirely to the Lukashenka rule is, arguably, a hyperbole. Lukashenka is no Stalin. Political repression in Belarus is real and harsh, but prior to 2020, only a small (comprising several hundred people) group that challenges Lukashenka's rule while being funded by foreign sources used to be targeted; most Belarusians did not feel threatened by repressions and were not by any means permeated by a paralyzing fear. Much like in Russia, a deficiency of mutual trust and self-organization does not derive from politics. The reverse is more accurate. The Russian sociologist Tatyana Vorozheikina suggested that the most important reason why Russian society craved for a strong leader – after a period of democratic idealism initiated under Perestroika – was that society became permeated with fear of itself. The public order was shattered as a result of the sudden infusion of freedom, and that was a scary outcome. The same formula would aptly describe the impressions that the Belarusian society internalized from the brief interlude with democracy in 1992–4.[13]

But if a deficit of horizontal ties that cement people into a community is the cause while authoritarianism is the effect (a cause-and-effect relationship that appears to be in full compliance with such an authority on democracy as Charles Tilly[14]), then two other factors analysed above, that is indistinct identity and economic dependency on Russia, only amplify the effect in question because they put additional emphasis on the style of leadership and order of things that would defend the fledgling polity against Russia's expansionism. In a nutshell, one must howl with the wolves!

[12] Yevgeny Babushkin, 'Andrei Konchalovsky: Moite Vymya pered Doikoi', An interview, *Snob*, 9 October 2012, https://snob.ru/selected/entry/53571/.

[13] Tatyana Vorozheikina, 'Samozashchita Kak Pervyi Shag k Solidarnosti', *Polit.Ru*, 18 August 2008, http://www.polit.ru/research/2008/08/18/vorogejkina.html.

[14] Charles Tilly, *Democracy* (Cambridge, MA: Cambridge University Press, 2007), chapter 4.

Back in 1994, the enthronement of Alexander Lukashenka was a natural response both to the deep-seated misgivings that Belarusians had about their future in the early 1990s and to a more latent call for national survival. At least initially the latter was not even a public call; rather, it manifested itself as a growing reluctance of the new political elite to be demoted back to provincial level. Be that as it may, Belarusians en masse craved a strongman, and he has come and delivered what many Belarusians wanted, to some degree altering their attitude to national independence.[15]

Alexander Baunov wrote at the height of Lukashenka's crackdown on post-election protests in mid-August 2020:

> At the beginning of his career General Franco ruled Spain as a conquered territory, towards the end – as a peaceful autocrat, relying on civilian bureaucracy ... Before our eyes, the Belarusian regime is undergoing a reverse transformation ... Now the main goal of the regime is not the preservation of the economy it inherited, not the strengthening of sovereignty, not authoritarian modernization, but the relentless persecution of bad citizens on behalf of good ones.[16]

While Baunov is certainly on target, one has to point out that 'good' and 'bad' citizens remarkably coincide with mutually antagonistic groups on two sides of the tenacious cultural divide in the Belarusian society, and that Lukashenka himself contributed to bridging the gap between them (see below) and resorted to institutionalized violence only in response to an overt challenge to his regime. This is what authoritarian leaders enjoying support of a part of society always do – a statement that does not excuse Lukashenka's wrong-doing but rather points to a de facto balance of power between those two groups in Belarusian society. Consequently, that Lukashenka retained support of one of these groups is noteworthy. Even the opposition-minded pollsters, whose samples of respondents cannot but be skewed towards the opposition-minded respondents, state that no less than 30 per cent of Belarusians continue to support Lukashenka. In the absence of any other prospective leader, this is quite a chunk of society. Just in 2017, Artyom Shraibman, the most popular opposition-minded analyst, described Lukashenka's rule as 'the most consolidated and adaptive authoritarian regime in the post-Soviet space and possibly in the entire world'. 'Belarusian

---

[15] Grigory Ioffe, *Understanding Belarus and How Western Foreign Policy Misses the Mark* (Lanham, MD: Rowman and Littlefield, 2008), chapter 5.

[16] Alexander Baunov, 'Svoyi i Chuzhiye v Belorusskom Proteste', *Moscow Carnegie Center*, 14 August 2020, https://carnegiemoscow.org/commentary/82482.

society remains largely pro-Russian, with a stable pro-European minority of 25–35%', asserted Shraibman.[17]

Resisting Russia's expansionism

Two other aspects of Lukashenka's rule are worth mentioning. First, Lukashenka is a gifted public politician who has never lost touch with however diminishing but a significant part of Belarusian electorate. His skills of a public politician have been repeatedly mentioned even by his harshest critics. Second, by way of being rooted in the Russo-centric Belarusian community, Lukashenka has been most effective in staving off Russian expansionism. During the period immediately preceding Lukashenka's enthronement, a critical mass of Belarusians imploring Russia to rescue them from economic chaos by incorporating them as five provinces into the Russian Federation was about to take shape. In the early 1990s, such appeals emanated from Belarus loud and clear, but then Lukashenka came to power, and they stopped. Subsequently, Lukashenka repelled dozens of Russian attacks on Belarus's sovereignty, ranging from arresting Russian oligarchs that used to be close to the Kremlin to an eviction of Russian ambassador who toured Belarus without advance notification and interfered in domestic affairs.

There has been no shortage of harsh statements on Lukashenka's part, like 'even Lenin and Stalin did not think of incorporating Belarus into Russia'.[18] Obviously, after Western sanctions have dramatically suppressed the freedom of Lukashenka's manoeuvre, clinging to Russia became the imperative of Belarus's economic survival. But even under such circumstances, Lukashenka contrives to stay away from most brazen adepts of Belarus's merger with Russia. Few, if any, Western observers pay attention.

For example, in September 2022, the Vitebsk Regional Administration cancelled the Vitebsk-based association named 'Russian Community' committed to nurturing Russian self-consciousness among its members and to promoting the Russian World concept.[19] And in October 2022, Ivan Kulyak, a Russian gymnast, was denied participation in the open championship of Belarus because earlier that year he was reprimanded by the ethics committee at the

---

[17] Artyom Shraibman, 'Fenomen Belorusskoi Gosudarstvennosti', *Moscow Carnegie Center*, 31 May 2017, https://carnegieendowment.org/2017/05/31/ru-pub-70099.

[18] 'Lukashenko: Dazhe Lenin i Stalin nr Dodumalis …', 21 August 2002, *News.ru*, https://www.newsru.com/world/21aug2002/lukashenko2.html.

[19] 'Vitebskiye Vlasti Likvidirovali Obshchestvennuyu Organizatsiyu, Prodvigavshuyu v Gorode Russkiq Mir', *Zerkalo*, 10 September 2022, https://news.zerkalo.io/life/21743.html.

World Cup competition in Doha, Qatar, for wearing a T-shirt with capital Z, which is a symbol of the Russian military operation in Ukraine.[20]

Moreover, just several years ago, from 2014 to 2020, Lukashenka was not merely rejecting overly close ties with Russia in the areas other than economic cooperation; he was moving toward a rapprochement with the Belarusian Westernizers, aka the opposition. This trend culminated in the three following episodes.

1. 25 March 2018: Public concert devoted to the centennial of the Belarusian People's Republic. While the open-air concert in the park attached to Minsk's Opera House was organized exclusively by opposition, the fact that the event was allowed by the authorities was a major deviation from acting solely in the interest of the Russo-centric side of the divide and of Russia itself.[21]

2. 12 May 2018: Opening of the monument to Tadeusz Kosciuszko in Merechiovshchina, Brest Oblast, the place of his birth. Symbolically, both the official green-red and the now unofficial white-red-white flags of Belarus were fluttering next to each other at that ceremony.[22]

3. 22 November 2019: Reburial of the remains of Konstanty Kalinowski in Vilnius, Lithuania, with the official Belarusian delegation headed by a vice-premier present at the event and delivering public remarks in honour of Kalinowski,[23] a leader of the 1863–4 anti-Russian uprising on Belarusian lands.

At the time of this writing (the end of 2022), all three episodes are perceived as if they took place in a different world. But that is because the imposition of Western sanctions on Minsk has more than undone the national consolidation implications of those events and literally pushed Belarus into the close embrace of Russia. But the aforementioned events did take place in reality. Moreover, the so-called soft Belarusization policy tacitly supported by the authorities resuscitated however fragile hopes for the Belarusian language eventually replacing Russian in everyday communication in Belarus. Also, the Minsk

[20] 'Rossiiskii Gimnast Zasvetilsya s Bukvoi Z …', *Zerkalo*, 19 October 2022, https://news.zerkalo.io/cel lar/24330.html.

[21] Grigory Ioffe, 'Belarus's Freedom Day: Post-Celebration Anxieties', *Eurasia Daily Monitor* 15, no. 56, 12 April 2018, https://jamestown.org/program/belaruss-freedom-day-post-celebration-anxieties/.

[22] Liubov Kasperovich, 'Asoba, yakaya abyadnala usikh', *Tut.by*, 12 May 2018, news.tut.by/ culture/592411.html.

[23] Liubov Kasperovich, 'Tysiachi liudei, BCHB flagi, ex-glava Belarusi i prezidenty: Kak proshlo perezakhoronenie Kalinovskogo', *Tut.by*, 22 November 2019, https://news.tut.by/culture/661 979.html.

Dialogue Council under the guidance of Yauhenii Preiherman organized two forums in Minsk with an abundance of Western and Russian analysts upholding Belarus's peaceful coexistence between Russia and the West. The council received financial support from Germany and organizational support from the Belarusian Ministry of foreign affairs, and Alexander Lukashenka delivered a speech at one of such events alongside such personalities as Alexander Wershbow and James Appaturai of NATO.[24]

In April 2019, a replacement of Mikhail Babich, Russia's ambassador to Minsk, captured public attention. Babich only served eight months in that position, but importantly he enjoyed the additional status of President Vladimir Putin's special envoy for the development of economic ties with Belarus. Some observers underscored the increased leverage of Minsk, if only because recalling a Russian ambassador for the officially articulated reason that Babich routinely confused Belarus with a federal district of Russia[25] was an event without a precedent. Lukashenka clearly stood in the way of such designs.

Last but not least, even the migration crisis that Minsk orchestrated in the Spring of 2021 at its border with Poland was arguably a desperate attempt to reclaim the West's attention, and seriousness with which he used to be treated as the leader of a polity separate from Russia. To some extent, the attempt worked when Angela Merkel herself telephoned Lukashenka on 15 November. However, the events that followed reinstated the West's conviction that Minsk is just a puppet state of the Kremlin. It would not be an exaggeration to claim that this conviction became a self-fulfilling prophesy.

Russia's Belarus policy is taking shape at long last

The legal basis for the Belarus–Russia reintegration is the Treaty on the Establishment of the Union State signed on 8 December 1999 by the heads of Belarus and Russia. In accordance with the treaty, Belarus and Russia have established goalposts, including the creation of a supranational governing body, single economic and customs space, common currency with a single currency-issuing centre, union-state citizenship, coordinated foreign and defence policy,

---

[24] International Forum, 'Eastern Europe: In Search of Security for All', Minsk 24 May 2018, https://presid ent.gov.by/en/events/international-forum-eastern-europe-in-search-of-security-for-all-18776.
[25] Grigory Ioffe, 'Belarus Builds Relations with Turkey as Russian Ambassador to Minsk Comes Under Fire', *Eurasia Daily Monitor* 16, no. 60, 26 April 2019.

unified legal system, coordinated social policy, security and crime control and so on. Altogether, the treaty consists of seventy-one articles.[26]

Two important observations are in order. While integration has indeed advanced in multiple areas, including mutual employment authorization and joint security arrangements, until recently it has not succeeded in several crucial areas: joint citizenship, supranational authorities on two-year rotation, common currency and a single economic space.

Back in 1999, the signing of the union treaty was even postponed from 2 April to 23 May; and two Russian officials who authored the project (Dmitry Ryurikov, Yeltsin's advisor, and Valentin Serov, a vice-premier) were fired because a certain provision of the project was identified as the way to make Lukashenka the head of the union state, if only for the time being. At that time, young, healthy and dynamic, Lukashenka was more popular than ageing and ailing Yeltsin – in Russia itself, definitely so outside Moscow and Saint Petersburg. It was Anatoly Chubais, then deputy prime minister of Russia, who uncovered that ploy and urged Yeltsin to change the project, which he did, and soon the enthronement of Vladimir Putin thwarted Lukashenka's Kremlin ambitions. Likewise, never implemented has been the idea of a common currency – in view of different weight of two national economies (Russia's GDP is thirty times larger than Belarus's and Russia's population is fifteen times larger) and due to obvious reluctance of Minsk to abide by the rules set by the Russia-based currency-issuing centre. The biggest impediment on the path of the single economic space's creation proved to be the reluctance of Russia to charge Russia's domestic prices on oil and natural gas sold to Belarus. The failure to fulfil these and some other provisions of the Union Treaty has been frequently used by critics declaring every now and then that the entire integration project was a fiasco.[27] That is certainly an exaggeration, as despite all odds, Russia and Belarus seem closer to each other on many levels than any two other world countries.

The history of developing and then endorsing twenty-eight roadmaps (renamed union state programmes) of Russia–Belarus integration is lengthy and intricate. On multiple occasions, this work was suspended.[28]

Work on the project to develop integration roadmaps intensified in 2019. This was the result of an umpteenth crisis in Belarusian-Russian relations that

---

[26] 'Dogovor o Sozdanii Soyuznogo Gosudarstva', 2023, https://soyuz.by/dogovor-o-sozdanii-soyuzn ogo-gosudarstva.

[27] Mikhail Sokolov, 'Rossiya Poglotit Belarus k 2024 Godu?', *Svoboda*, 20 September 2019, https://www.svoboda.org/a/30173067.html.

[28] 'Bylo 33 Karty, Stalo 28 Program: Kak Razvivalis Peregovory po Belorussko-Rossiiskoi Integratsii', *Zerkalo*, 10 September 2021, https://news.zerkalo.io/economics/2769.html.

came to a head by the end of 2018. Belarus was (once again) dissatisfied with Russian gas prices, restrictions on access to the Russian market for Belarusian goods and, most importantly, with the 'tax manoeuvre' in the Russian oil industry, as a result of which Belarus could lose more than $11 billion over six years. For its part, Russia stated that the solution to these issues could be found only after deepening integration within the framework of the Union State. At the very end of 2018, the then prime minister of the Russian Federation Dmitry Medvedev even stated that Belarus can count on subsidies from Russia only if the 1999 Union State Treaty with all its provisions is implemented: supranational authorities, a single currency, a common customs service and the like.

The Belarusian side reacted sharply to Medvedev's pronouncement. A few days later, Alexander Lukashenko announced that the roadmap with the aforementioned provisions had never been discussed. 'We are two sovereign states. Yes, we are promoting integration, but one that does not infringe on sovereignty of the other.'[29]

One has to point out, though, that the negotiations about the roadmaps were conducted in a secretive manner, and a complete list of all roadmaps, not to mention their content, has never been published.

It was this atmosphere of secrecy fraught with diminished Belarus's sovereignty that provoked protests in Minsk during the meetings between Lukashenka and Putin in Russia on three separate occasions in 2019. It is noteworthy that the Belarusian police acted with restraint, the actions were not dispersed, only the organizers were penalized – and then not right away. Because of this, many assumed that the protests in Minsk helped the Belarusian authorities to defend Belarus's sovereignty from Russia.

As a result, until the end of 2019, the parties did not sign anything, and work on finalizing the entire integration project was postponed until the next year. However, at the start of 2020, integration issues were back-burnered yet again both in Belarus and in Russia. In Belarus, they began to prepare for the new presidential elections, and the attention of the public quickly switched to that topic. In Russia, the authorities decided to 'amend' the Constitution and 'reset' Putin's presidential terms. According to an alternative project, Putin was expected to become president of the Union State so there would be no need to change the constitutional clause about term limits for Russia's president. In

---

[29] 'Lukashenko: My Nikakim Suverenitetom Ne Delimsya', *Belta.by*, 24 December 2019, https://www.belta.by/president/view/lukashenko-my-nikakim-suverenitetom-ne-delimsja-ni-rossija-ni-belarus-374011-2019/.

addition, the Covid-19 pandemic commenced, and that also turned the attention away from the integration issues.

Moreover, in February 2020, Alexander Lukashenko's pronouncements about Russia 'forcing' Belarus to integrate engaged attention; and in March, Belarusian foreign minister Vladimir Makei said that he sees no point in continuing to work with Russia on integration roadmaps until the issues related to deliveries of Russian oil to Belarus are resolved.[30]

The integration agenda resurfaced yet again after the presidential elections in Belarus and the largest protests and political crisis in the country's history that followed. Due to mass repressions, official Minsk ran afoul of the West, relations with which had reached an unprecedented high level just recently, in 2019–20. In the face of a serious political crisis and lacking international support, the Belarusian authorities turned to their eastern neighbour for help – and received a $1.5 billion loan. Already in September, the discussions about integration roadmaps resumed. Even so, it would take more than one year before all twenty-eight roadmaps, now renamed union state programmes, were approved on November 4, 2021.

Out of the twenty-eight programmes, the largest group, consisting of seven programmes, is devoted to finances, credit and currency; four programmes deal with sources of power, including oil, gas and nuclear energy; three programmes are devoted to information and information security; two to transport. The following areas are represented by one programme each: macroeconomics, taxes and custom duties, veterinary and phytosanitary control, agricultural policy, industrial policy, access to government procurement, consumers' protection, competition, accounting, labour, tourism, retail and public catering.

Considering that these programmes harmonize regulations within such a broad scope of activities, they indeed collectively amount to a carefully thought-out policy. This impression is enhanced by the developments in the military sphere wherein cooperation has been most advanced all along.

Military-industrial and security cooperation

This is the area wherein Russia and Belarus are truly joined at the hip. After the break-up of the Soviet Union, it did not take long for military reintegration

[30] 'Makei: Poka Net Smysla Rabotat And Dorozhnymi Kartami', *Sputnik.by*, 5 March 2020, https://sput nik.by/20200305/Makey-poka-net-smysla-rabotat-nad--dorozhnymi-kartami-1044103466.html.

between Russia and Belarus to kick in. The first bilateral agreement on military cooperation was signed as early as October 1993. Perhaps the most important area of cooperation is air defence. On 25 February 1994, the Ministries of Defence of the Russian Federation and the Republic of Belarus signed an agreement on the procedure for interaction between the combat duty forces and air defence systems.[31]

Russia owns two military bases in Belarus. One of them, in Gantsevichi (in the eastern part of Brest Oblast), is an early missile detection station whose perceived significance increased after the break-up of the Soviet Union and the subsequent loss of an identical military installation in Skrunda, Latvia. Another base is a submarine monitoring station in Vileika, Minsk Oblast (one hundred kilometres to the northwest of Minsk). Scores of Belarusian military personnel study in Russian schools, and most of the Belarusian army's ammunition is either Russian made or a product of Russia–Belarus industrial cooperation.

On 2 March 2021, the Ministries of Defence of the two countries signed a five-year strategic partnership program. On the same day, Lukashenka proposed to deploy Russian aircraft at Belarusian bases. On 5 March 2021 the ministers of defence of Russia and Belarus, Sergei Shoigu and Viktor Khrenin, agreed to establish three centres for joint training of the military.

According to the State Committee for Military Industry of the Republic of Belarus, 99 Belarusian enterprises supply 1,880 items of components and elements of weapons for 255 enterprises of the Russian military-industrial complex, and the share of supplies from Belarus is about 15 per cent.[32]

Russia and Belarus conduct regular joint military exercises. Russia's invasion of Ukraine began four days after the scheduled completion of 10–20 February 2022 drills titled *Soyuznaya Reshimost* (Allied Resolve), and Belarus's territory was repeatedly used for missile attacks on Ukraine – though just days prior to the beginning of Russia's military operations both, Belarus minister of foreign affairs and its minister of defence, solemnly claimed Ukraine would be never attacked from the north.

These claims, however, may not necessarily amount to deliberate disinformation. It may very well be that Belarusian authorities were not in

---

[31] 'Voyenno-Tekhnicheskoye Sotrudnichestvo Rossii i Belorussii', *Novyi Oboronnyi Zakaz* 6, no. 65 (2020), https://dfnc.ru/arhiv-zhurnalov/2020-6-65/voenno-tehnicheskoe-sotrudnichestvo-rossii-i-belorussii/.

[32] 'Belorusskii Eksport Vooruzhenii Rastyot: Glavnyi Pokupatel – Rossiya, *Voyenno-Politicheskoye Obozreniye*, 14 March 2019, https://web.archive.org/web/20210925143633/https://www.belvpo.com/101697.html/.

the know. In his 17 August 2023 interview to Diana Panchenko, Lukashenka confessed that prior to 22 February 2022, when Russia's assault on Ukraine began, only a general idea of such a possibility was discussed with him. While some commentators took his words at face value, others did not. However, in the discussion that followed, a well-informed opinion was shared by the Belarusian historian Siarhei Bogdan, according to which 'the analysis of the disposition, structure and head count of the Belarusian army both then [in 2021] and now indicates the absence of plans for an offensive war much more convincingly than the words of President Lukashenka'. Indeed, as Bogdan points out, by the fall of 2021, almost the entire south of Belarus had been demilitarized. When the war started, Bogdan continues, Belarus's border with Ukraine had to be covered by elite special operations units. The Belarusian army in general did not expand. Minsk delayed the formal creation of the Southern Operational Command for as long as it could. But Bogdan sees this more as a gimmick. He postulates that perhaps Russia's tactical nuclear weapons were deployed *because* the Belarusian government did not strengthen its army.

In a rebuttal to Bogdan, Yury Drakakhrust of Radio Liberty argues that the information presented by Bogdan is unknown to most. Nevertheless, Bogdan insisted on the opposite. He contended that this information was publicly available and could be found in the 2019 and 2020 yearbooks of the International Institute for Strategic Studies, as well as in the publications of Minsk Dialogue.

From this exchange, it seems that the information Bogdan cited, while available in open sources, was not widely sought after. And this seems to be the gist of the matter. Apparently, this lack of interest largely stemmed from the belief that Belarus had effectively become an extension of Russia and therefore should be treated accordingly. It seems that the joint warning from Poland, Latvia and Lithuania on 28 August – that their borders with Belarus may be closed entirely in the near future – follows the same logic. In this, Lithuania has already closed two of its six border crossings with Belarus and has voiced plans to close two more.[33]

The human aspect of close cooperation in the military sphere is important. Thus, out of nine top-ranking military leaders of Belarus, only two were born in Belarus, including one, Victor Khrenin, the current minister of defence, who, however, was raised and educated in Russia. Also, Victor Gulevich, in

---

[33] Grigory Ioffe, 'Is It Worth Isolating Belarus from the West?', *Russiapost*, 30 August 2023, https://russiapost.info/politics/isolating_belarus?fbclid=IwAR0pC1JgQxD7vEYgmZliST-QClgrvtjzmWlIUCsWy4d9tpZyLjr8qgogjvs.

charge of the General Staff of the Belarusian army, was born in Belarus but educated in Moscow and served in East Germany and in the Soviet Union's Transcaucasus Military District. Out of the remaining seven military leaders, four were born in Russia, one in Crimea, one in Georgia and one in Hungary, born into a family of a Soviet military. Valery Karbalevich of the Belarusian Service of Radio Liberty attributes the preponderance of non-Belarus-born high-ranking military officers to several factors, including what he called the janissary phenomenon whereby people without roots in their current country of service are more committed to the country's ruler than those with local roots – and constitutionally guaranteed inability to run for president due to birth outside Belarus.[34]

Discussion

In his foreword to the groundbreaking volume on hybrid warfare, Ambassador Fredrik Löjdquist suggested that a threat posed by hybrid warfare is a combination of capability, intent and opportunity that the source of that threat puts to use. The latter element, the opportunity, is 'presented by our own vulnerabilities' thanks to 'increased digitalization and dependencies but also under-investment in internal and external security'.[35] If one focuses on Russia as the source of threat and Belarus as its target, then within the Belarus–Russia duo, the opportunities presented by Belarus's vulnerabilities arguably eclipse and outweigh everything else, including capability and intent on Russia's part. Moreover, Belarus's vulnerabilities vis-à-vis Russia are more rudimentary than digitalization or under-investment in security. The most critical of these vulnerabilities is a lack of clear-cut national identity detached from that of Mother Russia. While this deficiency does not pertain to all Belarusians, it pertains to quite a few. Among other things, this means that Russia does not need hybrid warfare to subjugate Belarus, it just needs to exploit Belarus's utmost closeness to it and perhaps additionally ingratiate itself to a critical mass of Belarusians by making financial concessions to its junior ally and by doing that consistently over an extended period. It is

34 Dzmitry Gurnevich, 'Addanyya Kramlyu?', *Svaboda*, 3 November 2022, https://www.svaboda. org/a/32113573.html.

35 Fredrik Löjdquist, 'Hybrid Threats and Hybrid Warfare', in *Hybrid Warfare: Security and Asymmetric Conflict in International Relations*, ed. Mikael Weissman, Niklas Nilsson, et al. (London: I.B. Tauris, 2021), viii–ix.

noteworthy that with the beginning of Russia's onslaught on Ukraine, oil-and-gas price haggling as well as provisional bans on Belarusian food exports to Russia stopped, and Belarus partakes in Russia's import substitution programmes (meaning substituting import from the West) and receives loans with more ease than ever before.

Prior to the imposition of the European Union's sanctions on Belarus, Minsk tried to reinforce transit diversification. Thus, as of January 2020, Lukashenko held a vision whereby only 30–40 per cent of oil is purchased from Russia, whereas 30 per cent is purchased elsewhere and entering via Klaipeda and the remaining 30 per cent comes via Odesa. In 2019, rail passengers between Belarus and Lithuania amounted to 380,000, and 225,000 with Poland. Train traffic was suspended in 2020 due to the pandemic but not resumed thereafter. Following the imposition of punitive Western sanctions, Minsk eventually (in February 2021) signed an agreement with Russia about rerouting its refined oil exports to Russian ports. By early 2022, Belarus found itself in a semi-blockade maintained by all of its neighbours except Russia. Vilnius decided to stop transporting Belarusian potash through its territory altogether from 1 February 2022. The Lithuanian government acted on its own, as the US and EU sanctions did not require Vilnius to take such measures at the time. The semi-blockade and Minsk's resulting reliance on Russia compelled the Belarusian government to make unprecedented concessions to Moscow.

Pavel Matsukevich, a former Belarusian diplomat, now in exile, observed that back in 2021, prior to sanctions, Belarus's export of transportation and logistical services, a reliable measure of Belarus's connectedness to the outside world, was worth $4 billion; there were 37,000 entrepreneurs organized into 11,000 branches. Belarus has long been an open economy, with exports exceeding 60 per cent of its gross domestic product.

Now, to proceed with exports, with the Lithuanian and Latvian ports being cut off, Belarus has to use nineteen different Russian seaports and incur significant additional expenditures.[36] Whereas before the imposition of sanctions, the share of the European Union and Ukraine in Belarus's international trade exchange amounted to 40 per cent, today (autumn of 2023), it amounts to 5 per cent.[37]

---

[36] Ioffe, 'Is It Worth Isolating Belarus from the West?'.

[37] 'Posol v RF zayavil, chto dolia Yevropy I Ukrainy vo vneshnei torgovle Belorussii sostavliayet 5%', *TASS*, 9 September 2023, https://tass.ru/ekonomika/18692815.

Short of entering any reasonable discussion about the overall expediency and implications of sanctions, the point that is impossible to neglect in this specific context is that the West itself has made ties with Russia – that used to be substantial anyway – Belarus's only survival alternative. And so, if Belarus's blurred identity itself allows one to suggest that any hybrid Russia's policy towards Belarus would be redundant, Belarus's semi-blockade by the West only makes this suggestion more credible.

Besides, in Belarus, any political activity of the pro-Russian flank of the political scene has been firmly under president's thumb. This is different from Ukraine or Latvia and Estonia, where certain political affiliations took shape on that flank (like the Party of Regions in Ukraine or Krievu Partija in Latvia). In contrast, any such emerging structures in Belarus have been nipped in the bud, as Lukashenka has been willing to be the only and exclusive negotiating partner of Russia in Belarus. That has brought about a seeming contradiction: there are no organized pro-Russian political forces in the most Russified country in the post-Soviet area (aside from Russia itself). That in and of itself also deprived Russia of any potential to establish a hybrid policy as there are no organized structures on that policy's receiving end.

It may well be that the Western foreign policymakers made a mistake by exacerbating Belarus's multiple vulnerabilities through punitive sanctions on Belarus's exports to the West and through cutting off non-Russia channels of Belarus's vital exports, like through the Lithuanian seaport of Klaipeda. Instead of talking directly to Minsk, the West prefers to talk to Belarusian exiles in Vilnius who have insisted on sanctions and succeeded in enhancing their own livelihood but disregarded that of Belarusians at home. As Matsukevich put it, 'an uncompromising bet on sanctions pressure contradicts the leitmotif of the democratic forces' statements that one cannot equate the regime and Belarus, it is necessary to separate them. However, sanctions … are a blind executioner who does not make that distinction and … strikes mainly at Belarusians, not at the regime.'[38]

That means that not only ordinary Belarusians are suffering but their country now depends on Russia even more. Above all, that implies that the Western policymakers must eventually do their homework on Belarus and stop helping Russia to bloodlessly annex it.

---

[38] Pavel Matsukevich, 'Blagaya Zhest', *Tsentr Novykh Idei*, November 18, https://newbelarus.vision/puls-lenina73/.

Bibliography

Babushkin, Y. (2012), 'Andrei Konchalovsky: Moite Vymya pered Doikoi', An interview, *Snob*, 9 October. Available online: https://snob.ru/selected/entry/53571/ (accessed 16 November 2023).

Baunov, A. (2020), 'Svoyi i Chuzhiye v Belorusskom Proteste', *Moscow Carnegie Center*, 14 August. Available online: https://carnegiemoscow.org/commentary/82482 (accessed 16 November 2023).

Belta.by (2019), 'Lukashenko: My Nikakim Suverenitetom Ne Delimsya', *Belta.by*, 24 December. Available online: https://www.belta.by/president/view/lukashenko-my-nikakim-suverenitetom-ne-delimsja-ni-rossija-ni-belarus-374011-2019/ (accessed 16 November 2023).

Drakakhrust, Y. (2022), 'Tyya Nemnogiya, Khto Vystupaye Za Belarus …', *Svaboda*, 7 July. Available online: https://www.svaboda.org/a/31930149.html (accessed 16 November 2023).

Gurnevich, D. (2022), 'Addanyya Kramlyu?', *Svaboda*, 3 November. Available online: https://www.svaboda.org/a/32113573.html (accessed 16 November 2023).

International Forum (2018), 'Eastern Europe: In Search of Security for All', Minsk, 24 May. Available online: https://president.gov.by/en/events/international-forum-eastern-europe-in-search-of-security-for-all-18776 (accessed 16 November 2023).

Ioffe, G. (2008), *Understanding Belarus and How Western Foreign Policy Misses the Mark*, Lanham, MD: Rowman and Littlefield.

Ioffe, G. (2018), 'Belarus's Freedom Day: Post-Celebration Anxieties', *Eurasia Daily Monitor*, 15 (56), 12 April. Available online: https://jamestown.org/program/belaruss-freedom-day-post-celebration-anxieties/ (accessed 16 November 2023).

Ioffe, G. (2019), 'Belarus Builds Relations with Turkey as Russian Ambassador to Minsk Comes Under Fire', *Eurasia Daily Monitor*, 16 (60), 26 April.

Ioffe, G. (2019), 'Split Identity and a Tug-of-War for Belarus's Memory', *Jamestown Foundation*, 20 December. Available online: https://jamestown.org/program/84916/ (accessed 16 November 2023).

Ioffe, G. (2020), 'Belarus: Elections and Sovereignty', *Eurasia Daily Monitor*, 17 (111), 29 July. Available online: https://jamestown.org/program/belarus-elections-and-sovereignty/ (accessed 16 November 2023).

Ioffe, G. (2023), 'Is It Worth Isolating Belarus from the West?', *Russiapost*, 30 August. Available online: https://russiapost.info/politics/isolating_belarus?fbclid=IwAR0pC1JgQxD7vEYgmZliST-QClgrvtjzmWlIUCsWy4d9tpZyLjr8qgogjvs (accessed 16 November 2023).

Kasperovich, L. (2018), 'Asoba, yakaya abyadnala usikh', *Tut.by*, 12 May. Available online: news.tut.by/culture/592411.html.

Kasperovich, L. (2019), 'Tysiachi liudei, BCHB flagi, ex-glava Belarusi i prezidenty: Kak proshlo perezakhoronenie Kalinovskogo', *Tut.by*, 22 November. Available online: https://news.tut.by/culture/661979.html.

Lavnikevich, D. (2017), 'Belorusy Vybirayut Putina', *Gazeta.ru*, 21 May. Available online: https://www.gazeta.ru/politics/2017/05/21_a_10684145.shtml (accessed 16 November 2023).

Löjdquist, F. (2021), 'Hybrid Threats and Hybrid Warfare', in M. Weissmann, N. Nilsson, P. Thunholm, B. Palmertz (eds), *Hybrid Warfare: Security and Asymmetric Conflict in International Relations*, London: I.B. Tauris.

Matsukevich, P. (2022), 'Blagaya Zhest', *Tsentr Novykh Idei*, 18 November. Available online: https://newbelarus.vision/puls-lenina73/ (accessed 16 November 2023).

Melyantsov, D., and E. Artiomenko (2013), 'Geopoliticheskiye Predpochteniya Belorusov', *BISS*, Minsk, 19 April.

Myfin (2021), 'Vneshnayia Torgovlya Respubliki Belarus', 7 April. Available online: https://myfin.by/wiki/term/vneshnyaya-torgovlya-respubliki-belarus (accessed 16 November 2023).

News.ru (2002), 'Lukashenko: Dazhe Lenin i Stalin ne Dodumalis ...', 21 August, *News. ru*. Available online: https://www.newsru.com/world/21aug2002/lukashenko2.html (accessed 16 November 2023).

Novosti NISEPI (1999), 'Khotiat li belorusy v Rossiyu', *Novosti NISEPI*, 3 (13), September 1999. Available online: http://www.iiseps.org/?p=3125 (accessed 16 November 2023).

Novyi Oboronnyi Zakaz (2020), 'Voyenno-Tekhnicheskoye Sotrudnichestvo Rossii i Belorussii', *Novyi Oboronnyi Zakaz*, 6 (65). Available online: https://dfnc.ru/arhiv-zhurnalov/2020-6-65/voenno-tehnicheskoe-sotrudnichestvo-rossii-i-belorussii/ (accessed 16 November 2023).

Shraibman, A. (2017), 'Fenomen Belorusskoi Gosudarstvennosti', *Moscow Carnegie Center*, 31 May. Available online: https://carnegieendowment.org/2017/05/31/ru-pub-70099 (accessed 16 November 2023).

Sokolov, M. (2019), 'Rossiya Poglotit Belarus k 2024 Godu?', *Svoboda*, 20 September. Available online: https://www.svoboda.org/a/30173067.html (accessed 16 November 2023).

Sputnik.by (2020), 'Makei: Poka Net Smysla Rabotat Nad Dorozhnymi Kartami', *Sputnik.by*, 5 March 2020. Available online: https://sputnik.by/20200305/Makey-poka-net-smysla-rabotat-nad--dorozhnymi-kartami-1044103466.html (accessed 16 November 2023).

Svaboda (2022), 'Ranei Nam Raseya Byla Siabrem, a Taper Tam Putin', *Svaboda*, 7 October 2022. Available online: https://www.svaboda.org/a/32068637.html (accessed 16 November 2023).

Svoboda (2023), 'Dogovor o Sozdanii Soyuznogo Gosudarstva'. Available online: https://soyuz.by/dogovor-o-sozdanii-soyuznogo-gosudarstva (accessed 16 November 2023).

TASS (2023), 'Posol v RF zayavil, chto dolia Yevropy i Ukrainy vo vneshnei torgovle Belorussii sostavliayet 5%', *TASS*, 9 September. Available online: https://tass.ru/ekonomika/18692815 (accessed 16 November 2023).

Tilly, C. (2007), *Democracy*, Cambridge, MA: Cambridge University Press.

Vorozheikina, T. (2008), 'Samozashchita Kak Pervyi Shag k Solidarnosti', *Polit.Ru*, 18 August. Available online: http://www.polit.ru/research/2008/08/18/vorogejkina.html (accessed 16 November 2023).

Voyenno-Politicheskoye Obozreniye (2019), 'Belorusskii Eksport Vooruzhenii Rastyot: Glavnyi Pokupatel – Rossiya, *Voyenno-Politicheskoye Obozreniye*, 14 March. Available online: https://web.archive.org/web/20210925143633/https://www.belvpo. com/101697.html/.

YouTube (2022), 'Chto Dumayut Belorusy o Voine' [YouTube], *YouTube*, 6 July. Available online: https://www.youtube.com/watch?v=ralXfuzx7eE (accessed 16 November 2023).

Zerkalo (2021), 'Bylo 33 Karty, Stalo 28 Program: Kak Razvivalis Peregovory po Belorussko-Rossiiskoi Integratsii', *Zerkalo*, 10 September. Available online: https:// news.zerkalo.io/economics/2769.html (accessed 16 November 2023).

Zerkalo (2022), 'Kak Belorusy i Ukraintsy Proshchayut Vinovatykh', *Zerkalo*, 7 July. Available online: https://news.zerkalo.io/economics/17448.html?c (accessed 16 November 2023).

Zerlako (2022), 'Rossiiskii Gimnast Zasvetilsya s Bukvoi Z …', *Zerkalo*, 19 October. Available online: https://news.zerkalo.io/cellar/24330.html (accessed 16 November 2023).

Zerkalo (2022), 'Vitebskiye Vlasti Likvidirovali Obshchestvennuyu Organizatsiyu, Prodvigavshuyu v Gorode Russkii Mir', *Zerkalo*, 10 September. Available online: https://news.zerkalo.io/life/21743.html (accessed 16 November 2023).

4

Russia's influence operations in the Baltic states

Jānis Bērziņš

Introduction

After Russia's actions in Crimea and Eastern Ukraine, it became almost a consensus among think-tankers, policymakers and some scholars that the next Russian military action would happen in the Baltics. The underlying presupposition is that, first, the Russian president Vladimir Putin wants to recreate the Soviet Union; second, that invading and annexing the Baltic states is one of the necessary steps for achieving this objective; third, that the Russian-speaking population could be easily used to support subversive operations in a Crimea-like scenario. At the operational level, this was to be done by employing supposed Russian Hybrid Warfare tactics, which would be based on an alleged Gerasimov Doctrine.[1]

A serious problem with this assumption is that it projects falsified strategic objectives and military instruments to be employed by Russia which are based on a narrative created by the West. In other words, it ignores Russia's strategic culture and operational code. It is not the case to say that Russia has no interest in the Baltic states. On the contrary, the Baltics are constantly under non-kinetic attack by non-military and military instruments and agents. Among these are psychological, information, and influence operations, including by financing pseudo Non-Governmental Organizations controlled by the Russian government for achieving political goals, disinformation campaigns, and strong

---

[1] The Russians have their own concepts, based on their own military thought. They use the term Hybrid Warfare to refer to the allegedly American and NATO strategy of creating colour revolutions as destabilization operations in targeted countries. The Russian refer to their own way of warfare as 'New Generation Warfare'. For an analysis of the Russian way of warfare, see Bērziņš (2020).

military posturing near the Baltic states' borders. According to open sources, Russia's main strategic objective in the region is the Baltics leaving NATO and the European Union.

The Russian strategy for the Baltic states is multilayered and determined by the following factors: First, they are considered to be part of the West and, as such, they are part of the Russian grand strategy towards the West. Second, the independence of the Baltic states resulted in Russia losing strategic depth as the NATO's border is now just 160 km from St Petersburg. Third, the significant Russian-speaking population in Estonia and Latvia. Although Russia does not consider the Baltic states part of the Russian World (*Russkiy Mir*) the same does not apply to their Russian-speaking population. Russia has the obligation to protect the interests and the preservation of the Russian national cultural identity of the Russian compatriots abroad (Kremlin, 2020).

This enters into direct conflict with the process of Westernization faced by the Russian-speaking population in the Baltic states. This reduces Russia's leverage in the region, since the Russian-speaking population could be used as an instrument for political pressure and as part of destabilization and influence operations. In this sense, the escalation of the Russian war against Ukraine in February 2022 resulted in the culmination of Russia losing most of its instruments of direct influence in the Baltics. Since the traditional instruments lost their effectiveness, the operations have been focusing in discrediting the West and its values, including its political and economic model.

This chapter discusses the main features of Russia's influence operations in the Baltic states in the following areas: politics, economic and social issues, diplomatic instruments and information, and energy. This chapter mostly uses Latvia as its main case study because of the similarity of the Russian influence operations in the Baltic states.

Russia and the Baltic states: Finlandization

The Baltic states rightly consider the Soviet period to result from forced illegal occupation and their independence from the Soviet Union in 1991 as the reestablishment of the pre-Second World War republics. Russia considers the Baltics as newly independent states arising from the former Soviet Republics of Estonia, Latvia and Lithuania (Simindey, 2019). At the same time, Moscow understands that the relations between the Baltic states and Russia always have been difficult. They result from deep cultural, religious and historical differences, aggravated by new issues and frictions (Skachkov, 2018).

Although occupation and annexation are not part of the current Moscow's strategic objectives, it does not mean that Russia is not interested in the Baltic states. Quite the contrary, Russia believes to have a natural sphere of influence called the 'near abroad', encompassing the post-Soviet space. Since the Baltic states are firmly part of the West, Russia's main objective seems to maintain and, possibly, to increase its influence in the region to achieve a situation of 'finlandization' (Skachkov, 2018).

The term has Its origin in Finland's foreign policy of accommodating the Soviet Union's interests in Northern Europe, but at the same time maintaining non-bloc neutrality and democracy. In other words, by external realpolitik to maintain internally values.

The argumentation to justify the Baltic states' finlandization is economic. The Russian argue that 'although they are firmly part of NATO and the EU, their current economic and social indicators, pace of macroeconomic development and demographic trends mean these countries will likely be depopulated by the middle of this century'. The solution is to freeze NATO membership at the same time maintaining the EU status together with 'restorative [*sic*] Eurasian integration' (Voronov, 2019).

Therefore, the strategic objective, as in Clausewitz, is political. It is to push Latvia, Estonia and Lithuania from the Western sphere influence back to Russia's near abroad without militarily attacking, annexing and occupying these countries. This is to be done indirectly, by using democracy as a weapon. The Russian strategy has nine points (Nagorny and Shurygin, 2013):

1. The stimulation and support of armed actions by separatist groups with the objective of promoting chaos and territorial disintegration.
2. Polarization between the elite and society, resulting in a crisis of values followed by a process of reality-orientation to Western values.
3. Demoralization of the armed forces and military elite.
4. Strategic controlled degradation of the socio-economic situation.
5. Stimulation of a socio-political crisis.
6. Intensification of simultaneous forms and models of psychological warfare.
7. Incitement of mass panic, with the loss of confidence in key government institutions.
8. Defamation of political leaders who are not aligned with Russia's interests.
9. Annihilation of opportunities to form coalitions with foreign allies.

It is very difficult to engage in such influence operations without having something to explore. In other words, influence operations are effective to the extent that vulnerabilities in a society allow them to be effective. These vulnerabilities can only take advantage of realities being created by underlying trends. Therefore, the strategy is to exploit the endogenous fragilities of the subject under attack. Since the objective is political, influence operations are specifically based upon identifying the key audiences in a population, profiling those audience behaviours – both current and latent – and producing influence pathways to either encourage or mitigate a specific behaviour.

Taking into consideration the resistance of the Baltic states' population against establishing deeper ties with Russia, the narrative being exploited is not pro-Russia and pro-Eurasia. Instead, the main aim is to convince the population that the current alignment with the West, democracy as political model, NATO and EU membership are impeding them to achieve its full potential of development. Also, that the natural moral values of the Baltic states' population are different from the Western values and similar to the specific traditional values championed by Russia. The desirable outcome is populist anti-NATO, anti-European Union and anti-West politicians being democratically elected resulting in a natural re-alignment with Russia.

The success of these methods is directly dependent on the level of 'exit' found within a country. This can be understood by using A. Hirschmann's theoretical framework of voice, exit and loyalty. People can express discontent in two ways: one, by directly communicating their dissatisfaction by voice; other, by exiting – usually the result of a citizen becoming convinced that voicing has no results. The conclusion is that more voice is equal to more loyalty, but more exit means less loyalty. To exit makes sense in economics, as it is the way the market mechanism works. However, at the political level, it is associated with negative trends, as voice is the basis for political participation, therefore, for the democratic system to work. In this sense, the most radical form of exit is emigration (Hirschmann, 1970).

Hirschman went as far as analysing the effects of emigration in small states but did not touch the political nor the security implications of another kind of exit, the one that can be called internal exit. In this way, a logic theoretical development of Hirschman's framework is the case when instead of emigrating, people become, voluntarily or not, isolated from the political, economic, cultural and social system of the country where they live. Most of the times, it results from the combination of multiple factors, although the most important seems to be political and economic alienation. In this case, the level of loyalty to the country's macrostructures is negatively correlated to the population's level of internal exit. Thus, it is also correlated to the level of influence of foreign narratives championing the strategic interests of other countries.

There are signs that a significant gap exists between society and the government/state in Latvia and Lithuania but considerably less in Estonia. This is shown by the low level of society's trust in governmental institutions, which gives a fertile field for malign actors to engage in influence operations and achieve their strategic objectives. The implication for defence is that, in case of non-kinetic and hybrid operations, the attacker might even gain support from the local population to its strategic objectives, if they are properly formulated.[2]

In the Baltic states, Russia has been exploiting local agents of influence, namely non-governmental organizations, informal groups, journalists, academics, artists, opinion leaders, government officials who may or may not be aware they are being used as such. Although the Baltic states' governments have been closely following the developments of these influence operations, counteraction has been usually done by presenting the population with facts and critical information and by directly informing about such operations in clear language stating who is the attacker (if known), what are the objectives, what is the narrative and why it is not true. Until Russia's escalation in February 2022, with the exception of Lithuania, it included not prohibiting the broadcast of Russian television and radio, unless there were cases of hate speech and incitement for violence. With the escalation, many Russian television channels were forbidden in the three Baltic states.

The non-military threats for the Baltic states' security are the result of their endogenous fragilities and, in some cases, the clash between security and strategic objectives with political and economic interests. Their main political objective after independence was joining the West and its main institutions, namely the European Union, the OECD and NATO to distancing from Russian influence. Nevertheless, one of the main priorities of the post-independence economic policy, especially in Latvia, was to establish them as a bridge between East and West in finance and logistics/transit, with Russia inevitably being the main partner.

Since economics and politics are deeply interconnected, it was also inevitable that Russia maintained a certain degree of indirect influence. Although it was

---

[2] For a more profound discussion, see Janis Berzins and Victoria Vdovychenko, 'Willingness to Fight for Ukraine: Lessons for the Baltic States'. *BSR Policy Briefing* (2022).

never successful in diverting the path of political and economic integration with the West, Russia was using economic interests as an instrument to gain political influence and traction. After the Crimea's annexation, the focus has shifted to fomenting populist anti-West, anti-neoliberal globalization, anti-homosexualism and to pseudo-traditional values, anti-science, anti-vaccine and the like.

Russia's influence in the Baltic states

Russia has been engaging in influence operations in the Baltic states since independence in the beginning of the 1990s. Although these countries are quite different, they do not represent a uniform unity; the Russian influence operations have been following the same patterns. Therefore, it is possible to use Latvia as a case study to generalize the situation in the Baltic states. This section analyses the Russian influence operations in the political, economic and social, diplomatic and informational, and energy realms.

Political

Russia's attempts to influence Baltic politics may be divided in three levels. First, by supporting pro-Russian political parties, organizations, non-governmental organizations and individuals; second, by maintaining or trying to increasing its political influence over the local population; third, by influencing politicians and civil servants, mainly at the regional level.

In Latvia, the main pro-Russian political force was the political alliance Harmony. It started as Harmony Center in 2005 as the merger of the National Harmony Party with the Socialist Party of Latvia, the New Center, the Daugavpils City Party and the Social Democratic Party. In 2010 and 2011, following a consolidation process, the coalition became the Social Democratic Party Harmony. In 2009, the party signed a cooperation agreement with United Russia (Putin's party) and A Just Russia, which is considered a sub-party under the former. In 2011, the party signed a cooperation memorandum with the Chinese Communist Party. In 2015, it joined the European Socialist Party. In 2017, it broke the agreement with United Russia in a move to become more palatable for Latvian mainstream politics and to be included in the government's coalition. It's main political figure, Nils Ušakovs, was the mayor of Riga for ten years (2009–19).

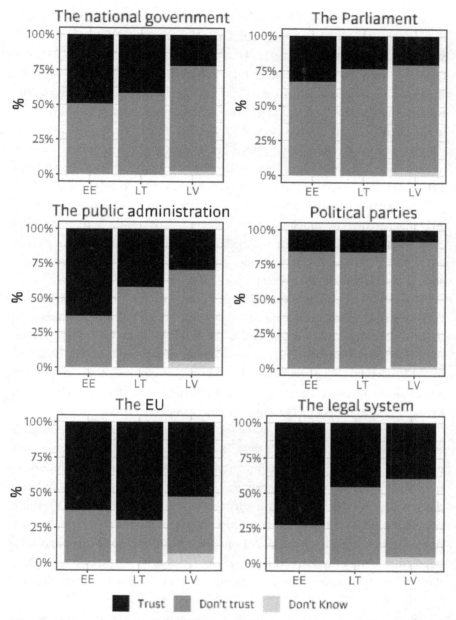

Figure 1 Trust in political institutions in the Baltic region. Own calculations based on the Eurobarometer 95.3, June–July 2021. EE = Estonia, LT = Lithuania, LV = Latvia.

Although it is not possible to affirm that Russia controls any political party in Latvia, many politicians have maintained close contact with Russian political actors. In an interview to the Russian radio station *Ekho Moskvi* in 2015, the former Russian ambassador to Latvia Viktor Kalyuzhny revealed that the Russian embassy had a plan for the Riga's city council to be governed by a pro-Russian coalition by 2009 and to get the majority of the seats in the Parliament in the 2010 elections.[3] In the same interview, Mr Kalyuzhny regretted that the plan worked for the Riga City Council but did not for the Parliament because his successor had other plans. He also mentioned telling Harmony's leader Jānis Urbanovičs to give space to new faces, probably referring to Nils Ušakovs. Both politicians denied the involvement in any plan from the Russian embassy.[4] Since 2017, the party has been publicly distancing from Russia and assuming a social-democratic profile to compete with ethnic Latvian parties, which are mostly conservative. It has a stable electorate, getting an average of 25 per cent of the seats in the Parliament. It never took part in the government coalition.

Russia's actions also have the objective to convince the local population that they are subject to discrimination and to delegitimize the political and economic model, including Latvia's alignment to the West. With Latvia's independence from the Soviet Union in 1991, all people who were citizens before 1940 and their descendants irrespective of their ethnic origin had their citizenship automatically restored. The people from the Soviet Union who moved to Latvia between 1940 and 1991 had to apply for citizenship.[5]

This created discontent and many felt insulted. Russia has been leveraging this discontent as part of its *Russkiy Mir* policy by allegedly supporting and protecting Russian speakers. In practical terms, Russia has been supporting initiatives to avoid Russian-speaking Latvians from fully integrating into the country. Nevertheless, it is a mistake to consider the Russian-speaking population in Latvia and in the Baltics as a fifth column ready to support Russian destabilization operations in the region. The identity of the Russian-speaking population is very diverse and most are not necessarily pro-Kremlin. In 2019, the Parliament approved a law granting automatic citizenship to all non-citizens'

---

[3] See Victor Kalyuzhny interview on the program 'Razbor Paleta',https://web.archive.org/web/2015031
    0000755/http://www.echo.msk.ru/sounds/1506612.html, in Russian. Accessed on 16 January 2024.
[4] See Urbanovičs un Ušakovs noliedz Krievijas 'programmas' īstenošanu Latvijā, https://skaties.lv/
    zinas/latvija/politika/urbanovics-un-usakovs-noliedz-krievijas-programmas-istenosanu- latvija in
    Latvian. Accessed on 16 January 2024.
[5] To receive full citizenship, each applicant need to pass tests to demonstrate Latvian language skills,
    the lyrics of their national anthem and basic knowledge of Latvian History; they are also required to
    swear loyalty to the Latvian state. The status of non-citizen entitles the same rights of a citizen with
    the exception of voting and working in the public sector.

children born after 1 January 2020, provided that the children's parents agreed to not seek citizenship of another country for their children and that the children did not already hold citizenship of another state.

Education is also a sensitive issue. After the independence from the USSR, Latvia maintained the Soviet dual language system of education, with schools in Latvian and in Russian language. Each one had its educational program and material resulting, in some cases, in a deep divergence of learning outcomes especially in disciplines as History. By 2002, the Latvian government initiated a program to protect the cultural heritage of minorities living in Latvia opening publicly financed schools in seven different languages.[6]

Starting with the school year 2019/2020, new rules applied for minority education. Before, 60 per cent of the studies were to be in Latvian and 40 per cent in the minority language. Between 2019/2020 and 2021/2022 there was a gradual transition until all disciplines were to be taught in Latvian with the exception of language and literature and disciplines related to the cultural and historical aspects of the minority group. The political party Harmony Center tried to block the initiative in the Parliament and later appealed to the president to not promulgate the law. There were protests organized by pro-Russian politicians such as Tatjana Ždanoka, but they failed to have any political impact.[7] The reform is following its planned course.

Russia also tried to use local pseudo-activists and 'governmental/non-governmental' organizations financed by the Kremlin to destabilize the country. Although the amount of financial resources is relatively small, they fuel the Kremlin's paranoia about the West, creating or exaggerating issues disconnected from reality to keep being financed. It is fair to conclude that they have the least interest in protecting minorities, since solving the issues they falsely claim to exist would make them irrelevant, and the pseudo-activists would become unemployed. They championed five initiatives with the objective of destabilizing Latvia in the past ten years: First, education in Russian as discussed above; second, Russian becoming the second official language in Latvia; third, automatically issuing citizenship for all non-citizens in Latvia; fourth, the autonomy of the region of Latgale and fifth, the morals and family initiative.

The initiative for Russian becoming Latvia's second official language had a double character. On the one hand, the objective was to revert the process

---

[6] Russian, Polish, Hebrew, Ukraine, Estonian, Lithuanian and Belorussian.
[7] See 'Protestā pret mācībām tikai latviski pulcējās 1500 cilvēki; bez starpgadījumiem', https://www.lsm.lv/raksts/zinas/latvija/protesta-pret-macibam-tikai-latviski-pulcejas-1500-cilveki-bez-starpgad ijumiem.a317696/, in Latvian. Accessed 16 January 2024.

of de-Russification Latvia has been passing through since independence, at least partially. With Russian as official language, the educational reform discussed above would not happen. Second, it was part of a broader strategy aiming to establish Russian as one of the European Union's official languages.[8] On 4 March 2011, the youth movement 'United Latvia' started collecting signatures in cooperation with the Association 'Native Language' to propose amendments on the Latvian constitution permitting Russian to become Latvia's second official language.[9] The political party For Human Rights in a United Latvia (since 2014 Latvian Russian Union) declared its support soon after.[10]

The petition with 12,533 signatures was submitted to the Central Election Commission in September 2011. Between 1 and 30 November 2011 an official signature gathering took place, when 187,378 signatures from the necessary 154,379 were collected. The proposal was sent to the president, who submitted it to the Parliament for consideration. Since the amendments were rejected, a national referendum had to take place. It happened on 18 February 2012.[11]

Some political parties tried to stop the action initiating a discussion about its legality, but the supreme court concluded that it was constitutional. The referendum result was 1,098,593 citizens with voting rights (70.73 per cent of the electoral college) taking part and was 821,722 (74.8 per cent) voting against and 273,347 (24.88 per cent) voting for. Although the Russian Ministry of Foreign Affairs protested stating that the results don't reflect reality because non-citizens were not allowed to vote. Nevertheless, if all non-citizens irrespectively of age (312,189 in 2012) were allowed to vote, the result would still be the same, only with a different proportion between 'against' and 'for'.[12]

On 4 September 2012, the political party For Human Rights in a United Latvia submitted to the Central Election Commission a petition with 12,686 signatures asking that as of 1 January 2014, all non-citizens should be granted

---

[8] A language may attain official status in the European Union if one of its member states recognizes it as one of its official languages.

[9] Until 2012 the Latvian law permitted that at least ten thousand citizens of Latvia with voting rights have the right to lodge a fully drawn-up draft law or draft amendments to the Constitution to the Central Election Commission, which will organize a referendum. The current redaction changed the number to 10 per cent of the citizens with voting rights.

[10] See https://web.archive.org/web/20150220171222/http://vienotalatvija.lv/index.php?limitstart=35&lang=lv and https://web.archive.org/web/20140815043533/http://zapchel.lv/?lang=ru&mode=archive&submode=year2011&page_id=11033.

[11] See https://www.cvk.lv/lv/parakstu-vaksanas/parakstu-vaksanas-lidz-2012-gadam/parakstuvaksana-par-grozijumu-satversme-ierosinasanu-2011-gada-novembris, in Latvian.

[12] In this case, it would have been 58.4 per cent against and 41.4 per cent for (own calculations based on data from the Central Election Commission and the Central Statistical Bureau of Latvia).

Latvian citizenship, unless submitting an application for keeping the status of non-citizen. Although the number of signatures was enough to initiate an official signature gathering, the Central Election Commission had doubts whether the proposed amendment was constitutional. The opinion of several institutions were asked to consider the issue including the chancellery of the president, the Legal Bureau of the Saeima (the Latvian Parliament), the Ministry of Justice, the Ministry of the Interior, the Ministry of Foreign Affairs, the Department of Public Law Sciences and the Department of International and European Law of the University of Latvia's Faculty of Law, the Riga Stradins University's Faculty of Law, Dr Mārtiņš Paparinskis from the Riga Graduate School of Law and international law expert. The submitters of the initiative also had the opportunity to express their opinion on the subject. On 1 November 2012, the Central Election Commission decided that the initiative should not be submitted for signature collection.[13]

While the Central Election Commission was discussing the legality of the citizenship initiative, the leader of the party 'Native Language' Vladimirs Lindermanis started championing the idea of an autonomous Latgale region. In a short interview for the Latvian news agency LETA published on 9 October 2012, he stated that 'it is possible to see that the rulers are doing everything to delay and forbid the referendum about citizenship. There must be an adequate answer and, I think, Latgale's autonomy still as part of Latvia is such answer.'[14]

On 5 December 2012, the Security Policy conducted a search at Lindermans' home, confiscating a computer, some CDs and some flash drives. The home of other activists also were searched and similar hardware confiscated. Three days later he went to the city of Daugavpils to lead a conference about Latgale's autonomy. Only few people attended the event. Harmony Center's leaders Jānis Urbanovičs said the idea to be unproductive and Nils Ušakovs called it a hallucination. Lacking support, the initiative died by itself.

Arguably, the most successful initiative to influence Latvian politics was the *Tikumība* (Morals) initiative. This is was a very significant case, since it united pro-Russian political agents and Latvian nationalists to fight for family values based

---

[13] See https://www.cvk.lv/lv/parakstu-vaksanas/parakstu-vaksanas-lidz-2012-gadam/parlikumproje kta-grozijumi-pilsonibas-likuma-ierosinasanu-2012, in Latvian.

[14] Author's translation from '*Redzam, ka valdošie grib aizliegt pilsonības referendumu, dara visu, lai novilcinātu laiku un beigās to vispār aizliegtu. Uz šādu rīcību jābūt kādai adekvātai atbildei un domāju, ka Latgales autonomija Latvijas sastāvā būtu šāda atbilde.*' See https://www.leta.lv/arch ive/search/?patern=vladimirs\%20lindermans&item=97CED278-2809-4C1C-BFD9-2D9581FA3 BFF&date=-7200,15 88194000&mode=wide&_fy=2012.

on myths created by Russian agents of influence. One of the most widespread falsehoods was the myth of infant rape and incest as a social tradition in Norway. It had two conduits. First, an interview of the famous anaesthesiologist Pēteris Kļava affirming that in Norway 'there are special classes for children learning how to recognize that their fathers crossed the limit' and 'this was a suggestion of a Norwegian minister, who said in an interview for a Russian publication that incest in Norway is a social tradition'.[15] Second, in a conference about gender equality and policy financed by Norway, the dean of Riga Stradiņš University's Faculty of Law stated that Norway is a pedophiles' paradise and the European Union is fighting for legalizing pedophilia.[16]

In 2013, the NGO 'Let's Save Our Children' started collecting signatures for a referendum with the objective to forbid the popularization of sex. It happened in the same time Russia approved a law for imposing money penalties for the popularization of homosexuality among minors. One year before, Russia approved two laws regulating spreading information against family values and blocking internet pages without a court decision. The referendum plans were not successful. Christian Latvians involved in the organization could not accept that its main leader was Vladimir Linderman.

Its success at the political level started after the former member of the Parliament Irina Cvetkova from Harmony witnessed a protest organized by the NGO Dzimtas (Family). After meeting with the organization's leadership, she proposed amending the Law for Children Protection to include forbidding sexual education or what they called the popularization of sex at schools, but failed to gain support from her own party. After leaving the party with another member, she was able to present the amendment for consideration with five colleagues from Zatlers' Reform Party. She backed the amendment's importance by affirming that in Norway incest is considered normal and is a social tradition. These allegations were backed by the documentary '*TransNorway*'. It shows non-gender kindergartens in Sweden, a Norwegian millionaire donating the equivalent of €3.2 million to champion homosexuality in schools, and families letting children to choose their own gender. These allegations are not supported by reality.

---

[15] See Peteris Klyava. Demokratiya s zapakhom pedofilii, https://web.archive.org/web/20190421031
037/https://www.mklat.lv/mnenie/24547-peteris-klyava-demokratiya-s-zapakhom-pedofilii, in Russian. Accessed 16 January 2024.

[16] Inese Liepiņa, 'RSU profesoram pārmet Norvēģijas nomelnošanu', Diena, 9 August 2017, https://www.diena.lv/raksts/latvija/zinas/rsu-profesoram-parmet-norvegijas-nomelnosanu-14178021. Accessed 31 January 2024.

In 2015, the Latvian Parliament approved an amendment to the Law of Education determining the removal of all immoral material from educational books. It had substantial support from the Latvian nationalistic party. They were also able to amend the constitution, including a definition of a Latvian family as a heterosexual couple with children.

In the past years, amendments in the citizenship and education laws and the estrangement among the Russian-speaking groups created by Russia's war against Ukraine drastically reduced the leverage of the usual points of influence. It resulted in Russia changing the focus towards the immorality and decadence of the West, anti-science, anti-vax, populist and against the Western political and economic models. Taking into consideration the globalization's disruptive character, there is a very fertile field that may be explored irrespectively of ethnic issues.

Economic and social instruments

The analysis of the economic platforms of all parties elected to the fifth to eighth Saeima (the Latvian Parliament) shows that the key economic sectors to be developed were transit, real estate and finance (Bērziņš, 2015). All three have been highly dependent on money from Russia and the Commonwealth of Independent States' countries, resulting in business interests being a significant conduit for Russian influence. Since part of these assets had shadowy origins, this also created a problem of reputation for Latvia because of allegations of money laundering and corruption.

In other words, favouring finance, real estate and transit resulted in deindustrialization, the shrinkage in the services sector through a lack of competitiveness resulting from the overvalued exchange rate and economic reorganization in favour of speculative and/or non-sustainable sectors as, for example, consumption of durable goods (Bērziņš, 2014). In other words, the competitiveness of the country has been based on low wages and not in the establishment of a complex economy based on high productivity sectors able to export high added-value goods. Although the country's economy grows and develops, in relation to other countries it results in a permanent process of insufficient development.

Nevertheless, Russia's possibilities for influencing Latvia by economic means is very limited. The majority of Latvia's external trade is with European Union and NATO member states. In 2019, 72 per cent of Latvia's exports were to European Union member states, whereas 11 per cent of exports were to non-European

Union NATO member states. The exports to Russia accounted for 9 per cent. At the same time, Latvia's imports to European Union member states accounted for 75 per cent of the total, while 8 per cent were from non-European Union NATO member states and 7 per cent from Russia. The transit sector, which has been mostly dependent on Russia, represented 8 per cent of Latvia's GDP. The national air carrier Air Baltic was responsible for 3 per cent.

For many years, Latvia has been accused of laundering money from Russia and the former Soviet Union. Nevertheless, since 2017 the country has been pressured by the United States to toughen its anti-laundering laws. American officials were surprised that five banks operating in Latvia were circumventing international sanctions against North Korea. Also, the penalties were insignificant and the leading local bank, ABLV, was left unpunished. The bank was accused of 'institutionalized money laundering' and the Bank of Latvia's governor was investigated for suspected bribery.[17] By mid-2019, the Latvian Saeima passed an anti-laundering law attempting to avoid being placed on a grey list by Moneyval.[18]

A popular narrative among the Latvian population is the idea of 'I love this land, but I hate this country'. Although Latvia's transition to a market economy might be considered a success, one of the economic policy's pillars has been low wages as a means for establishing competitiveness. This resulted in developing a low-complexity economy with low productivity producing low added-value goods. Therefore, economic growth has not resulted in improving relative living standards. On the contrary, it deepened wealth inequality and consequently increased the sentiment of relative deprivation among the population.[19] This was aggravated by the financial crisis of 2008. Absolute living standards decreased and because of the austerity policies a significant part of the population emigrated or developed some sort of resentment against the state and the political system. Thus, since its economic leverage is quite small, Russia has been focusing on discrediting the Western Financial Neoliberalism and Latvia's economic model. However, the Baltics have been implementing policies to solve these issues. Wages are increasing and sectors with high economic complexity such as IT are developing. The same applies to Estonia and Lithuania.

---

[17] See 'Latvia Passes Anti-Money Laundering Reform', *Financial Times*, 12 June 2019, https://www.ft.com/content/045c12a6-8de1-11e9-a1c1-51bf8f989972. Accessed 16 January 2024.

[18] Moneyval is a permanent monitoring body of the Council of Europe which is assessing compliance with the principal international standards to counter money laundering. See https://www.coe.int/en/web/moneyval.

[19] Relative deprivation refers is the subjective judgement that one is worse off or deprived of some state or thing in comparison to some standard. See Williams (2017).

Diplomatic and informational instruments

Russia's diplomatic and information actions in Latvia have the objective of debasing its credibility, specially within NATO, the European Union and the United States. There are five issues explored by Russia in its diplomatic efforts against Latvia. First, the notion of the Baltics liberated from fascism by the Red Army and voluntarily joining the USSR, instead of forcibly annexed. The most recent example is a series of tweets from the Russian Embassy in Latvia. They started in early July 2020, presenting the Russian interpretation about Latvia's occupation and annexation by the Soviet Union. It advances the idea that Latvia voluntarily joined the Soviet Union, denying it was annexed and occupied. It is part of the Russian efforts to establish a narrative victimizing the Soviet Union because of the inevitability of the Molotov–Ribbentrop Pact as a means for self-preservation and maintaining peace. Since 2002, there is a process of Russian 'passportization' ongoing in Latvia for two target groups.[20] The main target groups are non-citizens and people willing to receive a Russian pension.[21]

Taking into consideration that the idea of protecting compatriots abroad was used as an excuse for the Russian military intervention in Georgia and Ukraine, an increase of Russian citizens results in Russia having a stronger excuse to intervene in Latvia. Nevertheless, for many, taking the Russian citizenship was an economic decision to receiving a pension earlier and complement the regular income in Latvia and not allegiance and loyalty to Russia.

Third, Russian diplomats look to establishing contact with regional governments with the objective of renovating Soviet military memorials. At the same time, the Russian Embassy has been actively identifying and recruiting potential individuals and organizations with the potential for doing research and conservation work in this field, such as Russian history and culture clubs and groups of military archaeology. Russian information operations in Latvia have the objective of channelling the public opinion towards specific interpretations about specific issues within some social groups. The ultimate objective is to create and strengthen discontent about the current political, cultural and economic model and to increase the rejection of Western values (Bērziņš, 2018).

The main instruments are disinformation articles in Russian- and Latvian-language media, using social media (trolls) to spread fake news or share opinions

---

[20] In 2002, the acquisition of Russian citizenship was simplified for any citizen of the former Soviet Union, irrespective of the current country of residence.

[21] Until 2018, Russia kept the Soviet Union retirement age of fifty-five years for women and sixty years for men. In Latvia it is currently sixty-three years and six months to reach sixty-five by 2025.

usually about discrimination in Latvia, the Western society's moral decadence and how it is inherently rotten or agreeing with Russia's narratives. The main narratives used by Russia are the following (Bērziņš, 2018):

1. Russian-speaking minorities are marginalized and treated unfairly by the government.
2. The Baltic states are failed states and corruption is widespread.
3. EU membership resulted in economic and social underdevelopment. Latvia should follow its own path without foreign interference.
4. EU membership is tantamount to being a USSR republic.
5. NATO membership decreases the overall level of security because of possible Russian countermeasures.
6. Western values are corrupted. Tolerance towards homosexuals and other minorities is presented as the moral degradation of traditional family values.
7. There is no real democracy in the West. Politicians are puppets controlled by the financial system and work against the real interests of the population.
8. Fascism is glorified in the Baltics.

There are considerable efforts to characterize Latvia's History, society, culture and political system as neofascist. For example, the yearly Latvian SS Legion march is mischaracterized as an apology to Nazism. In reality, on 12 September 1950 the United States Displaced Persons Commission recognized that the Baltic SS legions did not share the German SS goals, ideology, activities and composition concluding that it would not be hostile to the American government. Latvians were fighting for Latvia's independence against totalitarian Soviet Union, which had occupied the country in 1940, liquidated its army, repressed civilians and repeatedly threatened with occupation.[22]

The focus of the anti-Western narrative is to show the decadence of the West. The issues range from economic and social problems till homosexuality and paedophilia being acceptable in the West. Although the governments of the Baltic states have been closely following the developments of these influence operations, counteraction is done by presenting the population with facts and critical information and by directly informing about such operations in clear

---

[22] For a historical analysis, see J. Tomasevskis, 'Latvian Legion: Controversial Points', 2016, https://web.archive.org/web/20210623060816/http://www.karamuzejs.lv/en/home/publications/JanisTomasevskis/sub.aspx. Accessed 16 January 2024.

language stating who is the attacker (if known), what are the objectives, what is the narrative and why it is not true (Bērziņš, 2018). Before the escalation of Russia's war against Ukraine, there was no prohibiting the broadcast of Russian television and radio, except some cases of hate speech and incitement for violence. Since February 2022, the Baltic states' media regulators forbade the retranslation of many channels in Russian language that were considered to spread Russian disinformation.

Energy

An important question to consider is Latvia's energetic security. This is of special relevance because of historical ties with Russia which deepened during the Soviet period. The first issue is Latvia's dependence on gas from Russia. The second is the Baltic states' connection to Russia's power grid. The third is the import of electricity from Russia. These factors would result in Latvia's strategic fragilities since Russia allegedly could turn off the electricity system in the Baltics or cut gas flows during the winter. As always, reality is more complex. Latvia has an underground gas storage facility with a capacity for 4.47 billion cubic metres in Inčukalns. From that, 2.3 billion cubic metres are of active utilization, or the equivalent to roughly two years of Latvia's consumption of natural gas. It is possible to increase the active reserves to 3.2 billion cubic metres. After the escalation of Russia's war against Ukraine, the Baltic states decided to increase their independence from Russian gas supplies. Latvia is considering constructing a terminal for importing liquified gas from other sources in Skulte and increasing gas reserves in Inčukalns. Estonia is close to finishing the construction of gas terminals in Paldiski and Tallinn, and Lithuania in Klaipeda.

Still, thirty years after leaving the Soviet Union, the Baltic states are synchronized to Russia's power grid to maintain stable power supplies and prevent blackouts. Some analysts believe that, in case of conflict, Russia could turn off the electricity to the Baltic states. Although technically possible, it would result in turning off the energy in Kaliningrad, in Russia's western region, including St Petersburg, and in a considerable part of Belarus.

The Baltic states have plans to completely disconnect from the Russian power grid and connect to the European power grid by 2025. Russia answered by launching a power plant in Kaliningrad to guarantee the region's self-supply and allegedly has plans to disconnect the Baltic states from the Russian power grid already in 2024. There are contingent plans to avoid any disruption from the Russian side by connecting to the European network.

Regarding Latvia's dependence on imports of electricity, in 2021 the country produced 5,817 million kilowatt/hour while the consumption was 7,382 million kilowatt/hour. In 2022, the production of energy was 4,951 million kilowatt/hour. In other words, Latvia might be nearly self-sufficient in electricity production depending on precipitation and volume of water in the rivers.

Final remarks

Non-kinetic instruments of warfare have been gaining significance in achieving military strategic objectives. At the same time, kinetic instruments might be used to achieve non-military strategic objectives, blurring the traditional division between military and non-military means of warfare. As a result, the first step to evaluate the instruments a country might use against an opponent is to determine its strategic objectives.

At least in open-source discussions, Russia's strategic goal in the Baltic states is to stimulate a process described in the literature as finlandization. It can be achieved by kinetic or non-kinetic means, although a combination is also possible. In the case of the Baltic states, Russia has chosen non-kinetic means until now. This is mostly the result of NATO reassurance and deterrence actions of the Baltic states' development of new defence capabilities. Therefore, one should not underestimate the relevance of military deterrence in the region. An important point to be taken into consideration is that the operationalization of non-kinetic warfare, especially information, psychological, and influence operations depend very much on the opponent's idiosyncratic fragilities. As a result, deterrence has to be mostly by denial. This means that it surpasses the mandate of the military and belongs to the political realm.

The Russian influence operations in the Baltic states have been following the methods and points discussed in the Russian military literature. Nevertheless, their success is low. Russia has been unable to exploit economic interests as a result of the orientation of the Latvian economy to the West. The fact that joining the European Union, NATO and, more recently, the OECD was among the most important objectives of the Baltics foreign policy, which resulted in the internal political actors having to adapt their interests, reducing Russia's economic and political leverage.

The political operations carried out by Russian agents of influence mostly failed with the exception of the morality initiative in Latvia. Diplomatic and information operations have been limited, therefore their effect has been also limited. There is a natural suspicion of the population about Russian intentions. At the same time, Russia is unable to present itself as an attractive and viable alternative to the West. This resulted in Russia changing its strategy from pro-Russian to anti-Western objectives. Because of the idiosyncrasies of the Neoliberal Western model of political and economic governance, the opportunities Russia can exploit in influence operations are plenty. The political elite has to make a sincere self-criticism to find where these fragilities are, to solve them and reduce the leverage of Russia and other possible malign actors.

Bibliography

Berzins, J., and V. Vdovychenko (2022), 'Willingness to Fight for Ukraine: Lessons for the Baltic States', *BSR Policy Briefing* 9/2022. Available online: https://www.centrumb alticum.org/files/5422/BSR_Policy_Briefing_9_2022.pdf (accessed 15 January 2024).

Bērziņš, J. (2014), 'Ignacio Rangel Visits Latvia: Crisis and the Political Economy of Duality', *Debatte: Journal of Contemporary Central and Eastern Europe*, 22 (1): 81–102.

Bērziņš, J. (2015), *Macroeconomic Policy, Business Cycles, and Neoliberalism in Latvia*, PhD Thesis, University of Latvia, Latvia. Available online: https://dspace.lu.lv/dsp ace/handle/7/28204.

Bērziņš, J. (2018), 'Integrating Resilience in Defense Planning against Information Warfare in the Post-Truth World', in V. Norman, S. Jayakumar and B. Ang (eds), *Drums: Distortions, Rumours, Untruths, Misinformation, and Smears*, Singapore: World Scientific.

Bērziņš, J. (2020), 'The Theory and Practice of New Generation Warfare: The Case of Ukraine and Syria', *Journal of Slavic Military Studies*, 33 (3): 355–80.

Hirschmann, A. (1970), *Exit, Voice, and Loyalty: Responses to Decline in Firms, Organizations, and States*, Cambridge, MA: Harvard University Press.

Kremlin (2020), 'Podpisan zakon o popravke k konstitutsii rossiyskoy federatsii' (The law on amendments to the constitution of the Russian federation), *Kremlin*. Available online: http://kremlin.ru/acts/news/62988.

'Latvia' Passes Anti-Money Laundering Reform' (2019), *Financial Times*, 12 June. Available online: https://www.ft.com/content/045c12a6-8de1-11e9-a1c1-51bf8f989 972 (accessed 16 January 2024).

Liepiņa, Inese (2017), 'RSU profesoram pārmet Norvēģijas nomelnošanu', Diena, 9 August. Available online: https://www.diena.lv/raksts/latvija/zinas/rsu-profesoram-parmet-norvegijas-nomelnosanu-14178021 (accessed 31 January 2024).

Nagorny, A., and V. Shurygin, eds (2013), *Defense Reform as an Integral Part of a Security Conception for the Russian Federation: A Systemic and Dynamic Evaluation*, Moscow: Izborsky Club.

Simindey, V. (2019), 'Etnopoliticheskaya model' postsovetskoy Latvii: Tendentsii i razvitiye' (The ethnopolitical model of post-Soviet Latvia: Trends and development), *Mezhdunarodnaya zhizn*, (3): 139–45.

Skachkov, A. (2018), 'Rossiya i Pribaltika: Prichiny krizisa' [Russia and the Baltics: The causes of crisis], *Mezhdunarodnaya zhizn*, (9): 204–14.

Tomasevskis, J. (2016), 'Latvian Legion: Controversial Points'. Available online: https://web.archive.org/web/20210623060816/http://www.karamuzejs.lv/en/home/publications/JanisTomasevskis/sub.aspx (accessed 16 January 2024).

Voronov, K. (2019), 'Strategii mezhdunarodnoy adaptatsii malykh stran, Satellizm vs. finlyandizatsiya' [Strategies for the international adaptation of small countries: Satellitism vs. finlandization], *Mezhdunarodnaya zhizn*, (5): 44–55.

Williams, R. M. (2017), 'Relative Deprivation', in L. A. Coser (ed.), *The Idea of Social Structure: Papers in Honor of Robert K. Merton,* New York: Routledge.

5

The vulnerable little brother: Opportunistic partnership and Serbia's exposure to Russia's spoiler tactics

Vuk Vuksanovic

Introduction

Serbia is not necessarily a neat fit for the hybrid warfare conceptual approach since it is engaged in its specific foreign policy of balancing and playing Western and non-Western powers against each other, with Russia being an important factor within the rubric of such foreign policy behaviour. Nevertheless, the case of Serbia is important in examining how Russia exercises its influence in partner countries, showing nuances of the local context.

The Serbian case shows that there is a role for the country-specific agency that is not just a blind object of Russian policies since there is also a local demand for the exercise of Russian power and influence. Serbia still offers insights into the way Moscow exercises its influence, as Russia is capable of opportunistically gaining influence at a low cost and in a low-risk fashion, successfully punching above its weight.

There are several arguments related to the Serbian case. In opposition to the conventional wisdom that portrays Serbo-Russian ties as a traditional alliance of two Slavic, Orthodox countries, this relationship is an opportunistic partnership rooted in current circumstances, where Russia uses ties with Serbia to gain a foothold in the Balkans, but more importantly, to gain leverage and bargaining power with the West. As opposed to that, Serbia uses Russia to leverage the West and get a better bargain with the West on the issue of Kosovo and the Serbian place in Western security architecture. It can also get the West to turn a blind eye to domestic transgressions of the illiberal regime in Belgrade.

In reality, in economic and security terms, Serbia's main partnerships, for better or worse, still revolve around the Western capitals. However, Russia still has three sources of influence in the Balkans that it uses effectively: (1) Energy dependence, (2) the unresolved Kosovo dispute – which puts Serbia in a state of political dependency on Russia because of Moscow's UN Security Council veto and (3) Russian popularity in the Serbian public opinion.[1]

These three areas tie Serbia and Russia together, but these are also the potential sources of vulnerability which Russia can use against Serbia if Moscow perceives that Belgrade is drifting too far westward. The energy dependence gives Moscow political leverage through potential energy blackmail which can upset Serbian economic growth. However, the salience of the Kosovo issue in Serbian domestic politics, alongside the enormous popularity of Russia and its president Vladimir Putin in Serbian public opinion, gives Russia the ability to politically disrupt Serbian leadership and potentially to cause its downfall. This would be done in case Serbian leadership would embark on a politically risky policy, like trying to resolve the Kosovo dispute in a fashion that excludes Russia or by joining Western sanctions against Russia. While Russia's ability for mischief in the Balkans is limited as it is bogged down in the Ukraine war, the theoretical possibility remains that Russia can exploit these openings to harm and leverage Serbia if deemed necessary.

The nature of Serbo-Russian relations

When one discusses the nature of Serbo-Russian relations, a popular explanation is that it is a traditional alliance between two Slavic, Orthodox nations that perseveres throughout centuries. However, this is a misleading description. In all historical iterations, the ties and political closeness between the two countries were always determined by the balance of power during the given historical era and by who were the elites in power in the two countries.[2] Moreover, it is also misleading to regard Russia's engagement with both Serbia and the Balkans as the continuation of the Tsarist or Soviet era, but Russian policies should be viewed

---

[1] Vuk Vuksanovic, 'Why Serbia Won't Stop Playing the Russia Card Any Time Soon', *Carnegie Endowement for International Peace*, 28 October 2019, https://carnegiemoscow.org/comment ary/80188.

[2] Vuk Vuksanovic, 'Serbs Are Not "Little Russians"', *The American Interest*, 26 July 2018, https://www.the-american-interest.com/2018/07/26/serbs-are-not-little-russians/.

in the modern, post-Cold war context.[3] One can say that the Serbo-Russian partnership is an opportunistic partnership rooted in more recent history.

In this partnership, Russia is using the opportunity to gain a foothold in the Balkans, using the power vacuum that has been present in the Balkans since the global financial crisis and the Eurozone crisis of 2008 when the Western attention, primarily the EU's, was diverted from the region.[4] While Russia is not willing to sacrifice too much for Serbia but by backing Serbia, Moscow believes that it is not only maintaining a presence in the region, but it is also regaining the status of European and global power that the West denied to Russia in the 1990s, including through its Balkan interventions.[5]

NATO's intervention against the Federal Republic of Yugoslavia during the Kosovo war of 1999 played a powerful role in fomenting this perception among Russian national security elites. This intervention symbolized the unipolar world where the United States is the rule-maker, and Russia is bypassed in the UN Security Council.[6] NATO's interventions in the Balkans, both in Bosnia in 1995[7] and in Kosovo in 1999, additionally strengthened Russia's security anxieties regarding NATO expansion, particularly since the Kosovo war took place the same year when the first tranche of NATO expansion took place. For Russians, this meant not only that NATO was expanding but that it transformed from being a purely defensive alliance.[8] The analogies between the Kosovo war of 1999 and the Second Chechnya War which Russia was waging that year also exacerbated Russian grievances over Western interventions in the Balkans.[9]

By opposing the Western policies in the region, Russia believes it is reclaiming great power status. However, it is more important for Moscow because it gains the bargaining chip and leverage with the West. This is particularly pronounced in the case of the Kosovo dispute. By backing the Serbian claim in the Kosovo dispute, Russia gets the pleasure of opposing Western unilateralism while using

[3] 'Russia in the Balkans – Panel 1 (The Balkans in Russia's Foreign Policy Strategy)', Russia in the Balkans conference, London School of Economics and Political Science, 13 March 2015, https://www.youtube.com/watch?v=z3QVJY3virc&t=2795s.

[4] Gordon N. Bardos, 'The Balkans, Post-Pax Americana', *The National Interest*, 1 October 2012, https://nationalinterest.org/commentary/the-balkans-post-pax-americana-7537.

[5] Barry Buzan and Ole Wæver, *Regions and Powers: The Structure of International Security* (Cambridge: Cambridge University Press, 2003), 430.

[6] Vuk Vuksanovic, 'Serbs Are Not "Little Russians"'.

[7] John J. Mearsheimer, 'Why the Ukraine Crisis Is the West's Fault: The Liberal Delusions That Provoked Putin', *Foreign Affairs* 93, no 5 (September/October 2014): 78.

[8] Fyodor Lukyanov, 'Putin's Foreign Policy: The Quest to Restore Russia's Rightful Place', *Foreign Affairs* 95, no 3 (May/June 2016): 33.

[9] Vuk Vuksanovic, 'An Unlikely Partnership in Trouble: Serbia and Azerbaijan', *Royal United Services Institute (RUSI)*, 19 August 2020, https://rusi.org/explore-our-research/publications/commentary/unlikely-partnership-trouble-serbia-and-azerbaijan.

the Kosovo precedent to deflect Western criticism whenever Russia imposes a loss of territory onto its neighbours in the post-Soviet space – invoking the Kosovo precedent in territorial disputes and conflicts in the post-Soviet space paid off for Moscow, as demonstrated by the independence of Abkhazia and South Ossetia after the Russo-Georgian war of 2008,[10] the 2014 annexation of Crimea[11] and the Russian claim on Donbass in 2022.[12]

The Russian role in Serbia's regional environment of the Balkans can be described as one of 'spoiler power', a power intent not on offering its version of geopolitical order to the region but intent on disrupting the policies of other powers, in this case, the West.[13] This role particularly came to the fore after the original Ukraine crisis of 2014, when the Russian foreign policy elite started to perceive the Balkans as 'Europe's soft underbelly', an area of Western vulnerability where Russia can instigate controlled crises that divert Western attention away from Ukraine and the post-Soviet space, giving Russia leverage.[14]

Serbia has a different expectation from this partnership. Serbian engagement with Russia is largely a product of two systemic realities that emerged in 2008 – the independence of Kosovo and the mentioned regional power vacuum that began with the financial crisis of 2008.[15] As Serbian elites felt disappointed and humiliated that the West unilaterally pushed Kosovo's independence without any concessions to Belgrade, Serbian leadership believed that the Russian veto in the UN Security Council would give Serbia a chance to get a better solution to the dispute in which Serbia is not a humiliated and sole looser of Kosovo saga.[16] In the words of former Serbian diplomat and Russia specialist Srećko Đukić, 'The balancing that began in 2008 started because of Kosovo ... We had to start balancing our relations with Russia primarily because of Kosovo. Balancing is

[10] Michael Kofman, 'The August War, Ten Years On: A Retrospective on the Russo-Georgian War', *War on the Rocks*, 17 August 2018, https://warontherocks.com/2018/08/the-august-war-ten-years-on-a-retrospective-on-the-russo-georgian-war/.

[11] Bojana Barlovac, 'Putin Says Kosovo Precedent Justifies Crimea Secession', *Balkan Insight*, 18 March 2014, https://balkaninsight.com/2014/03/18/crimea-secession-just-like-kosovo-putin/.

[12] 'Putin: Right to Recognise Donbas Republics Same as How Kosovo Got Recognition', *N1*, 18 March 2022, https://rs.n1info.com/english/news/putin-right-to-recognise-donbas-republics-same-as-how-kosovo-got- recognition/.

[13] Nikola Burazer, '[EWB Interview] Bechev: Russia Is Playing the "Spoiler" in Western Balkans', *European Western Balkans*, 28 November 2017, https://europeanwesternbalkans.com/2017/11/28/ewb-interview-bechev-russia- playing-spoiler-western-balkans/.

[14] Ivan Krastev, 'The Balkans Are the Soft Underbelly of Europe', *Financial Times*, 14 January 2015, https://www.ft.com/content/2287ba66-8489-11e4-bae9-00144feabdc0.

[15] Vuk Vuksanovic, 'Why Serbia Won't Stop Playing the Russia Card Any Time Soon'.

[16] Maxim Samorukov, 'Escaping the Kremlin's Embrace: Why Serbia Has Tired of Russian Support', *Carnegie Endowment for International Peace*, 22 January 2019, https://carnegiemoscow.org/commentary/78173.

in play because the West was pressing us severely as we could not find common ground with them on Kosovo.'[17]

The mentioned power vacuum in the Balkans originally started with the global financial crisis of 2008, and it only became deeper with the migrant crisis, Brexit and all the other crises which impacted the EU since then. In this systemic environment, Russia is more assertive in the region, while Belgrade is encouraged to hedge its bets by engaging Moscow and using it to leverage the West. Within that structural condition, 'balancing and playing off rival powers in order to reap short-term benefits at the expense of long-term public interest may well become the dominant foreign policy strategy for local elites'.[18]

This strategy became even more prevalent due to the worsening of ties between Russia and the West in the wake of the original Ukraine crisis of 2014. While most of the countries in the Balkans responded to this new security situation by trying to portray themselves as Western allies intent on suppressing Russian influence, Serbia upped the ante by playing and balancing Russia and the West.[19] Over time, Serbian leadership played the Russia card not just because of the Kosovo dispute or to extract concessions from the West but also because of domestic developments. Namely, under the leadership of incumbent president Aleksandar Vučić and its Serbian Progressive Party (SNS), Serbia experienced a steady democratic decline since 2012. The illiberal Serbian government saw Russia as a way to deter the West from criticizing its transgressions in Serbia.[20]

Sources of Russian influence in Serbia

Despite the Serbo-Russian partnership, Belgrade's most important economic and security partnerships are still with the West. While the EU integration process is lagging, Serbia is still an EU membership candidate. The EU remains Serbia's main economic partner. In total trade between 2010 and 2021, the EU was Serbia's main partner (EUR 30.28 billion), followed by the countries included in the Central European Free Trade Agreement (CEFTA) (EUR 4.67

---

[17] Vuk Vuksanovic, 'Systemic Pressures, Party Politics and Foreign Policy: Serbia between Russia and the West, 2008–2020' (PhD Thesis, London School of Economics and Political Science, 2021), p. 46.

[18] Dimitar Bechev, 'The Periphery of the Periphery: The Western Balkans and the Euro Crisis', *European Council on Foreign Relations (ECFR)*, 30 August 2012, p. 2, https://ecfr.eu/publication/the_periphery_of_the_periphery_the_western_balkans_and_the_euro_crisis/.

[19] Dimitar Bechev, *Rival Power: Russia in Southeast Europe* (New Haven, CT: Yale University Press, 2017), p. 82.

[20] Besnik Pula, 'The Budding Autocrats of the Balkans', Foreign Policy, 15 April 2016, https://foreignpolicy.com/2016/04/15/the-budding-autocrats-of-the-balkans-serbia-macedonia-montenegro/.

billion), a trade agreement implemented in Southeast Europe, China (EUR 30.28 billion) and Russia (EUR 2.37 billion).[21] In terms of exports, Russia is the third destination of Serbian exports (EUR 840 million) behind the EU (EUR 13.94 billion), CEFTA countries (EUR 3.4 billion) and in front of China (EUR 822 million).[22] Between 2010 and 2021, foreign direct investments (FDI) from the EU accounted for more than 63 per cent of total FDI coming to Serbia, reaching a total of EUR 19.1 billion.[23]

In terms of defence and security policy, Serbia's most important partnerships also remain in the West. Russia has no military presence in the region since it withdrew its peacekeepers from Bosnia and Herzegovina and Kosovo in 2003.[24] Serbia is geographically encircled by NATO member states. Serbia does not want to join NATO because of the legacy of NATO's bombing campaign of 1999. According to the public opinion surveys conducted in late 2022 by the Belgrade Centre for Security Policy (BCSP), 23.6 per cent of the population supports cooperation with NATO, with Serbia remaining a neutral state; those who are against both NATO membership and any cooperation with the alliance are a strong majority with 64.1 per cent. Those who favour NATO membership, with only 4.5 per cent, are almost negligible.[25]

However, Serbia is also a member of NATO's Partnership for Peace (PfP) programme since 2006. Within that programme, Serbia is implementing an Individual Partnership Action Plan (IPAP), the highest degree of cooperation that the non-member can have with NATO.[26] The NATO Military Liaison Office has been operating in Belgrade since 2006. The NATO staff employed at the Liasion Office have diplomatic immunity, and the Liasion Office is situated in the building of the Serbian Defence Ministry.[27] In contrast, Russia does not have these assets in Serbia. In 2020 there were talks that Russia would open a military office in Belgrade but this never happened.[28] Serbian-Russian

---

[21] 'Main Trade Partners of Serbia in 2021', *EU Delegation in the Republic of Serbia*, 19 October 2022, https://europa.rs/trade/?lang=en#.

[22] Ibid.

[23] Ibid.

[24] Alexander Nikitin, 'Partners in Peacekeeping', *North Atlantic Treaty Organization (NATO)*, 1 October 2004, https://www.nato.int/cps/en/natohq/opinions_21119.htm?selectedLocale=en.

[25] Vuk Vuksanovic, Luka Steric and Maja Bjelos, 'Public Perception of Serbian Foreign Policy in the Midst of the War in Ukraine', *Belgrade Centre for Security Policy (BCSP)*, December 2022, p. 12.

[26] 'Relations with Serbia', *North Atlantic Treaty Organization (NATO)*, 23 May 2022, https://www.nato.int/cps/en/natohq/topics_50100.htm.

[27] Vuk Velebit, 'Serbia and NATO: From Hostility to Close Cooperation', *European Western Balkans*, 15 November 2017, https://europeanwesternbalkans.com/2017/11/15/serbia-nato-hostility-close-cooperation/.

[28] 'Russia to Open Defence Ministry Office in Serbia in Push to Deepen Military Ties', *Reuters*, 20 October 2020, https://www.reuters.com/article/us-russia-serbia-idUSKBN2751SA.

humanitarian centre in the city of Niš, active since 2012, never got diplomatic status despite numerous Russian requests, and even its ability to operate in the future is under question because of the sanctions and pressures by the EU.[29] Serbian military holds more military drills with NATO than with Russia. In 2021, Serbia participated in fourteen exercises with NATO members and partners and four military exercises with Russia, while in 2019, Serbia held five exercises with Russia and twenty-three with NATO members.[30] After the war in Ukraine prompted Serbia to cancel all its international military drills, the Serbian government lifted that moratorium so that it could participate in the 'Platinum Wolf' military exercise with the US military.[31]

With that in mind, Russia effectively uses three instruments of influence in both Serbia and the Balkans. These three instruments include energy dependence, the already described unresolved Kosovo dispute and soft power, implying Russia's popularity among parts of the population.[32] Energy dependence is part of the Russian toolkit in Serbia and the Balkans. In 2008, Serbia sold to Russia's Gazprom the majority shares in Naftna Industrija Srbije (Petroleum Industry of Serbia, NIS), a Serbian multinational oil and gas company.[33] Former Serbian president Boris Tadić (2004–12), under whose watch the NIS acquisition took place, even admitted a few years later that this transaction was motivated not only by energy interests but also by political considerations. Namely, Belgrade took into account Moscow's protection of Kosovo, and Belgrade also hoped that the now defunct gas pipeline project South Stream would be constructed across Serbian territory.[34] On 1 January 2021, the Serbian branch of the Ruso-Turkish gas pipeline project TurkStream began operating in Serbia, affirming Serbian dependence on the Russian gas supply.[35] The gas link also allows Russia a

[29] 'Demostat Claims Belgrade Changing Status of Serbian-Russian Humanitarian Center', N1, 20 June 2022, https://rs.n1info.com/english/news/demostat-claims-belgrade-changing-status-of-serbian-russian-humanitarian-center/.

[30] Luka Steric, Maja Bjelos and Marija Ignjatijevic, 'Balkan Defence Monitor', *Belgrade Centre for Security Policy (BCSP)*, 14 March 2022, p. 37, https://bezbednost.org/publikacija/balkanski-monitor-odbrane/.

[31] Igor Mirosavljević, 'Through Military Exercise with NATO Members, Serbia Leans Towards Cooperation with the West', *European Western Balkans*, 27 April 2023, https://europeanwesternbalkans.com/2023/04/27/through-military-exercise-with-nato-members-serbia-leans-towards-cooperation-with-the-west/.

[32] Vuk Vuksanovic, 'Why Serbia Won't Stop Playing the Russia Card Any Time Soon'.

[33] Oleg Shchedrov, 'Serbia Signs Strategic Energy Deal with Russia'. *Reuters*, 25 January 2008, https://www.reuters.com/article/uk-russia-serbia-idUKL2515142420080125.

[34] 'Tadić uveren da će Južni tok biti izgrađen [Tadić is convinced that the South Stream will be built]', *N1*, 2 December 2014, https://rs.n1info.com/biznis/a16577-tadic-uveren-da-ce-juzni-tok-biti-izgradjen/.

[35] 'Russia's Gazprom Begins Gas Deliveries to Serbia, Bosnia via TurkStream Pipeline', *Reuters*, 1 January 2021, https://www.reuters.com/article/russia-turkey-gas-idUKL8N2JC08N.

political presence in the country via the Russia-leaning Socialist Party of Serbia (SPS), led by Serbia's foreign minister Ivica Dačić, with the director of Srbijagas Serbia's state-owned natural gas provider, Srbijagas Dušan Bajatović, also being from the ranks of the SPS.[36]

Regarding Kosovo, in the words of Serbian diplomat Dušan Spasojević, Russia 'did not exist as a factor in Serbian politics' until Kosovo started sliding towards independence.[37] However, the continued salience of the Kosovo dispute put Serbia in a state of political dependence on Russia and its protection in the UN Security Council.[38] Serbia's dependence can be felt in foreign policy and domestic politics. In foreign policy terms, as long as the Kosovo dispute dominates Belgrade's foreign policy agenda, Belgrade cannot do anything deemed an anti-Russian move. However, the salience of the Kosovo dispute also generates domestic consequences in Serbia, leading to the issue of Russian soft power.

Russian soft power in Serbia manifests itself in the form of enormous popularity that Russia has in Serbia. In a public opinion survey in late 2022, 50.5 per cent of respondents thought that Russia was Serbia's most important partner, as opposed to 19 per cent who claimed it was China and 18.3 per cent who thought it was the EU. In that same survey, when asked about the country's greatest friend, 65.8 per cent of Serbs thought it was Russia, whereas 27.5 per cent thought that Russia was only looking after its interests, not after Serbia. In that same category, only 14.2 per cent of Serbs considered the EU a friend of Serbia, while 56.3 per cent thought that the EU only cares about its interests.[39] This popularity is not the product of sincere Rusophilia but of Serbian memories of the 1990s and emotional frustration with Kosovo's independence.[40] Consequently, Serbian leaders avoid policies that are perceived as anti-Russian to avoid going against these pro-Russian sentiments while keeping the ability to win votes of both pro-Russian and pro-EU voters through

---

[36] Sergiu Mitrescu and Vuk Vuksanovic, 'The Wider Balkan Region at the Crossroads of a New Regional Energy Matrix', *New Strategy Center and Belgrade Centre for Security Policy*, October 2022, p. 30.

[37] 'Russia in the Balkans – Panel 4 (Soft Power)', Russia in the Balkans conference, London School of Economics and Political Science, 13 March 2015, https://www.youtube.com/watch?v=H_5GeTSIk08&t=3124s.

[38] Maxim Samorukov, 'Escaping the Kremlin's Embrace'.

[39] Vuk Vuksanovic, Srdjan Cvijic, and Maxim Samorukov, 'Beyond Sputnik and RT. How Does Russian Soft Power in Serbia Really Work?', *Belgrade Centre for Security Policy (BCSP)*, December 2022, p. 8.

[40] Vuk Vuksanovic, 'Russia Remains the Trump Card of Serbian Politics', *Carnegie Endowment for International Peace*, 17 June 2020, https://carnegiemoscow.org/commentary/82090.

foreign policy balancing, as the socio-economic welfare of Serbian citizens is still largely dependent on the EU.[41]

Russian soft power in Serbia is not just a product of the spontaneous emotional reaction of the Serbian public to Western policies. Russian definition of soft power is different from how the founder of the concept, American international relations theorist, Joseph Nye understood it as the ability of a country to influence others through attraction. As opposed to that, the Russian government believes soft power capital can be boosted through purposeful government policies and strategies.[42] However, most of the pro-Russia narrative does not originate from Russian sources. While radio Sputnik has a Serbian bureau that has operated since 2015, the RT channel in Serbo-Croatian did not open in 2015 as originally planned, showing the limits of Russian media presence.[43] It was only in 2022, to compensate for the closure of RT stations across Europe, that the RT decided to open a news portal in Serbian, with a news channel planned to follow in 2024.[44]

In Serbia, most of the pro-Russian narrative was distributed through the pro-government tabloids and the pro-government media precisely to profit from pro-Russian sentiments at home.[45] Tapping into these pro-Russian sentiments can also be used by the Serbian elites to build domestic legitimacy. In early 2019, during Vladimir Putin's visit to Belgrade, according to Serbian media, 120,000 people greeted Putin in front of the Orthodox Church of Saint Sava in Belgrade. However, as the Serbian government was faced with massive protests over the rule of law and media freedom, the ruling coalition in Serbia used Putin's visit to demonstrate to the opposition that it also could gather masses in the streets and match the protests.[46] Projecting the image of an all-powerful Russia by the Serbian government and pro-government media can also be used to deter the EU and the West from criticism of democratic backsliding. As Dimitar Bechev said, 'The scarier Putin is, the more leeway Balkan wannabe-Putins have.'[47]

[41] Ibid.
[42] Dimitar Bechev, *Rival Power*, 226.
[43] Vuk Vuksanovic, 'Systemic pressures, party politics and foreign policy', 226.
[44] 'RT Launches Local Website, Broadcasting in Serbia', *The Moscow Times*, 15 November 2022, https://www.themoscowtimes.com/2022/11/15/rt-launches-local-hub-in-serbia-a79380.
[45] Valerie Hopkins, 'In Balkans, Britain Rejoins Battle for Influence', *Politico*, 30 March 2018, https://www.politico.eu/article/balkans-bbc-britain-rejoins-battle-for-influence-russia-soft-power/.
[46] Vuk Vuksanovic, 'Why Serbia Won't Stop Playing the Russia Card Any Time Soon'.
[47] Dimitar Bechev, 'Russia's Foray into the Balkans: Who Is Really to Blame?', Foreign Policy Research Institute (FPRI), 12 October 2017, https://www.fpri.org/article/2017/10/russias-foray-balkans-really-blame/.

Ties that bind, but also vulnerabilities

However, all these three sources of Russian influence are simultaneously points of vulnerability. The points of vulnerability Russia can potentially use against Belgrade in case Serbian leadership embarks on policies deemed harmful to Russia's interest, like joining Western sanctions, trying to resolve the issue of Kosovo without Russian participation or trying full pivot towards the West.

The first point of vulnerability that Russia can use is energy which can disrupt economic stability in Serbia. The energy link with Russia tended to produce problems for Serbia even before the war in Ukraine. In October 2014, Vladimir Putin was a guest of honour at a military parade celebrating the seventieth anniversary of Belgrade's liberation from Nazi occupation. That same month, in response to an unpaid debt of USD 224 million towards Gazprom, Gazprom cut gas supplies to Serbia by 28 per cent, forcing Belgrade to tap into gas depot reserves from the village of Banatski Dvor.[48]

As the energy crisis began hitting Europe, Serbian president Vučić met Putin in Sochi in November 2021 to discuss the issue of gas prices for Serbia as the old supply contract was expiring. The deal was reached for the price of USD 270 per 1,000 cubic metres for six months, alongside the pledge that the amount of delivered gas would also increase during that period to match the fact that Serbian gas consumption had doubled at that point. It remains unknown if the deal implied Belgrade doing political counter-favours to Moscow, but this deal was a concession that Putin made to his Serbian counterpart for the heating season and the electoral cycle that Serbia was about to undertake in April 2022, showing the political leverage that Moscow has in Belgrade with gas supplies.[49]

In the wake of the Ukraine war, Russia began using energy and commodities to maintain its overseas partnerships by offering them at preferential prices.[50] As Russia was cutting off gas exports to EU members Finland, Poland and Bulgaria for their refusal to pay the Russian gas in roubles, Serbia and Russia reached a new agreement on gas prices in May 2022.[51] In a phone conversation, President Vučić and President Putin agreed to replace the old ten-year gas-supply contract

---

[48] 'Neće biti gasne krize' [There will not be a gas crisis], *RTS*, 31 October 2014, https://www.rts.rs/page/stories/sr/story/13/ekonomija/1738367/nece-biti-gasne-krize.html.

[49] Vuk Vuksanovic, 'Russia's Gas Gift to Serbia Comes with Strings Attached', *Euronews*, 4 December 2021, https://www.euronews.com/2021/12/04/russia-s-gas-gift-to-serbia-comes-with-strings-attached-view.

[50] Sergiu Mitrescu and Vuk Vuksanovic, 'The Wider Balkan Region at the Crossroads of a New Regional Energy Matrix', 31.

[51] Al Jazeera, 'Serbia secures gas deal with Putin, as West boycotts Russia', Al Jazeera, 29 May 2022, https://www.aljazeera.com/news/2022/5/29/serbia-ignores-eu-sanctions-secures-gas-deal-with-putin.

with a new three-year gas-supply contract with a pledge to deliver 2.2 billion cubic meters of gas annually with a price estimated between 340 and 350 per 1,000 cubic metres depending on the amount.[52]

However, it is not the energy blackmail that is the biggest concern of Serbian policymakers. The other two pillars of Russian influence that frighten Serbian leadership must be viewed in pair: the unresolved Kosovo dispute and Russian popularity in Serbia. It has already been said that due to the powerful pro-Russian narrative projected by the pro-government media and tabloids, Russian popularity in Serbia reached a surreal level. Some of Serbia's perceptions of Russia are highly unrealistic as a result. In public opinion surveys, 45.1 per cent of the respondents believed Russia will be the dominant power in the twenty-first century, 23.2 per cent think it will be China and 17.5 per cent believe it will be the United States.[53]

However, this has become a hindrance for Serbian leadership, giving Russia the means to disrupt them politically if the need arises. Serbian leaders got a taste of it between 2018 and 2020 when they believed that with the help of Donald Trump's administration in the United States, they could resolve the Kosovo dispute. This notion came to the fore in 2018 when the leadership of Serbs and Kosovo Albanians started exploring the idea of a land swap to resolve the Kosovo dispute. According to that idea, the Preševo Valley in southern Serbia, with an Albanian population, was supposed to join Kosovo, while the Serb-dominated municipalities in north Kosovo would join Serbia.[54] At the time, the US National Security Advisor John Bolton, quickly noted that the United States would not oppose the deal that Serbia and Kosovo reached on their own accord.[55] US president Donald Trump also followed by encouraging Kosovo and Serbia to seize the opportunity of a deal.[56]

The next step for Belgrade was to secure Moscow's backing after having Washington's, only to discover Moscow had its own plans. In October 2018, President Vučić visited Moscow to meet President Putin. The main purpose of the

---

[52] Tahla Ozturk, 'Serbia secures new 3-year deal with Russia for gas supply', Anadolu Agency, 29 May 2022, https://www.aa.com.tr/en/europe/serbia-secures-new-3-year-deal-with-russia-for-gas-supply/2600651.

[53] Vuksanovic, Cvijic, Samorukov, 'Beyond Sputnik and RT', 8.

[54] Guy Delauney, 'Kosovo-Serbia Talks: Why Land Swap Could Bridge Divide', *BBC*, 6 September 2018, https://www.bbc.com/news/world-europe-45423835.

[55] 'Bolton Says U.S. Won't Oppose Kosovo-Serbia Land Swap Deal', *Radio Free Europe*, 24 August 2018, https://www.rferl.org/a/bolton-says-u-s-won-t-oppose-kosovo-serbia-land-swap-deal/29451395.html.

[56] Andrew Gray, 'Trump Urges Kosovo to Seize Chance for Peace with Serbia', *Politico*, 18 December 2018, https://www.politico.eu/article/donald-trump-urges-kosovo-hashim-thaci-to-seize-chance-for-peace-with-serbia/.

visit was for Belgrade to secure Moscow's support for the land swap initiative and possible recognition of Kosovo by the Russian government. However, Vučić 'was given the cold shoulder' by Putin, and Putin's visit to Belgrade, originally planned for November 2018, was postponed.[57] When Putin visited Belgrade in January 2019 and received an impressive welcome from the crowd in front of Saint Sava Temple, Serbian leaders again tried to secure Putin's approval but to no avail. Serbian leadership realized that Russia was unwilling to accept a solution to the Kosovo dispute without its participation, as it would deny Russia the opportunity to ask for something in return in a great power bargain with the United States and push Serbia into the arms of the West.[58] More importantly, Russia's and Putin's popularity in Serbia became a potential threat to Serbian leadership because if Russia were to sabotage any agreement negotiated by the Serbian government, it would be perceived by the Serbian public as Russia being more mindful of Serbia's interests than the Serbian government.[59] This situation would be a political fiasco leading to the political destabilization of the Serbian regime or its downfall.

This resulted in a cooling down of Serbo-Russian ties during the entire year of 2020. When the Covid-19 pandemic reached Serbia, Russian medical aid was not greeted with the same enthusiasm and fanfare as it did with the Chinese aid, showing that Belgrade replaced Moscow with Beijing as its primary partner in the East.[60] In the summer of 2020, Serbia experienced violent anti-lockdown protests generated by the growing illiberalism and the government's concealment of data related to the pandemic, which resulted in the storming of the Parliament and a harsh response from the police. The pro-government media had their suspect for the riots. The pro-government tabloid *Kurir* accused the 'anti-European forces led by pro-Russian right-wingers organised the demolition of Belgrade', stressing that pro-Russian politicians, alongside anti-vaxxers and opponents of migrants and 5G technology wanted to disrupt the attempt to resolve the Kosovo dispute, with the Western help. The tabloid even cited as evidence of Russian involvement the presence of a random Russian woman at the protests interviewed by the Serbian TV crew.[61]

---

[57] Maxim Samorukov, 'Why Is Russia Hooked on the Kosovo Conflict?', *Südosteuropa Mitteilungen*, no. 2 (2019): 60.

[58] Samorukov, 'Escaping the Kremlin's Embrace'.

[59] Samorukov, 'Why Is Russia Hooked on the Kosovo Conflict?'; Vuksanovic, 'Russia Remains the Trump Card of Serbian Politics'.

[60] Vuk Vuksanovic, 'Belgrade Is Embracing China as It Ditches Its Russian Alliance', Reaction, 10 July 2020, https://reaction.life/belgrade-is-embracing-china-as-it-ditches-its-russian-alliance/.

[61] 'Udar na Srbiju: Desničarske proruske strane stoje iza protesta' [Attack on Serbia: Rightwing Pro-Russian Forces Are Behind the Protests], *Kurir*, 24 August 2020, https://www.kurir.rs/vesti/polit ika/3494521/udar-na-srbiju-desnicarske-proruske-snage-stoje-iza-protesta.

Another pro-government tabloid, *Alo*, accused the Russian 'deep state' and Russian intelligence services of being behind the protests, citing as proof the fact that the Serbian security service arrested a Ukrainian and a Kyrgyz citizen who participated in the demonstrations.[62] These stories continued even after the protests were done. Another tabloid *Srpski Telegraf*, wrote that the Russian deep state, without President Putin's approval, was plotting the overthrow of President Vučić by collaborating with Mlađan Đorđević, a minor opposition politician.[63] Even the more mainstream press, like the daily *Blic*, alleged that Russia was behind the protests in its drive to control the Balkans through the right-wing groups, state media and the Russian–Serbian Humanitarian Center in Niš.[64] The same propaganda machine that used to glorify Russia was now willing to scapegoat Russia, all with the purpose of inflating the Russian threat to curry favour with the West and to scale back some of Russia's popularity in the country.[65]

The crisis did not end there. In August 2020, Serbia announced the purchase of the Chinese anti-aircraft FK-3 missile system instead of the Russian S-300 system, a transaction that angered some Russian media.[66] As leaders of Serbia and Kosovo met in the White House to sign an economic normalization agreement under Trump's mediation, the spokeswoman of the Russian Foreign Ministry, Maria Zakharova, on social media likened Serbian president Vučić to Sharon Stone's explicit scene in the erotic thriller *Basic Instinct*, prompting an angry response from the Serbian side.[67] While this is a mere diplomatic gaffe, it took place at a time when the Serbo-Russian partnership was experiencing

---

[62] 'Ruski špijuni podstrekuju haos u Srbiji' [Russian Spies Incite Chaos in Serbia], PressReader, 10 July 2020, https://www.pressreader.com/serbia/alo/20200710/282041919423569.

[63] Đorđe Bojović (@bojovicdj), 'Russian Ambassador to Belgrade got "unpleasantly surprised" with the cover page of state-back tabloid @Srpski_Telegraf which claims that "Russian deep state is overthrowing Vučić"', Twitter, 23 July 2020, 11.16 am, https://twitter.com/bojovicdj/status/1286228733729353729.

[64] Marko Tašković, 'Moskva bi da kontroliše Balkan Amerikanci tvrde da Rusija stoji iza protesta u Beogradu i da koriste ekstremne desničare, dezinformacije i sajber-rat (Moscow Wants to Control the Balkans. Americans Claim that Russia is Behind the Protests in Belgrade and That They Are Using Extreme Rightwinges, Disinformation and Cyber Warfare)', *Blic*, 11 August 2020, https://www.blic.rs/vesti/politika/moskva-bi-da-kontrolise-balkan-amerikanci-tvrde-da-rusija-stoji-iza-protesta-u/ds34hhj?fbclid=IwAR1A1D8Zz2PT7CHpq38CCaMLnsaVmEzvni5QOUCk0PWOi86uZpEvaV3Zs1g.

[65] Vuk Vuksanovic, 'Belgrade's New Game: Scapegoating Russia and Courting Europe', *War on the Rocks*, 28 August 2020, https://warontherocks.com/2020/08/belgrades-new-game-scapegoating-russia-and-courting-europe/#.

[66] 'Russian Media Suggest Serbia Behaves as Divided Personality', *N1*, 10 August 2020, https://rs.n1info.com/english/news/a628258-russian-media-suggest-serbia-behaves-as-divided-personality/.

[67] Matthew Bodner, 'Russian Official Ignites Spat with Serbia over "Basic Instinct" Facebook Post', *NBC News*, 7 September 2020, https://www.nbcnews.com/news/world/russian-official-ignites-spat-serbia-over-basic-instinct-facebook-post-n1239460.

a severe downturn.[68] In that same period, Serbia cancelled its participation in Slavic Brotherhood 2020, a traditional trilateral military exercise with Russia and Belarus.[69]

The failed reelection of Donald Trump and the presidency of Joseph Biden forced Belgrade to reactivate some of its ties with Moscow.[70] However, the political vulnerability that comes along with Russia's popularity and unresolved Kosovo dispute remains in play, including in the background of the 2022 Russian invasion of Ukraine. A few days before the start of the invasion, President Vučić told the Serbian press: 'That is why our position is so difficult. Serbia has embarked on the European path, Serbia has always supported Ukraine's integrity, but on the other hand, some eighty-five percent of the people will always side with Russia no matter what happens. These are the facts I am faced with as the country's President.'[71] This statement omits the fact that most of the media in the country are directly or indirectly influenced by Vučić and his government, as well as that these media played no small part in inflating the already high Russian popularity. This reality is again haunting Serbian leadership as it cannot join the EU sanctions against Russia despite the potential European pressures due to fear that it could anger significant portions of the public or give Russia an opening to disrupt them by simply accusing them of betraying Serbo-Russian friendship.[72]

Indeed, the domestic terrain is fertile for Moscow to do so if it deems it necessary. In Serbia, 63 per cent of the population of Serbia blamed the West for the war in Ukraine, making it a global outlier by being in front of any other country that displayed pro-Russian sympathies in the ongoing war, including Senegal (52 per cent), Indonesia (50 per cent), Turkey (43 per cent), Nigeria (39 per cent), Moldova (35 per cent) and India (34 per cent).[73] The vast majority of Serbs oppose introducing sanctions against Russia, with 44.1 per cent being against it because Serbia experienced them in the 1990s, 24.3 per cent because

[68] Vuk Vuksanovic, 'Russia and Serbia: A Partnership Past Its Prime', *Royal United Service Institute (RUSI)*, 23 September 2020, https://rusi.org/explore-our-research/publications/commentary/russia-and-serbia-partnership-past-its-prime.

[69] 'Serbia Withdraws From Belarus Military Exercise, Citing EU Pressure', Radio Free Europe, 9 September 2020, https://www.rferl.org/a/serbia-withdraws-from-belarus-military-exercise-citing-eu-pressure/30829735.html.

[70] Vuk Vuksanovic, 'In Serbia, Russia Is Down but Not Out', *The National Interest*, 8 October 2021, https://nationalinterest.org/feature/serbia-russia-down-not-out-195004.

[71] '85% of Serbians Will Always Support Russia, No Matter What – Says President Vučić', *TASS*, 21 February 2022, https://tass.com/world/1407763.

[72] Una Hajdari, 'Pandering to Putin comes back to bite Serbia's Vučić', Politico, 7 March 2020, https://www.politico.eu/article/vladimir-putin-russia-serbia-aleksandar-vucic/.

[73] Vuksanovic, Cvijic, Samorukov, 'Beyond Sputnik and RT', 5.

they consider Russia to be Serbia's greatest friend and 11.8 per cent because of the Kosovo dispute.[74] Russian soft power capital, where the Serbs continue viewing Russia through the lens of their 1990s experience and salience of the Kosovo dispute, continues informing Belgrade's behaviour towards Moscow.

In the early stages of the war in April 2022, thousands of people gathered in Belgrade to support Russia and its war in Ukraine.[75] It remains unknown whether the Serbian government organized the gathering as some ploy to manipulate both Russia and the West or by the Russian government as a warning to the Serbian government about joining too close to the West. However, the gathering does show serious domestic impediments and the political vulnerability of Serbian elites to the Russian leadership. Instead of joining sanctions against Russia, Serbian leadership feels more comfortable using the ongoing war to profit domestically. This was done in April during the Serbian election cycle as Serbian president Vučić ran on a platform of being an experienced leader capable of leading the country in times of global uncertainty, as demonstrated by the electoral slogan 'Peace, Security, Vučić'.[76]

Conclusion – practical and academic implications

The case of Russian influence in Serbia gives practical insights for the future and scholarly wisdom on how Russian power manifests itself in individual countries. Hypothetically, while one could still envision a scenario in which Russia employs proxies, active measures and disinformation to cause a crisis in the Balkans that would harm the West, the Russian mischief capability is limited because of Western restrictive measures.[77] In June 2022, Russian foreign minister Sergei Lavrov was forced to give up on his visit to Belgrade as the European air space was closed for Russian airliners.[78] Equally important is that to stir trouble in the Balkans and Serbia, Moscow needs the backing of local players, and local

[74] Vuksanovic, Cvijic, Samorukov, 'Beyond Sputnik and RT', 11.

[75] 'Pro-Russia Serbs Protest in Belgrade to Support Russia and against NATO', *Euractiv*, 17 April 2022, https://www.euractiv.com/section/enlargement/news/pro-russia-serbs-protest-in-belgrade-to-support-russia-and-against-nato/.

[76] Misha Savic and Zoltan Simon, 'Putin Casts His Shadow Over Elections in Hungary and Serbia', *Bloomberg*, 2 April 2022, https://www.bloomberg.com/news/articles/2022-04-02/elections-in-hungary-and-serbia-are-overshadowed-by-war-in-ukraine.

[77] Dimitar Bechev, 'War Won't Be Coming Back to the Balkans', *War on the Rocks*, 24 March 2022, https://warontherocks.com/2022/03/war-wont-be-coming-back-to-the-balkans/.

[78] 'Lavrov Cancels Flight to Serbia after Countries Close Airspace, Interfax Reports', Reuters, 5 June 2022, https://www.reuters.com/world/europe/closed-airspace-forces-cancellation-russian-foreign-ministers-visit-serbia-ifax-2022-06-05/.

elites do not want to take any risks on behalf of Moscow.[79] In practical terms, the three levers of Russian influence in Serbia and the region remain energy, the unresolved Kosovo dispute and soft power.

The energy leverage, over time, will be less striking. The EU sanctions make it hard for Russia's Gazprom to operate in Serbia. In April 2022, the EU had to exempt Serbia from the fourth sanctions package against Russia that banned the EU companies from cooperating with a set of Russian firms, including Gazprom Neft and the subsidiaries in which Gazprom has stakes of over 50 per cent. This sanctions package would have prevented Serbia's NIS from importing oil through Jadranski naftovod (Adriatic Oil Pipeline) or JANAF in Croatia, through which 70 per cent of Serbian oil import comes.[80] In November, Serbia could no longer import Russian oil via JANAF because of the EU's ban on importing Russian seaborne oil, which forced Belgrade to change oil suppliers.[81] Some analysts even believe that the Russians will have to sell NIS sooner or later.[82] The Russian gas supply will remain in play, but Moscow's ability to use it as a weapon will be less pronounced as Serbia remains open to EU-backed projects on energy diversification, including storage and regasification unit (FSRU) in Alexandroupolis, Greece.[83]

However, the unresolved Kosovo dispute and Russian soft power will remain sources of Russian influence and Serbian vulnerability. This is one of the reasons why the EU is trying to push a final settlement between Serbia and Kosovo, including through the Franco-German proposal from early 2023, that implied Serbia accepting Kosovo's membership in the UN and international bodies and Kosovo forming an Association of Serbian Municipalities (ASM), an entity guaranteeing autonomy for Kosovo Serbs, all in the hope that the settlement would sever Belgrade's link with Moscow. However, the settlement remains elusive, and even if the deal is reached, it is a question mark whether Russia will try to sabotage it in opposition to an international agreement which excludes

[79] Bechev, 'War Won't Be Coming Back to the Balkans'; Maxim Samorukov, 'Why Is All Quiet on Russia's Western Balkan Front?', *Carnegie Politika*, 5 December 2022, https://carnegieendowment.org/politika/88547.

[80] Vladimir Spasić, 'Serbia to Be Exempt from EU's Sanctions against Russian Oil Firms', Balkan Green Energy News, 8 April 2022, https://balkangreenenergynews.com/serbia-to-be-exempt-from-eus-sanctions-against-russian-oil-firms/.

[81] Biagio Carrano, 'From November, the Flow of Russian Oil to Serbia Will Stop', *Serbian Monitor*, 22 August 2022, https://www.serbianmonitor.com/en/from-november-stop-russian-oil-serbia/.

[82] 'Kremlj je prilično zadovoljan Vučićem: Srpski predsednik čak i antiruske odluke usaglašava sa njima [The Kremlin is pretty satisfied with Vučić: Serbian President coordinates even the anti-Russian decision with them]', Nova S, 17 November 2022, https://nova.rs/vesti/politika/%D0%BAremlj-je-prilicno-zadovoljan-sa-vucicem-vucic-cak-i-anti-ruske-odluke-usaglasava-sa-njima/.

[83] Dimitar Bechev, 'Russia's So-Called 'Gas Weapon' Is Nothing but a Myth', Al Jazeera, 10 May 2022, https://www.aljazeera.com/opinions/2022/5/10/russias-so-called-gas-weapon-is-nothing-but-a.

Russia from the equation.[84] With that in mind, at this stage, it is not likely that Russia will employ these instruments against the Serbian government, as Belgrade allows Moscow to save face by showing that there are still those in the Balkans willing to do business with Russia.[85]

Indeed, so far, Russia never responded to the reports that Serbia supplied ammunition to Ukraine. However, the Serbian government remains mindful of Russophilic parts of the public since the government-controlled media do not report on this issue nor the intensified security cooperation with the West.[86] The episode, which clearly explains the nature of Serbo-Russian relations down the road, took place in early 2023 when reports emerged that the private Russian military outfit was recruiting Serbian citizens for fighting in Ukraine, prompting an angry public reaction from the Serbian government. There was no proof that the number of Serbs fighting was high nor that the Wagner Group had a robust presence in the country, but Moscow and Belgrade used this situation to their advantage. Moscow liked the fact that it could promote Wagner Group as a globally relevant military force and that the attention of the West was diverted from issues that are salient for Russia in Serbia, like the issues of sanctions and Kosovo. Meanwhile, the government in Belgrade could present itself to the West as a victim of Russian pressures that needed backing from the West.[87] Similarly, in late December 2023, as Serbian government was facing protests over electoral irregularities that also involved violence at certain point, Serbian government accused the West of fomenting a coloured revolution in Serbia while holding meetings with Russian Ambassador in Serbia.[88] Another proof how juggling between Russia and the West is used by the incumbent elites in Serbia for domestic political survival.

However, Russia can employ these instruments if the need arises. Serbian leadership could again try to smear Russia through its tabloid machinery, repeating the ploy from the 2020 anti-lockdown protests. In late April 2022, Serbian tabloids accused Russia of betraying Serbia after Putin justified the

[84] Vuk Vuksanović, 'Russia in the Balkans: Interests and Instruments', in *Europe and Russian on the Balkan Front: Geopolitics and Diplomacy in the EU's Backyard*, ed. Giorgio Fruscione (Milan: Istituto per gli Studi di Politica Internazionale ISPI, 2023), ch. 2.

[85] 'The Kremlin is pretty satisfied with Vučić.'

[86] 'Analyst: Washington, NATO Becoming Serbia's Primary Partners in Sphere of Defense', *Beta*, 15 June 2023, https://betabriefing.com/news/politics/23737-analyst-washington-nato-becoming-serbias-primary-partners-in-sphere-of-defense.

[87] Maxim Samorukov, 'What the Wagner Mercenaries' Row Reveals About Serbia's Relations with Russia', *Carnegie Politika*, 26 January 2023, https://carnegieendowment.org/politika/88885.

[88] 'Russia Says West Inciting Serbia Protests as Dozens Arrested', *Deutsche Welle (DW)*, 25 December 2023, https://www.dw.com/en/russia-says-west-inciting-serbia-protests-as-dozens-arrested/a-67821399.

annexation of Crimea and Donbass with Kosovo precedent.[89] The big problem is that even if Serbian leadership were to sever its partnership with Russia fully, it would not necessarily be a happy ending. The risk is that, in this case, the Serbian regime would use this opportunity to secure a blessing from the West and acquiescence to authoritarian policies at home.

In terms of academic implications, the Serbian case provides valuable insights. Serbia does not fit into the hybrid warfare literature that easily since we are talking about a country that has been open to engaging Russia to a certain extent within its foreign policy of hedging and balancing rival powers. Nevertheless, the Serbian case shows how, by inspecting local context and agency, one can infer the specific ways Russia exercises its influence on countries situated in grey areas between Russia and the West.

The usual approach to the issue of Russian influence mostly treated these countries and their ruling regimes as either helpless targets of Russian interference or proxies blindly following orders from Moscow. However, these countries have their own agency as the regimes and leaders ruling their countries have their own international and domestic agenda which informs their decision to engage Moscow. Countries like Serbia have their specific rationale for doing business with Russia. It is just that within these nuanced relationships, opportunities also emerge for Russia to push for its own agenda.

Bibliography

Al Jazeera (2022), 'Serbia Secures Gas Deal with Putin, as West Boycotts Russia', *Al Jazeera*, 29 May. Available online: https://www.aljazeera.com/news/2022/5/29/serbia-ignores-eu-sanctions-secures-gas-deal-with-putin (accessed 16 November 2023).

Bardos, G. N. (2012), 'The Balkans, Post-Pax Americana', *The National Interest*, 1 October. Available online: https://nationalinterest.org/commentary/the-balkans-post-pax-americana-7537 (accessed 16 November 2023).

Barlovac, B. (2014), 'Putin Says Kosovo Precedent Justifies Crimea Secession', *Balkan Insight*, 18 March. Available online: https://balkaninsight.com/2014/03/18/crimea-secession-just-like-kosovo-putin/ (accessed 16 November 2023).

Bechev, D. (2012), *The Periphery of the Periphery: The Western Balkans and the Euro Crisis*, European Council on Foreign Relations (ECFR), 30 August. Available

---

[89] Milica Stojanovic, 'Russian Ambassador to Serbia Denies Change in Putin's Kosovo Policy', *Balkan Insight*, 29 April 2022, https://balkaninsight.com/2022/04/29/russian-ambassador-to-serbia-denies-change-in-putins-kosovo-policy/.

online: https://ecfr.eu/publication/the_periphery_of_the_periphery_the_western_ balkans_and_the_euro_crisis/ (accessed 16 November 2023).

Bechev, D. (2017), *Rival Power: Russia in Southeast Europe*, New Haven, CT: Yale University Press.

Bechev, D. (2017), 'Russia's Foray into the Balkans: Who Is Really to Blame?', *Foreign Policy Research Institute (FPRI)*, 12 October. Available online: https://www.fpri.org/ article/2017/10/russias-foray-balkans-really-blame/ (accessed 16 November 2023).

Bechev, D. (2022), 'War Won't Be Coming Back to the Balkans', *War on the Rocks*, 24 March. Available online: https://warontherocks.com/2022/03/war-wont-be-com ing-back-to-the-balkans/ (accessed 16 November 2023).

Bechev, D. (2022), 'Russia's So-Called 'Gas Weapon' Is Nothing but a Myth', *Al Jazeera*, 10 May. Available online: https://www.aljazeera.com/opinions/2022/5/10/russias-so- called-gas-weapon-is-nothing-but-a (accessed 16 November 2023).

Beta (2023), 'Analyst: Washington, NATO Becoming Serbia's Primary Partners in Sphere of Defense', *Beta*, 15 June. Available online: https://betabriefing.com/news/ politics/23737-analyst-washington-nato-becoming-serbias-primary-partners-in-sph ere-of-defense (accessed 16 November 2023).

Bodner, M. (2020), 'Russian Official Ignites Spat with Serbia over "Basic Instinct" Facebook Post', *NBC News*, 7 September. Available online: https://www.nbcnews. com/news/world/russian-official-ignites-spat-serbia-over-basic-instinct-faceb ook-post-n1239460 (accessed 16 November 2023).

Bojović, D. (2020), 'Russian Ambassador to Belgrade Got "Unpleasantly Surprised" with the Cover Page of State-Back Tabloid @Srpski_Telegraf Which Claims That "Russian Deep State Is Overthrowing Vučić"', [Twitter] *Twitter*, 23 July, 11.16 am. Available online: https://twitter.com/bojovicdj/status/1286228733729353729 (accessed 16 November 2023).

Burazer, N. (2017), '[EWB Interview] Bechev: Russia Is Playing the "Spoiler"', in *Western Balkans*', *European Western Balkans*, 28 November. Available online: https:// europeanwesternbalkans.com/2017/11/28/ewb-interview-bechev-russia-playing- spoiler-western-balkans/ (accessed 16 November 2023).

Buzan, B., and Ole Wæver (2003), *Regions and Powers: The Structure of International Security*, Cambridge: Cambridge University Press.

Carrano, B. (2022), 'From November, the Flow of Russian Oil to Serbia Will Stop', *Serbian Monitor*, 22 August. Available online: https://www.serbianmonitor.com/en/ from-november-stop-russian-oil-serbia/ (accessed 16 November 2023).

Delauney, G. (2018), 'Kosovo-Serbia Talks: Why Land Swap Could Bridge Divide', *BBC*, 6 September. Available online: https://www.bbc.com/news/world-europe-45423835 (accessed 16 November 2023).

EU Delegation in the Republic of Serbia (2022), 'Main Trade Partners of Serbia in 2021', *EU Delegation in the Republic of Serbia*, 19 October 2022. Available online: https:// europa.rs/trade/?lang=en# (accessed 16 November 2023).

Euractiv (2022), 'Pro-Russia Serbs Protest in Belgrade to Support Russia and against NATO', *Euractiv*, 17 April. Available online: https://www.euractiv.com/section/enla rgement/news/pro-russia-serbs-protest-in-belgrade-to-support-russia-and-agai nst-nato/ (accessed 16 November 2023).

Gray, A. (2018), 'Trump Urges Kosovo to Seize Chance for Peace with Serbia', *Politico*, 18 December. Available online: https://www.politico.eu/article/donald-trump-urges-kosovo-hashim-thaci-to-seize-chance-for-peace-with-serbia/ (accessed 16 November 2023).

Hajdari, U. (2020), 'Pandering to Putin Comes Back to Bite Serbia's Vučić', *Politico*, 7 March. Available online: https://www.politico.eu/article/vladimir-putin-russia-ser bia-aleksandar-vucic/ (accessed 16 November 2023).

Hopkins, V. (2018), 'In Balkans, Britain Rejoins Battle for Influence', *Politico*, 30 March. Available online: https://www.politico.eu/article/balkans-bbc-britain-rejoins-bat tle-for-influence-russia-soft-power/ (accessed 16 November 2023).

Kofman, M. (2018), 'The August War, Ten Years On: A Retrospective on the Russo-Georgian War', *War on the Rocks*, 17 August. Available online: https://waronthero cks.com/2018/08/the-august-war-ten-years-on-a-retrospective-on-the-russo-georg ian-war/ (accessed 16 November 2023).

Krastev, I. (2015), 'The Balkans Are the Soft Underbelly of Europe', *Financial Times*, 14 January. Available online: https://www.ft.com/content/2287b a66-8489-11e4-bae9-00144feabdc0 (accessed 16 November 2023).

Kurir (2020), 'Udar na Srbiju: Desničarske proruske strane stoje iza protesta' [Attack on Serbia: Rightwing pro-Russian forces are behind the protests], *Kurir*, 24 August. Available online: https://www.kurir.rs/vesti/politika/3494521/udar-na-srbiju-desn icarske-proruske-snage-stoje-iza-protesta (accessed 16 November 2023).

Lukyanov, F. (2016), 'Putin's Foreign Policy: The Quest to Restore Russia's Rightful Place', *Foreign Affairs*, 95 (3): 33.

Mearsheimer, J. J. (2014), 'Why the Ukraine Crisis Is the West's Fault: The Liberal Delusions That Provoked Putin', *Foreign Affairs,* 93 (5): 78.

Mirosavljević, I. (2023), 'Through Military Exercise with NATO Members, Serbia Leans towards Cooperation with the West', *European Western Balkans*, 27 April. Available online: https://europeanwesternbalkans.com/2023/04/27/through-military-exerc ise-with-nato-members-serbia-leans-towards-cooperation-with-the-west/ (accessed 16 November 2023).

Mitrescu, S., and V. Vuksanovic (2022), 'The Wider Balkan Region at the Crossroads of a New Regional Energy Matrix', *New Strategy Center and Belgrade Centre for Security Policy*, October 2022. Available online: https://bezbednost.org/en/publicat ion/the-wider-balkan-region-at-the-crossroads-of-a-new-regional-energy-matrix/ (accessed 15 January 2024).

The Moscow Times (2022), 'RT Launches Local Website, Broadcasting in Serbia', *The Moscow Times*, 15 November. Available online: https://www.themoscowti

mes.com/2022/11/15/rt-launches-local-hub-in-serbia-a79380 (accessed 16 November 2023).

N1 (2014), 'Tadić uveren da će Južni tok biti izgrađen' [Tadić is convinced that the South Stream will be built], *N1*, 2 December. Available online: https://rs.n1info. com/biznis/a16577-tadic-uveren-da-ce-juzni-tok-biti-izgradjen/ (accessed 16 November 2023).

N1 (2020), 'Russian Media Suggest Serbia Behaves as Divided Personality', *N1*, 10 August. Available online: https://rs.n1info.com/english/news/a628258-russ ian-media-suggest-serbia-behaves-as-divided-personality/.

N1 (2022), 'Demostat Claims Belgrade Changing Status of Serbian-Russian Humanitarian Center', N1, 20 June. Available online: https://rs.n1info.com/english/ news/demostat-claims-belgrade-changing-status-of-serbian-russian-humanitarian- center/ (accessed 16 November 2023).

N1 (2022), 'Putin: Right to Recognise Donbas Republics Same as How Kosovo Got Recognition', *N1*, 18 March. Available online: https://rs.n1info.com/english/news/ putin-right-to-recognise-donbas-republics-same-as-how-kosovo-got-recognition/ (accessed 16 November 2023).

Nikitin, A. (2004), 'Partners in Peacekeeping', *North Atlantic Treaty Organization (NATO)*, 1 October. Available online: https://www.nato.int/cps/en/natohq/opinion s_21119.htm?selectedLocale=en (accessed 16 November 2023).

North Atlantic Treaty Organization (NATO) (2022), 'Relations with Serbia', *North Atlantic Treaty Organization (NATO)*, 23 May. Available online: https://www.nato. int/cps/en/natohq/topics_50100.htm (accessed 16 November 2023).

Nova S (2022), 'Kremlj je prilično zadovoljan Vučićem: Srpski predsednik čak i antiruske odluke usaglašava sa njima' [The Kremlin is pretty satisfied with Vučić: Serbian President coordinates even the anti-Russian decision with them]', *Nova S*, 17 November. Available online: https://nova.rs/vesti/politika/%D0%BAre mlj-je-prilicno-zadovoljan-sa-vucicem-vucic-cak-i-anti-ruske-odluke-usaglas ava-sa-njima/ (accessed 16 November 2023).

Ozturk, T. (2022), 'Serbia Secures New 3-Year Deal with Russia for Gas Supply', *Anadolu Agency*, 29 May. Available online: https://www.aa.com.tr/en/europe/ser bia-secures-new-3-year-deal-with-russia-for-gas-supply/2600651 (accessed 16 November 2023).

PressReader (2020), 'Ruski špijuni podstrekuju haos u Srbiji' [Russian Spies Incite Chaos in Serbia], *PressReader*, 10 July. Available online: https://www.pressreader. com/serbia/alo/20200710/282041919423569 (accessed 16 November 2023).

Pula, B. (2016), 'The Budding Autocrats of the Balkans', *Foreign Policy*, 15 April. Available online: https://foreignpolicy.com/2016/04/15/the-budding-autocr ats-of-the-balkans-serbia-macedonia-montenegro/ (accessed 16 November 2023).

Radio Free Europe (2018), 'Bolton Says U.S. Won't Oppose Kosovo-Serbia Land Swap Deal', *Radio Free Europe*, 24 August. Available online: https://www.rferl.org/a/bol

ton-says-u-s-won-t-oppose-kosovo-serbia-land-swap-deal/29451395.html (accessed 16 November 2023).

Radio Free Europe (2020), 'Serbia Withdraws from Belarus Military Exercise, Citing EU Pressure', *Radio Free Europe*, 9 September. Available online: https://www.rferl.org/a/serbia-withdraws-from-belarus-military-exercise-citing-eu-pressure/30829735.html (accessed 16 November 2023).

Reuters (2020), 'Russia to Open Defence Ministry Office in Serbia in Push to Deepen Military Ties', *Reuters*, 20 October. Available online: https://www.reuters.com/article/us-russia-serbia-idUSKBN2751SA (accessed 16 November 2023).

Reuters (2021), 'Russia's Gazprom Begins Gas Deliveries to Serbia, Bosnia via TurkStream Pipeline', *Reuters*, 1 January. Available online: https://www.reuters.com/article/russia-turkey-gas-idUKL8N2JC08N (accessed 16 November 2023).

Reuters (2022), 'Lavrov Cancels Flight to Serbia after Countries Close Airspace, Interfax Reports', *Reuters*, 5 June. Available online: https://www.reuters.com/world/europe/closed-airspace-forces-cancellation-russian-foreign-ministers-visit-serbia-ifax-2022-06-05/ (accessed 16 November 2023).

'Russia Says West Inciting Serbia Protests as Dozens Arrested', *Deutsche Welle (DW)*, 25 December 2023, https://www.dw.com/en/russia-says-west-inciting-serbia-protests-as-dozens-arrested/a-67821399.

RTS (2014), 'Neće biti gasne krize' [There will not be a gas crisis], *RTS*, 31 October. Available online: https://www.rts.rs/page/stories/sr/story/13/ekonomija/1738367/nece-biti-gasne-krize.html (accessed 16 November 2023).

Samorukov, M. (2019), 'Escaping the Kremlin's Embrace: Why Serbia Has Tired of Russian Support', *Carnegie Endowment for International Peace*, 22 January. Available online: https://carnegiemoscow.org/commentary/78173 (accessed 16 November 2023).

Samorukov, M. (2019), 'Why Is Russia Hooked on the Kosovo Conflict?', *Südosteuropa Mitteilungen*, Issue No. 2: 60. Available online: https://www.ceeol.com/search/article-detail?id=791315 (accessed 15 January 2024).

Samorukov, M. (2022), 'Why Is All Quiet on Russia's Western Balkan Front?', *Carnegie Politika*, 5 December. Available online: https://carnegieendowment.org/politika/88547 (accessed 16 November 2023).

Samorukov, M. (2023), 'What the Wagner Mercenaries' Row Reveals About Serbia's Relations with Russia', *Carnegie Politika*, 26 January. Available online: https://carnegieendowment.org/politika/88885 (accessed 16 November 2023).

Savic M., and Z. Simon (2022), 'Putin Casts His Shadow Over Elections in Hungary and Serbia', *Bloomberg*, 2 April. Available online: https://www.bloomberg.com/news/articles/2022-04-02/elections-in-hungary-and-serbia-are-overshadowed-by-war-in-ukraine (accessed 16 November 2023).

Shchedrov, O. (2008), 'Serbia Signs Strategic Energy Deal with Russia.' *Reuters*, 25 January. Available online: https://www.reuters.com/article/uk-russia-serbia-idUKL2515142420080125 (accessed 16 November 2023).

Spasić, V. (2022), 'Serbia to Be Exempt from EU's Sanctions against Russian Oil Firms', *Balkan Green Energy News*, 8 April. Available online: https://balkangreenenergyn ews.com/serbia-to-be-exempt-from-eus-sanctions-against-russian-oil-firms/ (accessed 16 November 2023).

Steric, L., M. Bjelos and M. Ignjatijevic (2022), 'Balkan Defence Monitor', *Belgrade Centre for Security Policy (BCSP)*, 14 March. Available online: https://bezbednost. org/publikacija/balkanski-monitor-odbrane/ (accessed 16 November 2023).

Stojanovic, M. (2022), 'Russian Ambassador to Serbia Denies Change in Putin's Kosovo Policy', *Balkan Insight*, 29 April. Available online: https://balkaninsight. com/2022/04/29/russian-ambassador-to-serbia-denies-change-in-putins-kosovo-pol icy/ (accessed 16 November 2023).

Tašković, M. (2020), 'Moskva bi da kontroliše Balkan Amerikanci tvrde da Rusija stoji iza protesta u Beogradu i da koriste ekstremne desničare, dezinformacije i sajber-rat' [Moscow wants to control the Balkans. Americans claim that Russia is behind the protests in Belgrade and that they are using extreme rightwinges, disinformation and cyber warfare], *Blic*, 11 August. Available online: https://www.blic.rs/vesti/polit ika/moskva-bi-da-kontrolise-balkan-amerikanci-tvrde-da-rusija-stoji-iza-prote sta-u/ds34hhj?fbclid=IwAR1A1D8Zz2PT7CHpq38CCaMLnsaVmEzvni5QOUCk 0PWOi86uZpEvaV3Zs1g (accessed 16 November 2023).

TASS (2022), '85% of Serbians Will Always Support Russia, No Matter What – Says President Vučić', *TASS*, 21 February. Available online: https://tass.com/world/1407 763 (accessed 16 November 2023).

Velebit, V. (2017), 'Serbia and NATO: From Hostility to Close Cooperation', *European Western Balkans*, 15 November. Available online: https://europeanwesternbalk ans.com/2017/11/15/serbia-nato-hostility-close-cooperation/ (accessed 16 November 2023).

Vuksanovic, V. (2018), 'Serbs Are Not "Little Russians"', *The American Interest*, 26 July. Available online: https://www.the-american-interest.com/2018/07/26/serbs-are-not-little-russians/ (accessed 16 November 2023).

Vuksanovic, V. (2019), 'Why Serbia Won't Stop Playing the Russia Card Any Time Soon', *Carnegie Endowment for International Peace*, 28 October. Available online: https:// carnegiemoscow.org/commentary/80188 (accessed 16 November 2023).

Vuksanovic, V. (2020), 'Russia Remains the Trump Card of Serbian Politics', *Carnegie Endowment for International Peace*, 17 June. Available online: https://carnegiemos cow.org/commentary/82090 (accessed 16 November 2023).

Vuksanovic, V. (2020), 'Belgrade Is Embracing China as It Ditches Its Russian Alliance', *Reaction*, 10 July. Available online: https://reaction.life/belgrade-is-embrac ing-china-as-it-ditches-its-russian-alliance/ (accessed 16 November 2023).

Vuksanovic, V. (2020), 'An Unlikely Partnership in Trouble: Serbia and Azerbaijan', *Royal United Services Institute (RUSI)*, 19 August. Available online: https://rusi.org/ explore-our-research/publications/commentary/unlikely-partnership-trouble-ser bia-and-azerbaijan (accessed 16 November 2023).

Vuksanovic, V. (2020), 'Belgrade's New Game: Scapegoating Russia and Courting Europe', *War on the Rocks*, 28 August. Available online: https://warontherocks. com/2020/08/belgrades-new-game-scapegoating-russia-and-courting-europe/# (accessed 16 November 2023).

Vuksanovic, V. (2020), 'Russia and Serbia: A Partnership Past Its Prime', *Royal United Service Institute (RUSI)*, 23 September. Available online: https://rusi.org/explore-our-research/publications/commentary/russia-and-serbia-partnership-past-its-prime (accessed 16 November 2023).

Vuksanovic, V. (2021), 'Systemic Pressures, Party Politics and Foreign Policy: Serbia between Russia and the West, 2008–2020', PhD Thesis, London School of Economics and Political Science.

Vuksanovic, V. (2021), 'In Serbia, Russia Is Down but Not Out', *The National Interest*, 8 October. Available online: https://nationalinterest.org/feature/serbia-rus sia-down-not-out-195004 (accessed 16 November 2023).

Vuksanovic, V. (2021), 'Russia's Gas Gift to Serbia Comes with Strings Attached', *Euronews*, 4 December. Available online: https://www.euronews.com/2021/12/04/ russia-s-gas-gift-to-serbia-comes-with-strings-attached-view (accessed 16 November 2023).

Vuksanovic, V., L. Steric and M. Bjelos (2022), 'Public Perception of Serbian Foreign Policy in the Midst of the War in Ukraine', *The Belgrade Centre for Security Policy (BCSP)*, December. Available online: https://bezbednost.org/en/publication/public-perception-of-serbian-foreign-policy-in-the-midst-of-the-war-in-ukraine/ (accessed 16 December 2023).

Vuksanovic, V., S. Cvijic and M. Samorukov (2022), 'Beyond Sputnik and RT. How Does Russian Soft Power in Serbia Really Work?', *Belgrade Centre for Security Policy (BCSP)*, December. Available online: https://bezbednost.org/en/publication/beyond-sputnik-and-rt-how-does-russian-soft-power-in-serbia-really-work/ (accessed 16 December 2023).

Vuksanović, V. (2023), 'Russia in the Balkans: Interests and Instruments', in G. Fruscione (ed.), *Europe and Russian on the Balkan Front: Geopolitics and Diplomacy in the EU's Backyard* (Milan: Istituto per gli Studi di Politica Internazionale ISPI).

YouTube (2015), 'Russia in the Balkans – Panel 1' ('The Balkans in Russia's Foreign Policy Strategy)' [YouTube], Russia in the Balkans conference, London School of Economics and Political Science, 13 March. Available online: https://www.youtube. com/watch?v=z3QVJY3virc&t=2795s (accessed 16 November 2023).

YouTube (2015), 'Russia in the Balkans – Panel 4 (Soft Power)' [YouTube], Russia in the Balkans conference, London School of Economics and Political Science, 13 March. Available online: https://www.youtube.com/watch?v=H_5GeTSIk08&t=3124s (accessed 16 November 2023).

6

'Kosovo is Serbia': A case study unpacking how Russia advances (shared) Russian and Serbian interests in the Balkans by shaping perceptions on Kosovo

Dorthe Bach Nyemann

Introduction

On January 2017, a train left Belgrade with Mitovicia in northern Kosovo as the final destination. This was the first (and last) train on the direct route between Serbia and Kosovo since the war in 1999. Serbia had acquired the train from Russia, and as it departed from Belgrade, it did not look like any regular train. Covering the whole exterior, the train had the quote 'Kosovo is Serbia' in no more than twenty languages in different sizes and shapes. Inside the train, icon-like images from Orthodox monasteries in Kosovo covered the walls and ceiling; the stewardesses' outfits were red, white and blue, following the Serbian flag. The train only made it to the Serbian border before it was stopped, and no direct line of transportation between Belgrade and the cities in Kosovo has since been re-established.[1]

The happening in 2017 encapsulates key elements of what this chapter aims to explain. Firstly, the quote 'Kosovo is Serbia' takes center stage in every influence campaign in Kosovo and Serbia. The image of Kosovo belonging to and *being* Serbia is enhanced by the Serbian government's policies and actions and promoted by different NGOs, local Serbian groups within Kosovo, the media and the Serbian Orthodox Church. The role of Russia in this campaign is not that easy to pinpoint. However, this chapter aims to show how and why Russia shapes and promotes the Serbian agenda, denying Kosovo the benefits and recognition

---

[1] BBC, 'Serbian Train Sparks Escalation in Tensions with Kosovo', 14 January 2017.

of statehood. The chapter will argue that Russia plays a two-level game to ensure its interests. One is the overt game of influencing the Serbian government and the international community on which policies to pursue regarding Kosovo. The other is more subtle. Russia also works to influence groups inside and outside Kosovo to keep the narrative of 'Kosovo is Serbia' vibrant and relevant. This happens regardless of the interests of the Serbian government.

In 2017, the train ride from Belgrade instantly sparked outrage, suspicion and divide within Kosovo. It provoked counteractions in Pristina and among the local population in northern Kosovo. The Serbian government circled rumours of mines placed on the tracks in Kosovo as the reason to stop the train before reaching the final destination. Growing tensions made the Kosovo government urge the EU and the United States to step in.[2] Achieving freedom of movement for Serbs and Kosovo Albanians, a part of the normalization package facilitated by the EU since 2011, was again off the table. The train ride incident highlights an inescapable dynamic in the Balkan region. With few efforts, due to the lack of agreement on statehood in Kosovo, Russia or Serbia can activate radical groups, reawake grievances, split the international community and create a situation of instability and alertness. This makes Kosovo a fertile ground for rivalry among the great powers and a space of opportunities for applying multiple tools of influence. The end state for Kosovo divides the EU and NATO countries, inflames the Balkan region and recommits Russia and Serbia as historical partners. It is hard to imagine what's not to like in this scenario seen from a Russian perspective.

This chapter will unpack the role of Russia in the relations between Kosovo and Serbia, covering the Russian two-level game regarding Kosovo. The chapter further addresses changes and possibilities for the three actors due to the war in Ukraine. Firstly, a brief introduction addressing the framework and methods of the analysis is in order.

Method and empirical data

This chapter builds on a mixture of fieldwork interviews and observations done in Pristina in 2021 and 2022, combined with the piecing together of a larger segment of literature done by local think tanks in Kosovo and international research institutes. The purpose of this approach is twofold: to draw a more comprehensive picture of how Russia tailors influence activities to a particular

---

[2] BBC, 'Serbian Train Sparks Escalation in Tensions with Kosovo'.

context and to include local voices in interpreting influence operations to better account for how they are perceived locally. The chapter draws on interviews with Florian Oehaja, former head of the Kosovar Centre for Security Studies (KCSS), now Kosovo's ambassador to North Macedonia; Lulzim Peci, Kosovar Institute for Policy Research and Development (KIPRED); and Jeta Krasniqi, Kosova Democratic Institute/Transparency International Kosovo. In December 2022, I interviewed Ramadan Ilazi of KCSS and several military and civilian advisors to the Kosovo government and security forces. These new interviews verify and add nuance to the findings of the field study in 2021 and explore possible changes in Russian behaviour since the war against Ukraine began. The chapter moreover builds on several articles from the Carnegie Moscow Centre by Maxim Samorukov, reports from NATO StratCom CoE and other sources, with the entire Balkans as the area of interest. Combining local perspectives with regional analyses provides a solid empirical foundation for the study. The research results were presented at two conferences: The Zagreb Security Forum 2022 to an academic audience and at a practitioner's Workshop on Countering disinformation organized by NATO Advisory & Liaison Team in Pristina in December 2022. Feedback from these forums has also influenced the final analysis.

How can a study of Russian influence operations best be approached? What are Russia's favoured means and methods? A pivotal work to turn to is a small book by James Sherr from 2013, *Hard Diplomacy and Soft Coercion – Russia's Influence Abroad*. The title captures Sherr's points about the Russian approach to influencing the Kosovo–Serbian relationship. According to Sherr, Russia uses its direct diplomatic power towards the states that are supposed to help Russia with their (common) interests. At the same time, Russia uses soft power towards different groups in societies Russia wants to influence, coercing the overall policies in Russia's favour. The Western reader recognizes the concept of soft power, described by Joseph Nye, as a power granted voluntarily due to the attraction that this power represents. According to Sherr, the Russian version is more instrumental and direct, less 'voluntary', and strengthened by covert activities.[3] Sherr lists five forms of influence characterizing the Putin era, focusing on the post-Soviet states: diplomacy, messaging, business, energy and humanitarian initiatives.[4] Russia uses its various forms of influence

[3] James Sherr, *Hard Diplomacy and Soft Coercion – Russia's Influence Abroad* (Washington, DC: Brookings Institution's Press/Chatham House., 2013), 1–2.
[4] James Sherr, *Hard Diplomacy and Soft Coercion – Russia's Influence Abroad*, 68.

without clear boundaries between the state and the private, the political and the economic, the legal and the criminal.[5] This blurring of roles, sectors and actors creates particular opportunities for Russia in the Balkans in line with Russia's experience in the post-Soviet space. According to Sherr, one of the Russian forms of influence is *business*. However, this research has not been able to uncover the connections, for example through media acquisitions, criminal networks, agreements on energy companies and the like, which could reveal complicated ties between Serbian and Russian society and state. Similarly, it has not been possible to uncover the role of intelligence services in operations that could severely impact the efficacy of Russian influence. Consequently, it is beyond the scope of this chapter to document the degree of coordination, systematization and orchestration of the different forms of Russian influence on the Serbian–Kosovo relationship – key elements to inform an analysis of the severity of a hybrid operation.[6] Instead, the chapter focuses on how a shared historical experience and source of humiliation, namely the bombing of Serbia by NATO in 1999, despite objections from Russia and the later ongoing struggle for independence of Kosovo against the will of both states, can be a source of continued and sustained alliance-building and disruption of momentum in an entire region. The Russian influence activities could well be viewed though a hybrid warfare lens, however, one of the weaknesses of a hybrid warfare perspective is the difficulty of studying the significant number of relevant variables and their interconnectedness in a specific context. Choosing to explore activities of hard diplomacy and soft coercion, as suggested by Sherr, provides the study with a more narrow scope. Still, this chapter only scratches the surface of the extended, complex interplay between the actors and proxies in Russia, Kosovo and Serbia. The study aims to provide the reader with a conceptual understanding of the Russian approach in the Balkans and critical images of how this unfolds in practice.

Russia's first level game: Hard diplomacy

Russia is experiencing severe difficulties maintaining a role in the Balkans. In 2009, Albania and Croatia became NATO members. In 2017, Montenegro

---

[5] James Sherr, *Hard Diplomacy and Soft Coercion – Russia's Influence Abroad*, 8.

[6] Dorthe B. Nyemann, 'Hybrid Warfare in the Baltics', in *Hybrid Warfare – Security and Asymmetric Conflict in International Relations*, ed. Weissmann, Nilsson, Palmertz and Thunholm (London: I.B Tauris, 2021), 197.

joined the Alliance despite the extensive efforts of Russia for this not to happen, including supporting an unsuccessful coup in 2016.[7] In 2020, North Macedonia joined the Alliance as well. Even Russia's closest ally in the region, Serbia, is a NATO partner. This also applies to Bosnia and Herzegovina. The situation is the same when it comes to the EU. The countries in the Balkans are all potential candidates or have association negotiations with the EU. Even though not all EU members recognize Kosovo as an independent state, including Spain, Greece, Romania, Slovakia and Cyprus, these negotiations also include Kosovo.

What can Russia do to stop these developments? Russia's best option is to keep a regional foothold in the Balkans through Serbia. A recent KCSS report concludes: 'Kosovo is Russia's bargaining chip to get what it wants from Serbia. Russia needs a friendly base in the Balkans, and no country is better positioned for this than Serbia. In turn, Serbia relies on Russia's diplomatic capacity to promote and protect its claims around Kosovo.'[8] Serbia is Russia's gateway to the Balkans. Kosovo is the obvious obstacle to the West's advance in the same region.

Russia and Serbia interconnect in the economy, energy, politics, religion, cultural heritage and military. Serbia has allowed Russia to control the Serbian oil and gas sector via Gazprom Neft, and Serbia imports much of its gas and oil from Russia.[9] Serbia supports Russia diplomatically. However, this became more tricky after the war in Ukraine started. Serbia hosts the Russian-Serbian Humanitarian Training Centre in Nis, Serbia. Established in 2012, the center focuses on humanitarian response and emergency assistance in natural disasters. Various sources claim that this is a front organization for a Russian intelligence outpost and a base of operations.[10] During the riots in northern Kosovo in December 2022, the centre again was accused of being a supply station from Russia to the Serbian rebels in Mitrovica.[11] Serbia has had a defense cooperation agreement with Russia since 2013, which allows soldiers from the two countries to train together regularly. Russia has donated six MiG-29 fighter jets, thirty T-72 tanks and thirty BRDM-2 armoured reconnaissance vehicles. Maintenance

[7] Savo Kentera, 'Russia's Role in the Balkans: The Case of Montenegro', *Digital Forensic Centre*, 2021, 15. https://dfcme.me/wp-content/uploads/Studija-ruski-uticaj-ENG-online-1.pdf.
[8] KCSS, 'Russian Influence in Kosovo – in the Shadows of Myth and Reality', 7 November 2020, 11.
[9] Maxim Samorukov, 'A Spoiler in the Balkans? Russia and the Final Resolution of the Kosovo Conflict', *Carnegie Moscow Centre*, 26 November 2019, 2.
[10] Maxim Samorukov, 'Fan Diplomacy in the Balkans', *Carnegie Moscow Center*, 8 July 2020; Vanja Dolapcev, 'The Bear Never Sleeps: The Position of the Serbian-Russian Humanitarian Centre in Nis', *European Western Balkans*, 24 December 2018.
[11] Zoya Sheftalovich, 'Russia Stoking Serbia-Kosovo Tensions to Distract from Ukraine, Pristina Says', *Politico*, 29 December 2022.

and service contracts linked to transferring additional MiG-29 and MI-17/35 helicopters interconnect Serbia and Russia further.[12]

Although Serbia and Russia have many common interests and support each other, Serbia is not necessarily an easy partner for Russia to control. Serbia simultaneously seeks benefits from the United States, the EU and China. Before the war in Ukraine in 2022, this gave Serbia greater room for manoeuvering in its foreign policy. Serbia receives substantial EU donations and has even contributed to several EU missions. Serbia has built relations with China regarding investments and loans in the Serbian national security sector, the energy sector, and the development of harbours and urban areas; it also received assistance from China in the early stages of Covid-19. There has also been institutionalized cooperation, such as inviting Serbia to participate in the Belt and Road initiative. Moreover, Belgrade hosts one of the largest Chinese cultural centres in Europe.[13] In spring 2022, China delivered a large number of surface-to-air missiles to Serbia and has previously provided combat drones to the Serbian defense. Serbia thus became the first state in Europe with Chinese missiles.[14]

For all the above reasons, committing Serbia to the Russian agenda is hard work. Russia, however, holds an essential advantage regarding its decisive role in international diplomacy. In the diplomatic sphere, the narrative 'Serbia is Kosovo' again takes center stage; Russia has consistently argued that Kosovo is part of Serbia and should remain so. Therefore, the diplomatic endeavour's main objective is to preserve the status quo of Kosovo's status. A more pragmatic approach from Belgrade regarding Kosovo's status would significantly reduce Russia's necessity as an ally of Serbia.[15]

Since 2010, the UN General Assembly has mandated the EU to negotiate solutions to the Kosovo–Serbia conflict. As a result, Russia is excluded from that negotiating table (KIPRED, 2020: 9).[16] Nevertheless, Russian diplomats need not worry too much, as five EU member states oppose Kosovo's independence. Thus, for a long period of time the EU single-handedly secured Russian interests

---

[12] Dimitar Bechev, *Russia's Strategic Interests and Tools of Influence in the Western Balkans* (Riga: NATO Strategic Communications Centre of Excellence, 2019), 14–15.

[13] Tena Prelec, *'Our Brothers', 'Our Saviours'. The Importance of Chinese Investment for the Serbian Government's Narrative of the Economic Rebound: Policy Paper* (Prague Security Studies, 2020), 12.

[14] Dusan Stojanovic, 'China Makes Semi-Secret Delivery of Missiles to Serbia', *AP*, 10 April 2022. https://apnews.com/article/russia-ukraine-europe-china-serbia-nato-682ab79c4239f14ecc1133ff5 c7addc9.

[15] KIPRED, 'Russia's Information Warfare towards Kosovo: Political Background and Manife-station: Special Policy Brief', October 2020, 3.

[16] KIPRED, 'Russia's Information Warfare towards Kosovo', 9.

concerning Kosovo's unresolved status. Just as Russian diplomats expected, the dialogue facilitated by the EU has turned out to be endless, with few results and no permanent solutions. Moreover, Russia secured a backdoor to the negotiations between the EU, Kosovo and Serbia by adopting a Strategic Partnership Agreement with Serbia in 2013, in parallel with Serbia signing the first agreement on normalizing the situation in Kosovo. Simultaneously, Russia significantly intensified its visits and exchanges with Serbia.[17]

In 2017, Serbian President Alexander Vučić initiated a new approach to the Kosovo issue. A proposal to swap selected territories with significant Serb and Albanian minorities and subsequently give Kosovo independence was put on the agenda. The seriousness of the proposal is hard to evaluate.[18] Discussions between the parties picked up during the Covid-19 period when many of the usual diplomatic exchanges were dormant. The Trump administration was eager to support this solution, hoping to finalize the Kosovo issue and gain a foreign policy victory.[19] This development was unfortunate for Russia as Russia could lose the bargaining chip that binds Russian and Serbian interests in the Balkans together. The opportunity for an agreement in Washington was missed and after 2020, Serbia again lost its appetite for a 'land swap'. This was a good news for Russia.

In recent years, Russia has intensified its lobbying against Kosovo's recognition, targeting specific states that have already recognized Kosovo to make them withdraw their recognition. Furthermore, Russia has sought to persuade states that have not yet recognized Kosovo not to do so. In 2017, Russia managed to convince Suriname, the smallest country in South America with about half a million inhabitants, to withdraw its recognition of Kosovo as an independent state. This happened at the same time as Suriname switched its military and economic partner from the United States to Russia and just before the first visit of Suriname's foreign minister to Russia and a planned visit to Suriname by a Russian business delegation.[20] The same pattern reoccurs in diplomatic relations with several other states. So far, more than ten states have suspended the recognition of Kosovo's statehood due to the successful joint diplomatic efforts

[17] KIPRED, 'Russia's Information Warfare towards Kosovo', 10.

[18] Bechev, *Russia's Strategic Interests and Tools of Influence in the Western Balkans*, 14.

[19] Maxim Samorukov, 'A Spoiler in the Balkans? Russia and the Final Resolution of the Kosovo Conflict', 2; Heather A. Conley and Dejana Saric, 'The Serbian-Kosovo Normalisation Process – a Temporary US Decoupling', 2021, *Center for Strategic and International Studies*, https://www.csis.org/analysis/serbia-kosovo-normalization-process-temporary-us-decoupling.

[20] Florian Qehaja, 'Acting against the Normalisation: Serbia's Diplomatic Offensive on Kosovo', in *Threats and Challenges to Kosovo's Sovereignty*, ed. David L. Philips and Lulzim Peci, New York: Columbia University., 48.

of Serbia and Russia.[21] In July 2023, Serbian president Alexandar Vučić met with the minister of foreign affairs of Suriname, Albert Ramdin. He emphasized that by withdrawing the recognition of Kosovo's independence, Suriname had become an example for more than twenty-five other countries that had subsequently done the same.[22]

Still, other countries have chosen not to recognize Kosovo at all. Many of these countries reside far away from Kosovo and lack political interests in the Balkan region; however, they cooperate strongly with Russia. Such a state is Angola, which continues to support Russia despite the war in Ukraine and has close collaboration on diamonds; mining and defence. Angola is now forging ties with Serbia, confirming that Kosovo belongs to Serbia.[23] These examples do not prove coercion or illegal methods on Russia's part, but they do suggest hard and direct diplomacy.

In parallel to diplomatic efforts, Russian and Serbian media have repeatedly published false stories about countries that have withdrawn recognition of Kosovo.[24] Following a dialogue with Kosovo, states such as Guinea-Bissau and Liberia have sent official letters explaining their recognition of Kosovo is still valid. In addition, Russia uses its diplomatic power to prevent Kosovo from joining different international organizations.[25] Moreover, Russia uses its position to delegitimize Kosovo's abilities for statehood in the international community. Russia often portrays Kosovo as violent towards Serb minorities and not protective and respectful of Orthodox shrines. Kosovo Albanian politicians are accused of working for Greater Albania and of inflaming ethnic conflicts through, according to Russia, irresponsible political statements.[26] Russia claims that the United States is turning the UN-mandated NATO mission in Kosovo, into a US tool and that the West is not respecting international norms on state sovereignty.[27]

---

[21] KIPRED, 'Russia's Information Warfare towards Kosovo', 4–11.
[22] Kosovo Online, 'Vucic: By Withdrawing the Recognition of Kosovo's Independence, Suriname Became an Example for Other Countries', 24 July 2023.
[23] *Telegraph*, 'Vucic Meet with Angolan Interior Minister Laborinho: We Will Always Support Serbia on the Issue of Kosovo',' 2022, https://www.telegraf.rs/english/3586774-vucic-meets-with-angolan-interior-minister-laborinho-we-will-always-support-serbia-on-the-issue-of-kosovo; Elliot Smith, 'Russia's Influence Is at Risk in the Southern African Nation of Angola as Voters Head to the Polls', *CNBC*, 2022, https://www.cnbc.com/2022/08/24/angola-election-russia-influence-at-risk-as-voters-head-to-the-polls.html.
[24] Qehaja, 'Acting against the Normalisation', 44–6.
[25] Qehaja, 'Acting against the Normalisation', 50.
[26] Samorukov, 'Fan Diplomacy in the Balkans'.
[27] KIPRED, 'Russia's Information Warfare towards Kosovo', 17.

The most vital power position for Russia in the diplomatic sphere is the permanent membership of the UN Security Council. Referring to UN Security Council Resolution 1244, Russia has consistently argued that Kosovo is an autonomous province of Serbia. In addition, Russia refuses to set a deadline for the conclusion of the negotiations between Serbia and Kosovo and maintains that Serbia's acceptance of an agreement is decisive for a settlement.[28] On 17 January 2019, more than 100,000 Serbs greeted Putin at an official visit to Belgrade. In this uplifting atmosphere, Putin announced Russia's view on the end state for Kosovo. He made it clear that Russia favours an agreement that satisfies Belgrade. However, Putin added a new twist to the Russian position: the UN Security Council must also confirm the deal.[29] This effectively gives Russia a veto over the agreement between the two warring parties. Russia will likely block any amendment to UNSCR 1244 to keep the situation unresolved. The Russian position on a solution for Kosovo has been stated several times since 2019.[30]

Russia's second-level game: Engaging the Serbian world from below

A large wall painting in the Serb district in Mitrocivia in northern Kosovo depicts the Serbian and Russian flags united in a tight knot. The Russian flag has Crimea, whereas the Serbian flag has Kosovo drawn on top. The message is clear: Crimea is Russia, like Kosovo is Serbia. Russia succeeded in reuniting with Crimea in time, and Serbia may be able to do the same.[31] Belgrade hosts a similar wall painting, excluding the Russian component. In Belgrade, the Serbian flag has four images of lost territories: Kosovo, Montenegro, Bosnia and Northern Macedonia.[32] The depicted places all host parts of the Serbian population. Important to note here is that the narratives and policies by Russia and Serbia on 'Kosovo is Serbia' must be understood as part of a broader framework. Serbia lacks more than being reunited with Kosovo, just like Russia wishes to reunite larger areas with Russia than just Crimea. With this in mind, Russian influence is, to

[28] KIPRED, 'Russia's Information Warfare towards Kosovo', 15.
[29] Conley and Saric, *The Serbian-Kosovo Normalisation Process*, 4.
[30] KCSS, 'Russian Influence in Kosovo', 12.
[31] Euractiv.com, 'Envoys from EU, US, Visit Northern Kosovo Serbs as Differences Resurface', 26 August 2022.
[32] A. Heil, M. Augustinovic and G. Katic, ' "Unity" Holiday Tests Sympathy, Balkan Tolerance for a New "Serbian World" ', *Radiofreeeurope*, 1 September 2021. https://www.rferl.org/a/serbia-flag-holi day-balkans/31460195.html

some extent, directed against Kosovo, trying to prevent normalization, spoiling Western plans, and keeping Serbia a close Ally. Hard diplomacy is essential to this endeavour. However, keeping the Serbian government in line with Russian interests also makes Russia inclined to focus on the broader situation for Serbia in the Balkans and use other more indirect approaches. These approaches are tailored to the Serb communities throughout the Balkans, not just Kosovo. The narrative is broader than the unification of Kosovo, focusing instead on the concept of a Serbian World.

'The Serbian World' is a term promoted among others, by right-wing Serbian historian Aleksandar Rakovic in 2020. According to him, a Serbian World already exists and will progress into the unification of Serbia, Republika Srpska and Montenegro.[33] The concept offers excellent opportunities to push Serbia towards Russian objectives. In promoting a Serbian World to different subgroups in the Serb community, Russia can instrumentalize its experiences establishing a Russian World in the post-Soviet space.[34] To some extent, Serbia has mirrored the Russian concept, although the Serbian World concept is not an official Serbian policy. Yet, there are many examples of vocal support by the government for different ideas and policies that serve its purpose.[35] The Serbian World combines the preservation of the cultural heritage of Serbs inside and outside the Serbian territory with the ambition that Belgrade should make decisions on issues of vital importance concerning Serbs and protect them wherever they live. Several government documents support this ambition as a policy towards Serbs in the region.[36]

Initiatives to promote the Serbian World focus primarily on wider Serbian influence in Montenegro and Republika Srpska, a Serb republic in Bosnia and Herzegovina. Still, they can also have significant implications for Kosovo.[37] In December 2022, confrontations arose between the Kosovo government and the northern province's local community after a long build-up of tensions. The situation escalated for a month, with roadblocks, blockades and demonstrations.

[33] Heil, Augustinovic, and Katic, '"Unity" Holiday Tests Sympathy, Balkan Tolerance for a New "Serbian World"'.

[34] Moritz Pieper, 'Russkiy Mir: The Geopolitics of Russian Compatriots Abroad', *Geopolitics*, 25, no. 3 (2020): 756–79.

[35] Nikola Dordevic, Serbian World – a Dangerous Idea? *Emerging Europe*, 27 July 2021, https://emerging-europe.com/news/serbian-world-a-dangerous-idea/.

[36] Digital Forensic Centre, 'The Serbian World – Originally Borrowed Concept – DFC Analysis of the Attempt to Merge Montenegro into the Serbian World', April 2021, 4.

[37] Heil, Augustinovic, and Katic, '"Unity" Holiday Tests Sympathy, Balkan Tolerance for a New "Serbian World"'; Global Voices, 'Spreading Misinformation about Kosovo Was Once Again Used as Part of the Election Strategy in Serbia', 21 May 2022; Conley and Saric, *The Serbian-Kosovo Normalisation Process*, 6.

Two borders between Serbia and Kosovo were closed, and the Serbian military took position on the Serbian side of the border, ready to defend its population in the Kosovo province.[38] The local Serb police and the local administration, supposed to provide 'law and order', left their jobs unwilling to enforce a law requiring Serbs to scrap Serbian-issued car license plates. To what extent these tensions were instigated by Serbia or supported directly by Russia is hard to say. However, in ending the confrontations, Serbian president Vučić demonstrated that Belgrade and not Pritisina controls and decides in the Serb community in Kosovo. Vucic resolved when to end the blockades in Mitrovica, when to establish a dialogue with the local Serb minority and how to move forward.[39]This incident portrays the dilemma for the Serbian government when pushing the agenda of a Serbian World.

On the one hand, the government gets legitimacy and public support when it acts with strength in neighbouring entities. On the other hand, right-wing groups with Russian sympathies and radical motives get to define goals for Serbia and reduce the room for new policies inwards and with international partners on which Serbia's future relies.[40] Serbia and Kosovo are hostages of the Russian agenda for the Balkans once more.

The 'Serbian World' concept is just one tool for Russia to engage and mobilize Serbian society across the Balkan states.[41] Serbia's Military Union has had meetings with the Russian Duma and Foreign Ministry and also with Russian veterans. The local branch in Kosovo of Vucic's political party, The Serbian List, has been attending meetings with and received direct support from Putin's party, United Russia, outside the control of the mother party in Serbia.[42] These direct contacts between members of Russian and Serbian society make it tricky for President Vucic to control patriotism in Serbian society and to work for Serbian interests that could contradict Russia's.[43] Russian soft power instrumentalized via contact with local subgroups can act as a soft coercer on Serbia not to abandon its policies on Kosovo nor to give up its support for Russia more broadly. One

[38] Sheftalovich, 'Russia Stoking Serbia-Kosovo Tensions to Distract from Ukraine, Pristina says."
[39] Fatos Bytyci, 'Serbs in Northern Kosovo to Start Removing Barricades from Thursday', *Reuters*, 28 December 2022.
[40] Heil, Augustinovic and Katic, '"Unity" Holiday Tests Sympathy, Balkan Tolerance for a New "Serbian World".
[41] KIPRED, 'Russia's Information Warfare towards Kosovo', 24.
[42] *The Geopost*, '"The Serbian List Met with Putin's United Russia" Party before the 2017 Local Elections in Kosovo', *The Geopost*, 6 March 2022. https://thegeopost.com/en/news/the-serbian-list-met-with-putins-united-russia-party-before-the-2017-local-elections-in-kosovo/
[43] Samorukov, 'A Spoiler in the Balkans? Russia and the Final Resolution of the Kosovo Conflict'.

of the most reliable sources of this instrumentation is the Orthodox Church community.

For Serbs, ethnicity and religious identity have almost identical meanings, which puts the Serbian Orthodox Church in an advantageous position to act as a medium for Russian soft power. The Serbian Orthodox Church and the Russian Orthodox Church have strong ties and are closely linked to each country's political system.[44] Orthodox churches and monasteries throughout Kosovo are landmarks of Serbias' historical heritage, cultural significance and contemporary right to the territories. These buildings mirror via their very presence that 'Kosovo is Serbia'. The religious heritage is even incorporated in the Serbian name for Kosovo, '*Kosovo and Metohija*'. The first part, 'Kosovo', refers to historical battles between the Serbian and the Ottoman Empire in 1389; the last part translates to land of monastic estates – a reference to the many estates owned by the Orthodox Church in the region. Both names show the significance of Kosovo to Serbian history and identity, the importance of preserving Orthodox Christianity and Serbia's willingness to make considerable sacrifices in this quest.

In 2018, Patriarch Irinej, leader of the Serbian Orthodox Church, led a delegation to Moscow. Here, he stressed that the Russian Orthodox Church is the spiritual center of all Orthodoxy. He also stressed that Serbs will always look to Russia for help and be the small boat tied to the big Russian ship.[45] Patriarch Irinej also touched upon similarities in the experiences of the Churches in Russia and Serbia. He reminded listeners that Slavic ancestors shed blood outside present-day Serbia to defend their Christian faith at Kosovo Polje. The reference emphasizes why Serbia must not abandon this territory. The parallel for Russia is Ukraine, which formed the core of the Kyiv Empire that gathered the Slavs and Christianized them.[46]

From a Russian point of view, the Orthodox Church is a powerful political tool.[47] The leader of the Russian Orthodox Church, Patriarch Kirill, is both a political and religious figure with powerful ties to the Kremlin. Kirill publicly describes Putin's ascension to power as a miracle of God, and the myth goes that Kirill secretly baptized Putin's father in 1952. These connections make Kirill's statements on Kosovo echo the will of Moscow's

---

44 KCSS, 'Russian Interference in Kosovo: How and Why?', 2017, 29.
45 Baskin, 'Unpacking Russia's Balkan Baggage', 69.
46 Christoph Mick, 'How Moscow Has Long Used the Historic Kyivan Rus State to Justify Expansionism', *The Conversation*, 8 March 2022, https://theconversation.com/how-moscow-has-long-used-the-historic-kyivan-rus-state-to-justify-expansionism-178092.
47 Conley and Saric, *The Serbian-Kosovo Normalisation Process*, 4.

leadership.[48] Kirill has publicly emphasized support for Kosovo Serbs and the funding of the restoration of churches in Kosovo, referring to the mistreatment of the holy sites and communities in Kosovo by the Kosovo administration.[49] In 2016, Kirill spoke in the Saviour Cathedral in Moscow, describing the similarities between Russia and Serbia:

> Our Church will never abandon her brothers who find themselves in a difficult position in Ukraine and will never turn her back on them. We will never agree to changes in the sacred canonical boundaries of our Church. For Kyiv is the spiritual cradle of Holy Rus in the same way as Mtskheta is to Georgia and Kosovo is *to Serbia*.[50]

In 2021, the Serbian minister of foreign affairs, Nikola Selakovic, visited the same cathedral in Moscow and met with Patriarch Kirill. At this meeting, Patriarch Kirill restated that the relations between the Russian Orthodox Church and the Serbian Orthodox Church are decisive regarding the overall ties between Russia and Serbia.[51] The mentioned examples represent only a fragment of a highly complex pattern of political and religious connections between Serbia and Russia – patterns exploitable for gains by Russia through the legitimacy of religious figures and arguments. The spiritual ties help the Russian policy softly coerce the Serbian government to stay on track with Russian interests.

A report from the European Parliament in 2021 concluded that the level of disinformation from the countries of Russia, Turkey and China is lower in Kosovo than in most other parts of the Balkan region.[52] Importantly, the report shows that influence operations from Russia are not aimed at the population of Kosovo as such, but instead at Serbs, who are motivated by the 'injustice' of the loss of Kosovo. This is not because of solid institutions or practices to counter disinformation present in Kosovo. A study on disinformation in Kosovo presented in November 2022 points to several vulnerabilities in Kosovo that could

[48] L. Sweeney and L. Stein, 'With His Luxury Watch and Murky Sovjet Past, Patriarch Kirill Is Putin's Spiritual Leader and Power Broker', *ABC News*, 21 January 2023.

[49] Srdjan Barisic, 'The Role of the Serbian and Russian Orthodox Churches in Shaping Governmental Policy', in *The Warp of the Serbian Identity*, ed. Sonja Biserko (Belgrade: Helsinki Committee for Human Rights in Serbia, 2016), 116.

[50] The Russian Orthodox Church, Department for External Church Relations, 'His Holiness Patriarch Kirill of Moscow and All Rus Addressed the Participants of the Gathering in the Church Assembly Hall of the Christ the Saviour Cathedral in Moscow', https://mospat.ru/en/news/48993/.

[51] The Republic of Serbia, Ministry of Foreign Affairs, 'Minister Selakovic and Patriarch Kirill: Relations between the Serbian Orthodox Church and the Russian Orthodox Church are key to the relations between Serbia and Russia', 16 April 2021. https://www.mfa.gov.rs/en/press-service/news/minister-selakovic-and-patriarch-kirill-relations-between-serbian-orthodox.

[52] Policy Department for External Relations, European Parliament, 'Mapping Fake News and Disinformation in the Western Balkans and Identifying Ways to Effectively Counter Them', 2021, 26.

potentially be exploited for disinformation and a lack of capacity to intercept and mediate it.[53] The fact that Russia makes little use of these vulnerabilities suggests that influence operations aimed towards the broader society in Kosovo have little value for Russia (as well as China or Turkey). Directly targeting the Serbian audience is far more effective and relevant. Sputnik Serbia is the leading platform for distributing pro-Russian narratives about Kosovo to the entire Serbian community.[54] In an interview in 2021, the executive director of KIPRED, Lulzim Peci, called it a tool for the *"Russian diplomatic war against Kosovo."*

Another media promoting Russian narratives to Serbs is RT International (RT.com). An article from RT International from October 23, 2021, about two Russian diplomats expelled from Kosovo states: *"Kosovo's de facto government is illegitimate, and its expulsion of two Russian diplomats in UN affairs has no legal validity."* The article's purpose is to remind the reader of Kosovo's lack of statehood and, thus, that Kosovo cannot expel foreign diplomats. The article ends by summarizing NATO's actions in 1999 as a pro-Albanian intervention. These ideas are repeated in other Kosovo-related articles on the RT website, generally focusing on undermining the authority and neutrality of public institutions in Kosovo, ethnic tensions, and the idea of creating a Greater Albania. These narratives come very close to Russian official statements undermining the legitimacy of the Kosovo administration and Kosovo as an independent, capable state, as discussed earlier. According to the NATO StratCom CoE report, the pro-Russian narratives are not limited to Russian-controlled media such as Sputnik Serbia or RT. Instead, the narratives are primarily pushed and disputed by local Serbian media.[55] Activities on the Serbian media platforms suggest identical mechanisms as that of the Orthodox Church and even the activities of the Serbian government itself. Serbia is not a victim of Russian influence. It is primarily a voluntary partner with an agenda similar to Russia's. Serbia's willful and long ongoing partaken promoting the Russian agenda in the Balkans has cornered the Serbian government on the Kosovo question. Consequently, the cheap points of popularity in Serb communities in Serbia and Kosovo that the Orthodox Church and Serbian government have enjoyed over the years continue to provide Russia with tools to spoil progress in the Balkans, sow discord in the EU and NATO, and stir low-level conflicts.

---

[53] Albana Rexha, 'Vulnerability Index of Disinformation in Kosovo', *Democracy Plus*, 2022.
[54] Dimitar Bechev, 'Hedging Its Bets: Serbia between Russia and the EU', *Carnegie Europe*, 19 January 2023, 3; NDI (National Democratic Institute), 'Kosovo: Post-Election Analysis of February 2021 Parliamentary Elections', 2021, 10.; Interviews in Kosovo 2021.
[55] NATO Strategic Communications Centre of Excellence, 2019: 25.

The war in Ukraine is a game-changer – does Kosovo get a second chance?

In November 2022, Russia launched a new Serbian-language service in Serbia called RT Balkan. It also announced its plans to start a local language broadcast in Serbia by 2024. The first tweet from the chief editor of the new platform read, 'Kosovo is Serbia'. This tweet's narrative and timing, amid growing tensions in the northern provinces of Kosovo at that time, make it obvious to interpret this initiative as yet another Russian initiative further to inflame tensions, alertness and instability in Kosovo – acting once more as the genuine spoiler. The EU countries already in March 2022 had blocked RT International as part of sanctions against Russia. Therefore, before the launch, Serbia was heavily criticized and under international pressure for allowing Russian propaganda and disinformation to spread from Serbia. This, however, did not make Serbia change its mind. RT Balkan was launched as planned despite the novel situation with a war in Ukraine.[56] Same old – same old, one could argue.

Suppose this image of RT reporting from Serbia encapsulates the Russian and Serbian relationship and the role of Kosovo post-February 2022. Then, the conclusion to this chapter writes itself: Russia continues to exploit possibilities to steer conflict in the Balkans by keeping Serbia dependent on Russia. Promoting the narrative 'Kosovo is Serbia' through hard diplomacy and as part of the Serbian World ideology still serves Russian purposes. Serbia and Russia tie an even tighter knot, sealing the common destiny as states being humiliated and lacking the respect of Western powers. They continue to share the common dream of uniting the lost territories and people to a Serbian or a Russian World.

Russia may wish to play the same game with Serbia as it has for more than a decade, but how about Serbia? Is it trying to strike a new balance in its foreign policy? An overview of actions taken by Serbia in 2022 does not show significant policy changes. Serbia has refused to follow the Western sanctions towards Russia. Flights from Russia still land in Belgrade in 2023, and Russians can enter Serbia visa-free and even move their businesses here to avoid sanctions. Data from numerous polls show that most Serbs still see Russia as the best ally and desired partner for Serbia. Asked in June 2022, 72 per cent of Serbs believe Russia was forced to start the war in Ukraine because of NATO enlargement.[57]

---

[56] Bne IntelliNews, 'Russian Propaganda Outlet RT Launches Serbia Service Amid Hike in Tensions with Kosovo', 16 November 2022.
[57] Bechev, 'Hedging Its Bets: Serbia Between Russia and the EU', 2–3.

Excusing his act as a matter of necessity, Vucic signed a new deal on energy with Russia in May 2022. In August 2022, the minister of interior and defense, Vulin, met with Russian Foreign Minister Lavrov in Moscow and announced, 'Serbia does not forget the centuries-old brotherhood with Russia'.[58] One has to be a skilled diplomat to read any signs of changes in this list of post-February 2022 policies and statements.

Giving Serbia some credit, it has supported several UN General Assembly resolutions during 2022 condemning Russian aggression against Ukraine. Serbia has also refused to let the Wagner group or other Russian military companies recruit Serbian volunteers. Many commentators interpret this as part of policy changes by Serbia. Still, already in 2015, Serbia prohibited nationals from volunteering in Syria or fighting in the Donbas region – so there is no news here. The same goes for the statements by Vucic that Serbia respects Ukraine's territorial integrity and sovereignty. This has been the official policy since 2008. These statements are vital arguments for Serbia to continue claiming that 'Kosovo is Serbia'. Russia is fully aware that this is the official Serbian policy and has therefore played subgroups outside the Serbian government to promote Russian views on this issue.[59] Serbia has intensified negotiations with other international actors since 2022 to avoid dependency on Russia. However, identifying fundamental policy changes towards Kosovo due to the war in Ukraine has not been possible.

Serbia may try to keep close and good relations with Russia and continue its policies on Kosovo despite the changing international environment. Still, changes at a much larger scale are starting to affect the dynamics in the Balkans. The EU, NATO and the United States are investing significantly to pressure Serbia and Kosovo to finalize the road to normalization. The goal for the Western actors is to reach an agreement that does not force Serbia or other unwilling states to recognize Kosovo as a sovereign state. Instead, Serbia could be pushed to accept Kosovo as a member of the international community and for the two states to coexist without mutual recognition. NATO, the EU, the United States and individual Western partners now weigh in on the Balkans with both soft and hard power. The seriousness of a hostile Russia has empowered these actors to act in greater cohesion and to move beyond 'petty discussions' that have torn

58 Bechev, 'Hedging Its Bets: Serbia Between Russia and the EU', 3.
59 Maxim Samorukov, 'What the Wagner Mercenaries' row Reveals about Serbia's Relations with Russia', *Carnegie Endowment for International Peace*, 26 January 2023.

the region or reflect internal concerns in those European states that still refuse to recognize Kosovos statehood.

Political realism may seize this moment amid a growing rivalry and the war in Ukraine. Consequently, more unity of Western forces may do what it takes to resolve the situation between Serbia and Kosovo more permanently. The construct of the former Yugoslavia withstood for decades due to the balance of power between the United States and USSR overlaying all other power dynamics. The same can reoccur in the Balkans, allowing Kosovo to become an independent state, including a protected autonomous Serb minority. In early 2023, Serbia still is not on board that train, and the actions by Serbia in the first year of the war are in no way convincing that Serbia is changing its course. However, it is still early days for the international pressure to make Serbia choose a new destination going West. The war in Ukraine and all the power struggles in the global system that follow from this could be dominant variables to undo the narrative 'Kosovo is Serbia' to a new 'Kosovo and Serbia'.

Bibliography

Barisic, S. (2016), 'The Role of the Serbian and Russian Orthodox Churches in Shaping Governmental Policy' in S. Biserko (ed.), *The Warp of the Serbian Identity*, 105–28. Belgrade: Helsinki Committee for Human Rights in Serbia.

Baskin, M. (2018), 'Unpacking Russia's Balkan Baggage', in David L. Philips and Lulzim Peci (eds), *Threats and Challenges to Kosovo's Sovereignty*, 55–71, The Institute for the Study of Human Rights at Columbia University in co-operation with the Kosovar Institute for Policy Research and Development (KIPRED) in Prishtina. Available online: https://www.kipred.org/repository/docs/ThreatsAndChallenges_Vers-FIN_60835.pdf (accessed 16 November 2023).

BBC (2017), 'Serbian Train Sparks Escalation in Tensions with Kosovo', *BBC*, 14 January. Available online: https://www.bbc.com/news/world-europe-38625872 (accessed 16 November 2023).

Bechev, D. (2019), *Russia's Strategic Interests and Tools of Influence in the Western Balkans*. Riga: NATO Strategic Communications Centre of Excellence, 14–15.

Bechev, D. (2023), 'Hedging Its Bets: Serbia between Russia and the EU', *Carnegie Europe*, 19 January 2023. Available online: https://carnegieeurope.eu/2023/01/19/hedging-its-bets-serbia-between-russia-and-eu-pub-88819 (accessed 16 December 2023).

Bne IntelliNews (2022), 'Russian Propaganda Outlet RT Launches Serbia Service Amid Hike in Tensions with Kosovo', 16 November.

Bytyci, F. (2022), 'Serbs in Northern Kosovo to Start Removing Barricades from Thursday', *Reuters*, 28 December. Available online: https://www.reuters.com/world/europe/kosovo-put-detained-serb-under-house-arrest-possibly-easing-stand off-2022-12-28/ (accessed 16 December 2023).

Conley, H. A., and D. Saric (2021), 'The Serbian-Kosovo Normalisation Process – a Temporary US Decoupling', *Center for Strategic and International Studies*. Available online: https://www.csis.org/analysis/serbia-kosovo-normalization-process-temporary-us-decoupling (accessed 16 November 2023).

Digital Forensic Centre (2021), 'The Serbian World – Originally Borrowed Concept – DFC Analysis of the Attempt to Merge Montenegro into the Serbian World', *Digital Forensic Centre*, April. Available online: https://dfc.me/en/the-serbian-world-origina lly-borrowed-concept/ (accessed 16 December 2023).

Dolapcev, Vanja. (2018), 'The Bear Never Sleeps: The Position of the Serbian-Russian Humanitarian Centre in Nis', *European Western Balkans*, 24 December. Available online: https://europeanwesternbalkans.com/2018/12/24/bear-never-sleeps-posit ion-serbian-russian-humanitarian-centre-nis/ (accessed 16 December 2023).

Dordevic, N. (2021), Serbian World – a Dangerous Idea? *Emerging Europe*, 27 July. Available online: https://emerging-europe.com/news/serbian-world-a-danger ous-idea/ (accessed 16 December 2023).

Euractiv.com (2022), 'Envoys from EU, US, visit Northern Kosovo Serbs as differences resurface', *euractiv.com*, 26 August. Available online: https://www.euractiv.com/sect ion/enlargement/news/envoys-from-eu-us-visit-northern-kosovo-serbs-as-differen ces-resurface/ (accessed 16 December 2023).

The Geopost (2022), '"The Serbian List Met with Putin's United Russia" Party before the 2017 Local Elections in Kosovo', *The Geopost*, 6 March. Available online: https://thegeopost.com/en/news/the-serbian-list-met-with-putins-united-russia-party-bef ore-the-2017-local-elections-in-kosovo/ (accessed 16 December 2023).

Global Voices (2022), 'Spreading Misinformation about Kosovo Was Once Again Used as Part of the Election Strategy in Serbia', 21 May. Available online: https://globalvoi ces.org/2022/05/31/spreading-misinformation-about-kosovo-was-once-again-use d-as-part-of-election-strategy-in-serbia/ (accessed 16 December 2023).

Heil, A., M. Augustinovic and G. Katic (2021), '"Unity" Holiday Tests Sympathy, Balkan Tolerance for a New "Serbian World"', *Radiofreeeurope*, 14 September. Available online: https://www.rferl.org/a/serbia-flag-holiday-balkans/31460195.html (accessed 16 December 2023).

Kallaba, Pëllumb (2017), 'Russian Interference in Kosovo: How and Why?', Kosovar Centre for Security Studies (KCSS).

Kentera, S. (2021), 'Russia's Role in the Balkans: The Case of Montenegro', *Digital Forensic Centre*. Available online: https://dfc.me/en/dfc-study-russias-role-in-the-balkans-the-case-of-montenegro/ (accessed 16 December 2023).

KIPRED (2020), 'Russia's Information Warfare towards Kosovo: Political Background and Manifestation: Special Policy Brief', *KIPRED*, October. Available online: https://

www.kipred.org/repository/docs/Russia_-_Kosovo_Political_Background_-_Eng_-_Fin_616233.pdf (accessed 16 Deceber 2023).

Kosovo Online (2023), 'Vucic: By Withdrawing the Recognition of Kosovo's Independence, Suriname Became an Example for Other Countries', *Kosovo Online*, 24 July. Available online: https://www.kosovo-online.com/en/news/politics/vucic-withdrawing-recognition-kosovos-independence-suriname-became-example-other (accessed 16 December 2023).

Mick, C. (2022), 'How Moscow Has Long Used the Historic Kyivan Rus State to Justify Expansionism', *The Conversation*, 8 March. Available online: https://theconversation.com/how-moscow-has-long-used-the-historic-kyivan-rus-state-to-justify-expansionism-178092 (accessed 16 December 2023).

National Democratic Institute (2021), 'Kosovo: Post-Election Analysis of February 2021 Parliamentary Elections', *National Democratic Institute*, 29 April. Available online: https://www.ndi.org/publications/kosovo-post-election-analysis-february-2021-parliamentary-elections (accessed 16 November 2023).

Nyemann, D. B. (2021), 'Hybrid Warfare in the Baltics', in M. Weissmann, N. Nilsson, P. Thunholm and B. Palmertz (eds), *Hybrid Warfare: Security and Asymmetric Conflict in International Relations*, London: I.B. Tauris.

Peci, L. (2020), *Russia's Information Warfare towards Kosovo: Political Background and Manifestation*, KIPRED. Available online: https://kipred.org/repository/docs/Russia_-_Kosovo_Political_Background_-_Eng_-_Fin_616233.pdf (accessed 16 November 2023).

Pieper, M. (2020), 'Russkiy Mir: The Geopolitics of Russian Compatriots Abroad', *Geopolitics*, 25 (3): 756–79.

Policy Department for External Relations, European Parliament (2021), 'Mapping Fake News and Disinformation in the Western Balkans and Identifying Ways to Effectively Counter Them'. *Policy Department for External Relations, European Parliament*. Available online: https://www.europarl.europa.eu/thinktank/en/document/EXPO_STU(2020)653621 (accessed 16 November 2023).

Philips, D. L., and L. Peci (eds) (2018), *Threats and Challenges to Kosovo's Sovereignty*, Columbia University, Prishtina–New York. Available online: https://www.kipred.org/repository/docs/ThreatsAndChallenges_Vers-FIN_60835.pdf (accessed 16 November 2023).

Prelec, T. (2020), ' "Our Brothers," "Our Saviours." The Importance of Chinese Investment for the Serbian Government's Narrative of the Economic Rebound', Policy Paper, *Prague Security Studies*.

Qehaja, F. (2018), 'Acting against the Normalisation: Serbia's Diplomatic Offensive on Kosovo', in David L. Philips and Lulzim Peci (eds), *Threats and Challenges to Kosovo's Sovereignty*, Columbia University, Prishtina–New York.

The Republic of Serbia, Ministry of Foreign Affairs (2021), 'Minister Selakovic and Patriarch Kirill: Relations between the Serbian Orthodox Church and the Russian Orthodox Church Are Key to the Relations between Serbia and Russia', *The Republic*

of Serbia, Ministry of Foreign Affairs, 16 April. Available online: https://www.mfa.gov.
rs/en/press-service/news/minister-selakovic-and-patriarch-kirill-relations-between-
serbian-orthodox (accessed 16 November 2023).

Rexha, A. (2022), *Vulnerability Index of Disinformation in Kosovo, Democracy Plus*.
Available online: https://dplus.org/wp-content/uploads/2022/11/ENG_Index-of-Dis
information.pdf?fbclid=IwAR3TPQ9i01l1wcVv60SuhTKGMYD8OU3z1ylCmN6Z
8PCQPVThmjCkU18W_qE (accessed 16 December 2023).

The Russian Orthodox Church (2016), 'His Holiness Patriarch Kirill of Moscow and All
Rus Addressed the Participants of the Gathering in the Church Assembly Hall of the
Christ the Saviour Cathedral in Moscow Department for External Church Relations',
The Russian Orthodox Church. Available online: https://mospat.ru/en/news/48993/
(accessed 16 November 2023).

Samorukov, M. (2019), 'A Spoiler in the Balkans? Russia and the Final Resolution of the
Kosovo Conflict', *Carnegie Moscow Centre*, 26 November. Available online: https://
carnegieendowment.org/2019/11/26/spoiler-in-balkans-russia-and-final-resolut
ion-of-kosovo-conflict-pub-80429 (accessed 16 December 2023).

Samorukov, M. (2020), 'Fan Diplomacy in the Balkans', *Carnegie Moscow Center*, 8
July. Available online: https://carnegieendowment.org/2019/11/26/spoiler-in-
balkans-russia-and-final-resolution-of-kosovo-conflict-pub-80429 (accessed 16
December 2023).

Samorukov, M. (2023), 'What the Wagner Mercenaries' Row Reveals about Serbia's
Relations with Russia', *Carnegie Endowment for International Peace*, 26 January.
Available online: https://carnegieendowment.org/politika/88885 (accessed 16
December 2023).

Sheftalovich, Z. (2022), 'Russia Stoking Serbia-Kosovo Tensions to Distract from
Ukraine, Pristina Says', *Politico*, 29 December. Available online: https://www.politico.
eu/article/russia-stoking-serbia-kosovo-tensions-distract-from-ukraine-pristina-bes
nik-bislimi/ (accessed 16 November 2023).

Sherr, J. (2013), *Hard Diplomacy and Soft Coercion – Russia's Influence Abroad*,
Washington, DC: Brookings Institution's Press/Chatham House.

Smith, E. (2022), 'Russia's Influence Is at Risk in the Southern African Nation
of Angola as Voters Head to the Polls', *CNBC*. Available online: https://
www.cnbc.com/2022/08/24/angola-election-russia-influence-at-risk-as-vot
ers-head-to-the-polls.html (accessed 16 November 2023).

Stojanovic, D. (2022), 'China Makes Semi-Secret Delivery of Missiles to Serbia', *AP*, 10
April. Available online: https://apnews.com/article/russia-ukraine-europe-china-ser
bia-nato-682ab79c4239f14ecc1133ff5c7addc9.

Sweeney, L., and L. Stein (2023), 'With His Luxury Watch and Murky Soviet Past,
Patriarch Kirill Is Putin's Spiritual Leader and Power Broker', *ABC News*, 21 January.
Available online: https://www.abc.net.au/news/2023-01-22/meet-patriarch-kirill-
orthodox-church-leader-and-putin-ally/101858322 (accessed 16 November 2023).

Telegraph (2022), 'Vucic Meet with Angolan Interior Minister Laborinho: We Will Always Support Serbia on the Issue of Kosovo', *Telegraph*. Available online: https://www.telegraf.rs/english/3586774-vucic-meets-with-angolan-interior-minister-laborinho-we-will-always-support-serbia-on-the-issue-of-kosovo (accessed 16 November 2023).

Vllasi, Elis (2020), 'Russian Influence in Kosovo – in the Shadows of Myth and Reality', Kosovar Centre for Security Studies (KCSS), 7 November.

7

Beyond cyber and disinformation: Russian hybrid warfare tactics in Georgia

Kornely Kakachia and Shota Kakabadze

Introduction

Since its independence, Georgia has been one of the most vocally independent countries among the Soviet Union's successor states. Located at the crossroads of Asia and Europe, it has an important economic and security role for the wider Black Sea region and European neighbourhood as an important transit route between Central Asia and Europe that bypasses Russia. Over the centuries, Georgia was the object of rivalry between the Persian, Ottoman and Russian Empires, before being eventually annexed by Russia in the nineteenth century. Since emerging from the collapsing Soviet Union as an independent state in 1991, Georgia has again become an arena for conflicting interests. Increasing Western (mostly the EU and the United States) economic and political influence in the country has long been a source of concern for neighbouring Russia, as have Georgia's aspirations to join NATO and the EU. As a frontline state in the 'gray zone', outside the safety of NATO's security umbrella, Georgia faces the daunting tasks of pursuing Euro-Atlantic integration, strengthening its democratic resilience, preserving sovereignty and avoiding Russian aggression – all at the same time.[1]

Given this conflict of interests, Georgian governments were unsuccessful in balancing between the Russian Federation and the West. President Saakashvili, who started his presidency on the promise that he would balance between

---

[1] Tracey German and Kornely Kakachia, 'Achieving Security as a Small State', in *Georgias Foreign Policy in 21 Century: Challenges for a Small State*, dd. Tracey German, Stephan Jones and Kornely Kakachia (London: I.B. Tauris, 2022).

Russian Federation and the West,[2] eventually became the target of the Kremlin's military aggression against Georgia in August 2008. Even the change to the more *pragmatic* approach towards Russia of the government that came in Georgia after 2012 yielded no results.[3] As of this writing, two territories of the country remain under the Russian occupation and there exists no diplomatic relations between the Kremlin and Tbilisi. Russian Federation is being perceived by many Georgians as a number one threat to the country[4] and any step from the government that could be interpreted as a compromise on declared foreign policy priorities is met by social tensions and protests.[5]

Yet, despite the complicated relationship, the economic cooperation and trade between the two has been steadily on a rise for the last decade.[6] The level of dependence of Georgia's economy on its northern neighbour has reached to the level that is considered alarming by many.[7] Increasing reliance on the Russian market has substantially increased Georgia's vulnerability and susceptibility to Russian influence.

The full-scale military invasion launched by the Russian Federation into the neighbouring Ukraine in February 2022 has dramatically changed the security paradigm in the wider Black Sea region and the Eastern Europe in general. It has even further aggravated the security challenges coming from Russia for European Union's Eastern neighbours. Countries like Georgia, Ukraine or Moldova which are not covered by the NATO Security umbrella remain vulnerable not only to threats posed by hybrid warfare but also to the use of the conventional hard power.

However, proceeding to detailed analysis of the threats and specific vulnerabilities posed by the Russian hybrid warfare to Georgia, it is important to provide a working definition of the concept that will be applied in this chapter. There exists no agreement in the scholarship on how to exactly define the concept

---

[2] Margarita Antidze, 'Georgian Leader Wants Better Ties with Russia', *Reuters*, 8 January 2008, https://www.reuters.com/article/us-georgia-election-saakshvili-idUSL0727751420080107.

[3] Kornely Kakachia, Salome Minesashvili and Levan Kakhishvili, 'Change and Continuity in the Foreign Policies of Small States: Elite Perceptions and Georgia's Foreign Policy towards Russia', *Europe-Asia Studies* 70, no. 5 (2018): 814–31, doi: https://doi.org/10.1080/09668136.2018.1480751.

[4] 'Public Opinion Survey Residents of Georgia March 2022', The International Republican Institute – Georgia, March 2022, https://www.iri.org/wp-content/uploads/2022/04/IRI-Poll-Presentation-Geor gia-March2022_Final.pdf.

[5] 'Protesters in Tbilisi Decry Georgian Government's Inadequate Support for Ukraine', *Radio Free Europe/Radio Liberty*, 1 March 2022, https://www.rferl.org/a/ukraine-invasion-tbilisi-protest-geor gia/31731006.html.

[6] 'Georgia's Economic Dependence on Russia: Trends and Threats', *Transparency International Georgia*, 4 May 2020, https://transparency.ge/en/blog/georgias-economic-dependence-russia-tre nds-and-threats.

[7] 'Georgia's Economic Dependence on Russia'.

of hybrid war.[8] In Russian military doctrines, unlike Western counterparts, it is understood as a type of war and not simply just another tool of state's foreign policy. For the Kremlin it denotes a type of the war rather than an instrument.[9] It implies the mix of conventional, economic, cyber, psychological and diplomatic means of conducting a war.

Following Reichborn-Kjennerud and Cullen, hybrid warfare model can be defined as being built on several characteristics: 'It is asymmetric and multi-modal along a horizontal and a vertical axis, and to varying degrees shares an increased emphasis on creativity, ambiguity, and the cognitive elements of war.'[10] The actor engaged in the hybrid warfare tactics uses all the instruments of power (military, economic, informational, societal, etc.) simultaneously to target opponent's vulnerabilities and achieve its desired goal. In other words, hybrid threats and hybrid warfare, through the variety of means from the threat of war to the propaganda, target opposing societies rather than combatants.[11]

This chapter engages in the analysis of Russian hybrid activities in Georgia that take place in several domains: ideological, informational, cyber and, through proxy forces in South Ossetia and Abkhazia, security. Combination of these elements has been a basis of Kremlin's projection of its influence in the neighbouring country. As Georgia has been the subject of Russian hybrid warfare tactics from the very start, as sort of 'testing ground', this case is of particular importance, if one wishes to examine the Kremlin's operations in the grey zone.[12] The second part of the chapter examines specific vulnerabilities that Georgian society is facing and what are the state's capacities to mitigate these challenges. Finally, it offers lessons that can be drawn from the case of Georgia and its wider applicability.

Overview of Russian hybrid methods and influence in the state's national context

Russian successful annexation of Crimea without applying conventional military tools in 2014 came as a surprise to many in the West, and since then,

---

[8] Erik Reichborn-Kjennerud and Patrick Cullen, 'What Is Hybrid Warfare?', Policy Brief [1/2016], *Norwegian Institute of International Affairs*, 2016, https://nupi.brage.unit.no/nupi-xmlui/bitstream/handle/11250/2380867/NUPI_Policy_Brief_1_Reichborn_Kjennerud_Cullen.pdf.

[9] Mason Clark, 'Russian Hybrid Warfare', Institute for the Study of War, September 2020, https://www.jstor.org/stable/resrep26547.1.

[10] Reichborn-Kjennerud and Cullen, 'What Is Hybrid Warfare?'.

[11] Niklas Nilsson et al., 'Security Challenges in the Grey Zone: Hybrid Threats and Hybrid Warfare', in *Hybrid Warfare*, ed. Mikale Weissmann et al. (London: I.B. Tauris, 2021), Ch. 1. p. 2.

[12] Niklas Nilsson. *Russian Hybrid Tactics in Georgia* (Washington, DC: Central Asia-Caucasus Institute & Silk Road Studies Program, 2018), 7.

it has been regarded as a considerable threat to other countries.[13] This case of effective application of non-military instruments and misinformation has led to hybrid warfare as the concept is gaining popularity and becoming the focus of the academic or strategic analysis.[14] Western academia usually accredits Russian hybrid war strategies to General Valery Gerasimov. His speech was published in 2013, where he argued that the line between peace and war was blurred and that new types of war now included the application of informational, political, economic, cyber, humanitarian and other methods.[15] As Russian military capabilities are considerably weaker, in comparison to the United States and its allies, the Kremlin prefers to operate in the grey zone – 'below the threshold of armed attack or use of force'[16] with the strong emphasis on information operations. This suggests that Russian hybrid activities and involvement in other countries takes place in various domains at the same time.

Hence, while examining Kremlin's strategy, it is important to analyse different fields of contestation where subversive activities are unfolding. In case of Georgia, Nilsson suggests dividing 'toolbox' of Russian hybrid tactics against Georgia into military, diplomatic, economic, subversive and informational.[17] This chapter focuses on cyber and informational domains as the most intensive fields of Russian activities in Georgia.

Cyber domain

The phenomenon of the hybrid warfare existed long before the so-called Gerasimov's doctrine or events unfolding in Ukraine in 2014. Crimean annexation is not the first instance when the Russian Federation has used nonconventional military methods as a part of its larger strategy. For instance, despite not being officially confirmed, it is accepted by the international community, that the Kremlin was behind the massive cyberattack against Estonia in 2007.[18] However, the case of Russian invasion of Georgia in August

---

[13] Renz Bettina and Hanna Smith, '"Hybrid Warfare" as an Operational Approach to War – a New War-Winning Formula?', in *Russia and Hybrid Warfare – Going Beyond the Label*, ed. Renz Bettina and Hanna Smith, Aleksanteri Papers, no. 1/2016 (Helsinki: Kikimora Publications, 2016), ch. 1, p. 2.

[14] Bettina and Smith, '"Hybrid Warfare" as an Operational Approach to War'.

[15] Fabian Sandor, 'The Russian Hybrid Warfare Strategy – Neither Russian Nor Strategy', *Defense & Security Analysis* 35, no. 3 (July 2019): 308–25; 311.

[16] G. Alexander Crowther, 'NATO and hybrid warfare Seeking a concept to define the challenge from Russia', in *Hybrid Warfare*, edited by Mikale Weissmann et al. (I.B. Tauris, 2021), Ch. 2. p. 31.

[17] Nilsson. *Russian Hybrid Tactics in Georgia*, 23.

[18] Sandor, 'The Russian Hybrid Warfare Strategy – Neither Russian Nor Strategy', 308–25; 311.

2008 is more telling in this regard. Already, in July of 2008, Georgian government websites were subject of coordinated cyberattacks coming from Russia. This marked the important precedent in international relations, as it was the first time ever, when the cyberaggression was later accompanied by the use of traditional military force.[19] These developments of coordinated attacks both in cyber and physical domains make the case of Russo-Georgian five-day War the first of this kind. An interesting aspect of these cyberattacks also was the fact that it was well coordinated with the overall Russian military strategy against Georgia in August of 2008. More specifically, some argue that there was a political decision not to attack critical infrastructure of the country and the aggression in the cyberspace also followed this strategy – sending a message that it could do so if wished.[20] This suggests that Russian activities in the cyber domain can serve two purposes: inflicting the actual damage, as it was the case of Estonia or Georgia; or it can be used to simply demonstrate the power. The latter was what happened in 2014 when Sweden experienced cyberattacks from Russia after Stockholm's consideration of joining NATO in response to annexation of Crimea.[21]

Ideological domain

Hybrid methods and influence of the Russian Federation go to several directions at the same time. For Georgian context especially relevant is ideological and informational domain which involves the projection to neighbouring countries what Morozov calls *paleoconservatism* – politicizing culture and using it as an instrument in the ongoing *civilizational struggle*.[22] It implies that the Russian civilizational discourse, despite being articulated as different and standing in contrast to the West, in fact is largely dependent on the latter. Due to the inability of creating an alternative ideological platform, the Kremlin's criticism of the West is based in accusing Europe of abandoning true values.[23] Values – that are based on Christianity and conservatism. Even after Russia's invasion of Ukraine, the West remained the key target of Russian disinformation campaign, with more emphasis to projecting it as an unreliable partner.[24]

[19] David Hollis, 'Cyberwar Case Study: Georgia 2008', *Small Wars Journal* (6 January 2011): 2, https://smallwarsjournal.com/jrnl/art/cyberwar-case-study-georgia-2008.
[20] Hollis, 'Cyberwar Case Study: Georgia 2008', 4.
[21] Sandor, 'The Russian Hybrid Warfare Strategy – Neither Russian Nor Strategy', 308–25; 312.
[22] Viacheslav Morozov, *Russia's Postcolonial Identity: A Subaltern Empire in a Eurocentric World* (London: Palgrave Macmillan London, 2015), doi: https://doi.org/10.1057/9781137409300.
[23] Morozov, *Russia's Postcolonial Identity*, 117–19.
[24] Tatia Chikhladze and Shota Shiukashvili, 'Pro-Russian Disinformation Narratives in Georgia Since Russia's Full-scale Invasion of Ukraine', *Caucasus Analytical Digest* no. 135 (2023): 3.

This conservative turn in Russian politics has become especially apparent after Putin's return to the president's office in 2012. According to Sharafutdinova, as Putin assumed the post for the third time, there was a need of a new niche for him to claim that would strengthen his authority,[25] especially amidst 2011–13 protests. In this context, the image of Russia as a defender of traditional values appeared, that served not only domestic purposes but also for more aggressive, value-based foreign policy. This conservative discourse is supported by the relevant legislation, for example, the so-called *Gay Propaganda Law* and *Anti- blasphemy Law* adopted together in 2013 which helps the Kremlin to position globally as the alternative civilizational pole of attraction.

Russian Federation is a secular state. Yet, once politics are closely examined, it immediately becomes clear to the observer that the Russian Orthodox Church (ROC) is far more advantageous in positions in relation to other religious institutions and plays the vital role in the Russian national identity discourse.[26] It is one of the key pillars of the Kremlin's hybrid warfare strategy in its so-called near abroad. This reliance on orthodox Christianity hints to its bordering countries that their orthodox history and culture places them on Moscow's side rather than part of the Western civilization. Russian foreign minister, Sergey Lavrov, has even argued that one of the main reasons why the West had distanced itself from Russia was orthodox Christianity – the latter's return to its traditional values.[27] Curanovic, in her book identifies several points around which goals and ideas of the Russian state and the ROC correlate. She argues that for both the post-Soviet space is considered as the sphere of essential interests of Russia; both the Kremlin and the Church see Russia belonging to the Eurasian/Orthodox civilization; and most importantly, their goals correlate in seeking conservative/strategic alliances with India, China or Iran and in seeing multipolar geopolitical and civilizational global order as the most desirable.[28]

---

[25] Gulnaz Sharafutdinova, 'The Pussy Riot Affair and Putin's Démarche from Sovereign Democracy to Sovereign Morality', *Nationalities Papers* 42, no. 4 (2014): 615–21.

[26] For instance, Curanovic notes that respondents in Russia, when asked '*whether they are "Orthodox"?*' give their answer for the most part thinking, '*yes, I am Russian*'. Alicja Curanović, *The Religious Factor in Russia's Foreign Policy: Keeping God on Our Side* (London: Routledge, 2012), 62.

[27] S. 'Lavrov: Zapad Otdaljaetsja Ot Rossii iz-za ee Vozvrata K Pravoslaviju', *Pravoslavie.ru*, 5 July 2014, https://pravoslavie.ru/71250.html.

[28] Curanovic, *The Religious Factor in Russia's Foreign Policy*, 138.

Informational domain

In the later years, Russian methods have evolved into what can be described as a *positional warfare*, where the objective truth loses its importance, and it all comes down to having the power over the information. Paul and Matthews called this *firehose of falsehood*, arguing that Russian misinformation campaign and propaganda is high-volume and multichannel; it is rapid, continuous and repetitive; it lacks commitment to objective reality; and it lacks commitment to consistency.[29] These four points suggest that Russian misinformation is not so much about making lies believable, but simply about inflicting chaos and making people question the reality.

In case of countries like Georgia, this approach feeds on anti-Western sentiments that is aggravated by the country's slow progress on its Euro-Atlantic integration.[30] In this discourse Europe and the United States are depicted as the global forces that are externally imposing their will on Georgia.[31] After 2008 August war, this pressure on Georgia from the Russian Federation has considerably increased. The existence of constant military presence in the occupied territories and the fear of the conflict breaking out again, remains an inseparable part of the Russian hybrid warfare against Georgia. Psychological pressure of the possible intervention in the future, for example of Ukraine, is used by pro-Russian political actors to support their arguments in favour of Georgia's military neutrality and subsequently, if successful, achieving the Kremlin's geopolitical goal without even using conventional methods of war.

Georgia's vulnerabilities, Russian approaches and methods to target them and estimated impact

Hybrid warfare can be described as containing two types of approaches. It either intends to shorten the conflict or to prolong it in time. The first approach relies on the element of surprise, while the second strategy is focused on proxy forces and drawing population into the conflict. Yet, it needs to be noted that

[29] Christopher Paul and Miriam Matthews, 'The Russian "Firehose of Falsehood" Propaganda Model', *Rand Corporation* 2, no. 7 (2016): 1–10.

[30] Shota Ghvineria, 'shidasakhelmts'ipoebrivi sisust'eebis rusul iaraghad ktsevis hibriduli st'rat'egia sakartvelosa da uk'rainis magalitze', in *hibriduli omebis anat'omia*, ed. Tinatin Khidasheli (Tbilisi: Palitra L Publishing, 2021), 235.

[31] 'Alt-Right Inaugurates Anti-Liberal, Russia-Friendly Party', Civil.ge, 20 October 2021, https://civil.ge/archives/456863.

both approaches have their weaknesses. It is not always possible to rely on unexpected moves as they wear out over time, while trying to prolong the war via hybrid methods can be very costly in the long run.[32] Although this feature makes operationalizing the concept very difficult, as the definition of success becomes rather vague,[33] in case of Russian strategy towards Georgia and specific methods that are applied, one can still argue that the Kremlin's approach is focused on prolonging the conflict in time in order to maintain the leverage over Tbilisi. These methods are aimed at undermining country's pro-Western foreign policy by increasing the feeling of vulnerability to Russian aggression without applying conventional military tactics. Specific vulnerabilities which are targeted by the Russian hybrid warfare tactics can be identified in the following domains: *ideological, Soviet nostalgia, misinformation, borderization and cyberspace.*

Vulnerabilities in the ideological domain

While there are no official diplomatic relations between the Russian Federation and Georgia there are several institutions, NGOs and media outlets which project Russian normative discourse in Georgia. They serve as potential actors which intentionally or unintentionally help the Kremlin to target specific vulnerabilities in the country. The most prominent out of these actors is the Georgian Orthodox Church (GOC) which shares many common values with the Russian counterpart. Despite officially supporting the state's pro-European foreign policy, several high-ranking clergymen and groups associated with the GOC have been actively involved in anti-Western propaganda.

The GOC and its interpretation of Christianity creates pockets of vulnerabilities for Russian influence. More specifically, Georgian society considers itself as religious with the majority (up to 85 per cent) belonging to the GOC.[34] The GOC itself is trusted or fully trusted by more than 80 per cent of Georgians.[35] These figures highlight the potential influence this institution holds over Georgian society. And since the GOC shares value systems with its

---

[32] Bettina and Smith, ' "Hybrid Warfare" as an Operational Approach to War', ch. 1, p. 4.

[33] Bettina and Smith, ' "Hybrid Warfare" as an Operational Approach to War', ch. 1, p. 4.

[34] 'RELGNEW: Which Religion or Denomination, if Any, Do You Consider Yourself Belong To?', *Caucasus Barometer*, 2020, https://www.caucasusbarometer.org/en/cb2020ge/RELGNEW/.

[35] 'TRUGOCH: Level of trust in Georgian Orthodox church', *Caucasus Barometer*, 2013, https://caucas usbarometer.org/en/cb2013ge/TRUGOCH/.

Russian counterpart,[36] it serves as a potential transmitter of the hybrid threats coming from the Kremlin. This is further aggravated by the fact that support for conservative and so-called traditional values is still considerably high among many Georgians. For instance, the survey right after the 17 May 2013 events, when thousands of believers mobilized by the GOC have attacked the LGBTQI+ community–organized flash mob, shows that 45 per cent of Tbilisi residents polled, believed that the Church should be intolerant towards sexual minorities. Furthermore, 50 per cent of those polled, believed that physical violence was acceptable in case the group endangers national values.[37] These numbers suggest that Georgian society is vulnerable to the Russian civilizational narrative, in which the West is portrayed as perverted, with degraded traditional values and most of all, the children are in need of protection from this 'influence'. Appeal to traditional values and especially to the alleged dangers from LGBTQI+ rights has a potential of increasing anti-Western sentiments and even igniting major social tensions.

Discourse articulated around the idea of *defending traditional values* reflects Russian conservative narrative and it could potentially have an impact on state's decision-making process even on the long-established consensus on Georgia's foreign policy. For instance, in 2014, as Georgian Parliament was supposed to adopt anti-discrimination bill to make a progress on European integration, it met a serious opposition from the GOC and groups associated with it. The leaders of the Orthodox community were not happy with the inclusion of words *sexual orientation* and *gender identity* in the bill, and the Patriarch called the Parliament to reject the proposed legislation.[38] Archpriest Theordore Gignadze, popular clergyman who appears often on different talk shows and gives public lectures at various universities, while commenting about the bill, remarked:

> This law is dangerous for Georgia's future. Where there is no Christ, we have nothing to do there On the example of Holland, we can easily see what are the problems that this law implies. 50 years ago lifestyle in this country was radically different. Families were patriarchal and traditions were respected.
>
> Today, propaganda of same-sex marriages and depravity is going on. Paedophilia and incest have almost become the norm. ... This law will be the beginning of

---

[36] Shota Kakabadze and Andrey Makarychev, 'A Tale of Two Orthodoxies: Europe in Religious Discourses of Russia and Georgia', *Ethnopolitics* 17, no. 5 (2018): 485–502, doi: https://doi.org/10.1080/17449057.2018.1495367.

[37] CRRC, 'Survey on the May 17th Events in Tbilisi', CRRC, 26 August 2013, http://www.crrccenters.org/2088/Survey-on-the-May-17th-Events-in-Tbilisi.

[38] 'p'at'riarki p'arlament's: gadadet ant'idisk'riminatsiuli k'anonp'roekt'is migheba', *Tabula*, 28 April 2014, https://tabula.ge/ge/news/562797-patriarki-parlaments-gadadet-antidiskriminatsiuli.

planting poison in humans' consciousness and these sins will gradually become norms among us.[39]

This shows the points of intersection with Russian civilizational discourse, which is focused on nodal points of the West imposing 'perversion' upon Orthodox societies. In the end, the Georgian Parliament still adopted the bill, angering the GOC.

Soviet nostalgia as a potential source of vulnerability

The GOC is the largest but not the only actor engaged in spreading Russian civilizational narrative in Georgia. There are organizations and individuals in Georgia which have direct connections to the Kremlin and are actively spreading Russian misinformation. As of this writing, there are seventy-six registered organizations in Georgia, which serve the purpose of *normalizing* relations with Russia. However, out of this seventy-six, sixty-five have acquired a passive status from the Revenue Services, meaning they have not been financially active for at least past two years.[40] However, some of the organizations have been very active in public, appealing not only to the conservative sentiments discussed above but also to the Soviet nostalgia that is still felt among older and economically less well-off Georgians.

According to a 2017 survey, 42 per cent of Georgians find the collapse of the USSR to be a bad thing for their country.[41] Especially this longing for the Soviet period is felt in the birthplace of Stalin, in Gori.[42] The ethnic background of the tyrant has special role in the memory of the post-Soviet Georgia, as Stalin, who spoke Russian with a heavy Georgian accent, was a source of national pride. The fact that the 'father' of all nations that defeated Nazi Germany was Georgian overshadows any other discussion of his crimes or role in ending the existence of the Georgia's first republic.[43]

[39] 'ras mogvit'ans ant'idisk'riminatsiuli k'anoni', *Kviris Palitra*, 5 May 2014, https://kvirispalitra.ge/arti cle/21570-ras-mogvitans-antidiskriminaciuli-kanoni/.

[40] 'vis da rat'om sjera sakartvelosa da rusetis k'etilmezoblobis?', iFact.ge, 21 July 2022, https://www. ifact.ge/kultura3/?fbclid=IwAR3E5IIUPXAh8hdnKNwJRMXcRkwD-pT0FnVqlCLn9gnLzWiB SxaNoOEJgug.

[41] 'USSRDISS: Has dissolution of the Soviet Union been a good/bad thing for Georgia?', Caucasus Barometer, 2017, https://caucasusbarometer.org/en/na2017ge/USSRDISS/.

[42] Giorgi Lomsadze, 'Missing the USSR, Even in Georgia', Eurasianet, 7 November 2017, https://eur asianet.org/missing-the-ussr-even-in-georgia

[43] Giorgi Maisuradze, *chak'et'ili sazogadoeba da misi darajebi* (Tbilisi: Bakur Sulakauri Publishing, 2011), 73.

This feeling of nostalgia for 'good old times' serves another source of Russia's hybrid influence. In this regard, there are attempts to celebrate the Victory Day (9 May) in a similar manner as they do in Moscow. In 2017, the first time ever, the march of The Immortal Regiment (Bessmertniy Polk) was held.[44] It is a movement, established by President Putin in 2007 and used as an ideological weapon to avoid 'falsification' of the history of the Second World War.

Vulnerabilities in misinformation domain

Social media and television became another important source of spreading Russian misinformation and narratives which later became important tools in the hybrid warfare. The most notorious of which in Georgia is Alt Info that started broadcasting after being banned from Facebook in January 2021. Overall, Georgian legislation on freedom of expression is very liberal and closer to the American *market of ideas* model than its European counterpart. This makes it easier even for channels like Alt Info, whose message is *Stay tuned. Don't switch to the liberast*[45] *channels* to freely broadcast and be available to subscribers on the internet television providers.[46] The TV channel reports on news from across Europe and the United States framing it in the Manichean language of struggle between 'perverted liberal West' and 'traditional, conservative' Russia-led world order. Interestingly, main ideologues and frequent guests of this channel share support for President Trump's cause in his fight against 'globalists'.[47] What needs also to be noted is that the group behind Alt Info has close contacts with one of the main ideologues of the modern Russian alt-right and neo-Eurasianism, Alexander Dugin, who has often appeared on the channel and even shared some of their content on his personal Facebook page.[48]

Alt Info later officially registered as a political party titled Conservative Movement/Alt Info whose declared purpose is defining a special status of the Orthodox Christianity in the Georgian legislation, banning 'foreign intervention' in media and education and legislative control of foreign-funded organizations in the country.[49] One of the leaders of the party has even stated

[44] 'vis da rat'om sjera sakartvelosa da rusetis k'etilmezoblobis?'.
[45] 'Liberast' is a term made up of combining words 'liberal' and 'pedarast' (slur word used for gay men in Russia).
[46] Shota Kincha, 'Georgia's Trump-loving alt-right begin broadcasting on TV', *OC Media*, 11 February 2021, https://oc-media.org/features/georgias-trump-loving-alt-right-begin-broadcasting-on-tv/.
[47] Kincha, 'Georgia's Trump-loving alt-right begin broadcasting on TV'.
[48] 'Activities of the "Conservative Movement/Alt Info" in the Regions of Georgia', *International Society for Fair Elections and Democracy*, 11 July 2021, https://isfed.ge/geo/blogi/220711014334test
[49] 'Activities of the "Conservative Movement/Alt Info" in the Regions of Georgia'.

that he did not believe in democracy and did not condemn violence.[50] The party has been actively setting up infrastructure in the regions, and unlike other major Georgian political parties, investing a lot in maintaining large presence in the regions during the period between elections.[51] And in the country where income distribution remains unequal and Gini Coefficient is still quite high,[52] population in the rural areas remain the most vulnerable and susceptible to Russia's hybrid warfare.

Borderization domain

Since the August War of 2008, Russian Federation keeps violating the ceasefire agreement and maintaining military presence in two occupied territories of Georgia. This allows the Kremlin to maintain the leverage over Georgia and keep the country under check. Since 2013, Russian Federation has activated borderization policy in these territories, which implies installation of fences and other dividing barriers along the administrative border between Georgia and Tskhinvali Region (South Ossetia) and Abkhazia.

In addition to very practical and tactical purpose which would let the Russian army move in deeper into Georgia, borderization allows Russian Federation to demoralize the Georgian society and undermine the state. In other words, borderization or *creeping occupation*, as it is referred sometimes, reflects the so-called Gerasimov's Doctrine about the new methods of war.[53] It gives an ability to conduct war without using direct military force. Most importantly, it also undermines the Georgian government by presenting it as weak and powerless to put up the resistance to these processes.[54] Creeping occupation is also directed against Georgia's Euro-Atlantic foreign policy by projecting it as damaging to the country's territorial integrity and not contributing to the solution of these territorial problems.[55]

[50] 'Russians Are Fleeing to the Country Putin Invaded before Ukraine', *Vice News*, 16 April 2022, https://www.youtube.com/watch?v=HO11wuBcLDU.

[51] 'Activities of the "Conservative Movement/Alt Info" in the Regions of Georgia'.

[52] 'Poverty and Gini Coefficients', *National Statistics Office of Georgia*, 2021, https://www.geostat.ge/en/modules/categories/192/living-conditions.

[53] Joseph Larsen, 'Deterring Russia's Borderization of Georgia', GIP Commentary Issue #18, *Georgian Institute of Politics*, September 2017, http://gip.ge/wp-content/uploads/2017/09/Commentary18.pdf, 4.

[54] Kornely Kakachia, How the West Should Respond to Russia's "Borderization" in Georgia. PONARS Eurasia Policy Memo No. 523, April 2018, https://www.ponarseurasia.org/how-the-west-should-respond-to-russia-s-borderization-in-georgia/.

[55] Natia Seskuria, 'Russia's "Hybrid Aggression" against Georgia: The Use of Local and External Tools', *Center for Strategic and International Studies*, 21 September 2021, https://www.csis.org/analysis/russias-hybrid-aggression-against-georgia-use-local-and-external-tools.

Vulnerabilities in cyber domain

Georgia is vulnerable to cyber espionage and hacker attacks. For example, in 2011 some Georgian websites were infected with an information-stealing Trojan leading to infecting 390 computers, 70 per cent of which were from Georgia.[56] The infected devices were under full control of the Trojan, allowing it to steal information from individuals, government and other entities. These challenges are further aggravated by the fact that despite being recognized as a threat to Georgia's national security, still a lot needs to be done to properly address these vulnerabilities. Especially problematic in this regard is a mismatch between the state's declared policy and insufficient budget. Due to the high costs, some of the government computers still run on unlicensed and pirated software.[57] These vulnerabilities also emerge from poor security measures of Georgian services that host most of the local websites. These weak protection measures have led to a successful massive cyberattack on Georgia, once again reactivating calls for stronger defence and resilience in this domain.[58]

In conclusion, Russian hybrid warfare strategy in Georgia is focused on specific vulnerabilities that emerge from conservative sentiments, soviet nostalgia, misinformation, creeping occupation and cyber domain. The Kremlin's actions in these directions directly reflect the main ideas outlined in infamous Gerasimov's speech in 2013.

Georgian state's capacity for agency and its room for manoeuvre in the context of Russia's hybrid strategy

Considering its strategic geographical location – a gateway between Europe and Asia, and most importantly, as an alternative transit corridor bypassing Russia – Georgia falls within the sphere of vital interest of large regional players. This makes the Black Sea country a primary target of Russian hybrid warfare. As it was already mentioned, the latter implies a combination of various means and tools that go beyond conventional methods. Therefore, the state strategy in response to these challenges must be multisectoral and focused on several levels

---

[56] Khatuna Mshvidobadze, 'Georgia Cyber Barometer Report', *Georgian Foundation for Strategic and International Studies*, 2015, https://gfsis.org.ge/files/library/pdf/2423.pdf, 32.
[57] Mshvidobadze, 'Georgia Cyber Barometer Report', 34–5.
[58] Khatuna Mshvidobadze, 'Massive Cyberattacks on Georgia Calls For Defense and Resilience', *Rondeli Foundation*, 1 November 2019, https://gfsis.org.ge/blog/view/996.

at the same time. Georgia needs a comprehensive de-risking strategy that will be aimed at countering Russian assertiveness in the region.[59]

Georgian Ministry of Defense's Strategic Defense Review (SDR) for 2021–5 identifies Russian hybrid activities as one of the main threats. These activities include borderization or so-called creeping occupation, cyberattacks, spread of propaganda and misinformation which serves discreditation of the country's pro-Western foreign policy.[60] In order to better assess state's capacity and agency to manoeuvre in the context of Russia's hybrid warfare, one needs to examine each of these domains in details.

Informational domain

Starting with the misinformation, as pro-Russian rhetoric remains very unpopular among Georgians, Russian strategy is focused on spreading skepticism and mistrust in Georgia's pro-Western foreign policy goals.[61] This requires from the state more active engagement with the information domain to counterbalance Russian *firehose of falsehood*. Situation is especially dire in the regions populated with ethnic minorities as Russian-language media remains the most widely used source of information.[62]

However, despite the acknowledgement of the threats which are posed by the Russian hybrid warfare methods, there is no coordinated actions and the framework from the government aimed at countering these influences.[63] There is also apparent lack of transparency and accountability of respective institutions working in this field.[64]

[59] Kornely Kakachia, Bidzina Lebanidze and Salome Kandelaki, 'De-risking Russia: Pathways to Enhanced Resilience for Georgia' Policy Paper No. 39, Georgian Institute of Politics (2023): 19–21.

[60] 'Strategic Defence Review', Ministry of Defense of Georgia, 2021, https://mod.gov.ge/uploads/upl oad_new/tavdacvis_strategiuli_mimoxilva.pdf.

[61] Nino Bolkvadze, 'How Russia Targets the Cognitive Domain to Achieve its Strategic Goals in Georgia', in *Georgia's Information Environment through the Lens of Russia's Influence*, ed. Nino Bolkvadze et al. (Riga: NATO Strategic Communications Centre of Excellence, 2021), 42, https://stratcomcoe.org/pdfjs/?file=/publications/download/A4_new.pdf?zoom=page-fit.

[62] Kuprashvili, Natia, 'Characteristics of the Information Domains of the Georgian Information Environment', in *Georgia's Information Environment through the Lens of Russia's Influence*, ed. Nino Bolkvadze et al. (Riga: NATO Strategic Communications Centre of Excellence, 2021), 52, https://stratcomcoe.org/pdfjs/?file=/publications/download/A4_new.pdf?zoom=page-fit.

[63] Tinatin Tsomaia and Ana Keshelashvili, 'How to Respond to Information Operations while Preserving Commitment to Free Speech and the Free Flow of Ideas?', in *Georgia's Information Environment through the Lens of Russia's Influence*, ed. Nino Bolkvadze et al. (Riga: NATO Strategic Communications Centre of Excellence, 2021), 120, https://stratcomcoe.org/pdfjs/?file=/publicati ons/download/A4_new.pdf?zoom=page-fit.

[64] Tsomaia and Ana Keshelashvili, 'How to Respond to Information Operations while Preserving Commitment to Free Speech and the Free Flow of Ideas?'.

Creeping occupation

Borderization remains one of the most difficult challenges which the Georgian state needs to address. Russian action of illegally constructing border demarcations continues as it does not cause major international backlash despite being damaging enough to undermine Georgian state sovereignty and stability as well as cause demoralization in the society.[65]

In this context its Western allies and their support remains a key element of Georgia's strategy in countering unwanted foreign influence. For example, the European Union Monitoring Mission (EUMM) – a civilian monitoring mission deployed at the administrative borders of occupied territories, remains the only credible actor that can record instances of *creeping occupation*. It also needs to be mentioned that, as of this writing, in violation to the cease fire agreement, Abkhazian and South Ossetian de facto authorities do not allow the EUMM to cross the dividing line. Therefore, Georgian authorities need to be more active in lobbying increasing Western involvement in these issues, especially in the context of Russian invasion of Ukraine and increasing involvement of the allies in the region.

Cyber domain

After the experience of 2008 August War, Georgian authorities took several major steps to address the challenges in the cyber domain. In 2010, the Data Exchange Agency was created, which was tasked with unifying government network in Georgia and developing e-governance.[66] In 2013, Georgian president signed the first Cyber Security Strategy and the Cyber Security Action Plan of Georgia. Since then, it has been updated twice, the latest being issued in 2021 and outlined the government strategy for the years 2021–4. The strategy has four main goals: it aims to accomplish increasing cyberculture in the society; strengthening the cybersecurity resilience and partnership between state and private sector; developing cyber capacities; and strengthening the role of Georgia on the international arena as a safe and protected country.[67]

---

[65] Larsen, 'Deterring Russia's Borderization of Georgia', 6.

[66] Khatuna Mshvidobadze, 'The Global Cyber Domain and New Challenges', Expert Opinion, *Georgian Foundation for Strategic and International Studies*, 2013, https://gfsis.org.ge/publications/view-opinion-paper/11, 8.

[67] 'sakartvelos k'iberusaprtkhoebis 2021 – 2024 ts'lebis erovnuli st'rat'egiisa da misi samokmedo gegmis damt'k'itsebis shesakheb', *Legislative Herald of Georgia*, 30 September 2021. https://matsne.gov.ge/ka/document/view/5263611?publication=0.

However, to what extent Georgia is successful in implementing effective cybersecurity measures at the nationwide level very much depends on how well functions and responsibilities are divided between state agencies responsible for cyber policy. Georgia is also missing well-defined mechanisms for information exchange and mechanisms of cooperation between the agencies as well as a comprehensive list of critical infrastructure.[68]

However, regardless of the domain, the State's capacity and agency to address threats coming from the Russian hybrid warfare strategy is considerably constrained by the overall low trust in state institutions. According to opinion polls, the percentage of people who trust (moderately or fully) the judicial system in Georgia are 13 per cent and 4 per cent, respectively, while distrust and fully distrust – 20 per cent and 17 percent. Trust level (fully trust and trust) for the Parliament is 16 per cent, and those who fully trust executive government is only 4 per cent.[69] Such low trust in state institutions considerably limits the ability of the respective institutions to mitigate the impact of Russian misinformation and subversive activities. Distrust leads to suspicion on how much the respective institutions are able to protect state's security, thus, increasing the feeling of vulnerability among the population and contributing to demoralization.

In such context of low trust of the state institutions in public, Georgia's resilience to the Russian hybrid strategy depends very much on its strong commitment to Euro-Atlantic foreign policy and close cooperation with its Western allies. Deepening its relations with the United States and continuing integration into NATO and the European Union remains a priority for Georgia as it is the only variable security guarantee amidst Russia's aggressive hybrid strategies. Support and expertise of its Western allies will have a deceiving impact on Georgia's resilience and ability to hinder subversive activities coming from the Kremlin.

Georgia's resilience and challenges to counter malign foreign influence

Although Georgian strategic documents recognize the threats posed by Russian hybrid warfare tactics, the state's overall strategy on countering these

---

[68] Mari Malvenishvili and Nini Balarjishvili, 'Cybersecurity Reform in Georgia: Existing Challenges, International Practice and Recommendations', *Institute for Development of Freedom of Information*, 2020, https://idfi.ge/en/cyber_security_reform_in_georgia_existing_challenges_international_practice_and_recommendations.

[69] 'TRUCR Trust – Court system', 'TRUPARL: Trust – Parliament', 'TRUEXEC: Trust – Executive Government', *Caucasus Barometer*, 2019, https://caucasusbarometer.org/en/cb2019ge/TRUCRTS/.

challenges remain underdeveloped and inconsistent. Georgia so far has been rather passive in its engagement with the resilience approach. The country has neither unified legislation nor a unified strategic approach towards resilience-building.[70] There exists a lack of coordination between the different agencies and between the state and non-state actors. Yet, certain policies have been implemented over the last decade, which were aimed at mitigating the potential vulnerabilities.

Georgian strategy to counter Russian misinformation campaign can be described as that of giving a priority to the freedom of expression over limiting certain media outlets. It stands closer to the American model rather than continental counterpart and implies wider understanding of the freedom of expression. It is only in 2019 that the Law of Georgia on Broadcasting was introduced which requires Georgian television stations to establish self-regulation mechanisms, but online and print media are exempt from this rule,[71] making it a breeding ground for misinformation and propaganda.

However, as Georgia remains a hybrid type of democracy, protection of the freedom of expression is vital for its future development. Any legislation introducing regulation in this regard, might be turned into a tool in the hands of the ruling party to suppress critical voices. In other words, while spread of misinformation and propaganda coming from Russia is being recognized by the Georgian government as a threat to national security, there exists no concrete strategy on how these threats are to be addressed.[72] This picture is further complicated by nonexistence of best practices of partnership and cooperation between civil society, non-state and state stake holders.

To address the vulnerability created by the nostalgia for the USSR, in 2011, the Georgian Parliament adopted a set of legislation known as *Liberty Charter* or *tavisuplebis kart'ia* in Georgian. The goal of the bill was to regulate the employment of the people associated with the Soviet secret services in the government offices and eradicating street names, symbols, monuments, and so on which were representing the Communist regime. However, the impact of this

---

[70] Kornely Kakachia, Bidzina Lebanidze, Salome Kandelaki. "National Resilience Strategy for Georgia: Lessons from NATO, EU and beyond," Policy Paper No. 33, *Georgian Institute of Politics*, December 2022. https://gip.ge/publication-post/national-resilience-strategy-for-georgia-lessons-from-nato-eu-and-beyond/

[71] Tsomaia and Keshelashvili, 'How to Respond to Information Operations while Preserving Commitment to Free Speech and the Free Flow of Ideas?'.

[72] Tsomaia and Keshelashvili, 'How to Respond to Information Operations while Preserving Commitment to Free Speech and the Free Flow of Ideas?'.

legislation remains still questionable as even the authors of the bill themselves have called it more symbolic rather than practical.[73]

Due to the experience of August 2008 war, Georgian state has been more consistent and relatively more successful in cyber domain. Before the military conflict with Russia, Georgian internet traffic passed through the northern neighbour. After the war, however, 90 per cent of the traffic goes through the fibre-optic line that comes through the Black Sea from Varna to Poti. Georgia has also established the Computer Emergency Response Team (CERT) that wars 24/7. The CERT is working on monitoring Georgian cyberspace and takes actions, if necessary.[74]

Nonetheless, considering Georgia's economic and military capabilities, its resilience towards Russian hybrid warfare tactics is largely dependent to the level of its partnership with the NATO allies. After the annexation of Crimea in 2014, the NATO has recognized the threats of hybrid war and has developed strategy on how to address these challenges. In 2016, it was publicly stated that a hybrid attack against one or more members of the alliance will be considered as an attack on all and the famous fifth article would be invoked. In 2018, NATO leaders reached an agreement about setting up a special support team, which would provide assistance to the Allies in preparing against hybrid activities.[75] However, this cooperation in countering hybrid threats go beyond NATO members. The Alliance is engaged in close cooperation with Georgian respective authorities to enhance country's resilience and capabilities, especially in the domain of cybersecurity.[76]

To sum up, while Georgian strategic documents recognize hybrid war as a threat, especially dangers of Russian misinformation campaign and cyberattacks, there exists no clear strategic vision on how these challenges are to be addressed. In this context, of critical importance is close coordination and cooperation with Western allies. Considering Georgia is not a member of NATO, and it is not covered by the security umbrella of the Alliance, bilateral partnership with Western partners has vital importance.

---

[73] Nino Kharadze, 'Parliamentma Tavisuplebis Qartia Miigho', *Radio Liberty*, 31 May 2011, https://www.radiotavisupleba.ge/a/24210559.html.

[74] Mshvidobadze, 'The Global Cyber Domain and New Challenges', 9.

[75] 'NATO's response to hybrid threats', North Atlantic Treaty Organization, 21 June 2022, https://www.nato.int/cps/en/natohq/topics_156338.htm

[76] Nino Chichua, 2022, 'ap'at'urai: sakartvelos roli evrop'is energomomaragebistvis upro mnishvnelovani gakhda', Netgazeti, 20 April 2022, https://netgazeti.ge/news/606424/

Conclusion

Examining the case of Georgia is an important element of the study of Russian hybrid strategies. It was one of the very first testing points when unconventional tactics along with traditional military forces were applied against another sovereign state. Cyberattacks against Georgia just a couple of weeks before the invasion outlined what future conflicts were going to look like.

Currently, Georgia, along with Ukraine and Moldova, remains one of the primary targets of Russia's aggressive foreign policy and hybrid activities. All three countries have been experiencing territorial conflicts with Russia-backed separatists, cyberattacks and have been susceptible to misinformation and propaganda coming from the Kremlin. All these domains are part of the hybrid war strategies as the latter implies a type of war which is a mix of both conventional and unconventional methods. Russian activities combine all the instruments of power and their application at the same time.

In case of Georgia these main domains are informational and ideological, mostly relying on conservative discourse and anti-Western skepticism as well as referring to the Soviet nostalgia. Kremlin's activities in this regard have drastically increased after the 2012 conservative turn in Russia, as President Putin has been engaged in actively positioning his country as the defender of traditional values and the *last bastion* of conservatism. These nodal points have become a major element around which Russian hybrid warfare in the domains of information articulates. Georgian actors who are transmitting this narrative, instead of publicly calling for pro-Russian foreign policy, due to its unpopularity, are more focused on sowing distrusts and skepticism in Western allies by portraying them as *perverted* and *degraded*. Russian hybrid war strategy in information domain is also focused on the feeling of nostalgia for the Soviet times. In this respect, the memory politics and remembrance of the Second World War as well as an image of Stalin as a Georgian, play a major role.

The existence of territories outside the control of the official Tbilisi, where Russian military presence is maintained, is one more important tool in the hands of the Kremlin to exert psychological pressure on Georgian society. *Creeping occupation* and the inability of Georgian authorities to prevent kidnaping of its citizens by the de facto regimes creates a feeling of helplessness and vulnerability among Georgians. It also undermines the Georgian state and the government by portraying it as impotent to protect its citizens and territorial integrity.

These characteristics of Russian hybrid war tactics illustrate that the approach to the challenges also need to be multisectoral and multilayered. Focus on one specific instrument of power and attempts to counterbalance implies a danger of overlooking other levels and domains of the Kremlin's subversive activities in the neighbouring countries. Therefore, the approach should be focused simultaneously on every domain and there needs to be a coordinated long-term strategy that alleviate potential threats coming from these tactics of the opponent. Despite several major steps that were taken towards strengthening cybersecurity and increasing resilience in this direction since the attacks of 2008, Georgian state remains quite vulnerable to foreign interference.

As the country remains outside of the NATO security umbrella or any similar defensive alliance, Georgia alone would not be able to counter Russian hybrid tactics. For economically and militarily less well-off countries, Western allies and their commitment to countering Kremlin's aggression is of vital importance. Close partnership with NATO and the European Union is fundamental pillar for Georgia's resilience to hybrid threats and subversive activities. Having said that, it also largely depends on how proactive is Georgia in seeking those security guarantees as well as on close cooperation between the private, non-state and state stakeholders, in order to avoid becoming Russia's next target after the failed *Blitzkrieg* in Ukraine.

Bibliography

Antidze, M. (2008), 'Georgian Leader Wants Better Ties with Russia', *Reuters*, 8 January. Available online: https://www.reuters.com/article/us-georgia-election-saakshvili-idUSL0727751420080107 (accessed 16 November 2023).

Bettina, R., and H. Smith (2016), '"Hybrid Warfare" as an Operational Approach to War – a New War-Winning Formula?', in Renz Bettina and Hanna Smith (eds), *Russia and Hybrid Warfare – Going Beyond the Label*, Aleksanteri Papers, no. 1/2016, ch. 1, p. 2, Helsinki: Kikimora Publications.

Bolkvadze, N. (2021), 'How Russia Targets the Cognitive Domain to Achieve Its Strategic Goals in Georgia', in N. Bolkvadze et al. (eds), *Georgia's Information Environment through the Lens of Russia's Influence*, 42, Riga: NATO Strategic Communications Centre of Excellence.

Caucasus Barometer (2017), 'USSRDISS: Has Dissolution of the Soviet Union Been a Good/Bad Thing for Georgia?', *Caucasus Barometer*. Available online: https://caucasusbarometer.org/en/na2017ge/USSRDISS/ (accessed 16 November 2023).

Caucasus Barometer (2019), 'TRUCR Trust – Court system', 'TRUPARL: Trust – Parliament', 'TRUEXEC: Trust – Executive government', *Caucasus Barometer*. Available online: https://caucasusbarometer.org/en/cb2019ge/TRUCRTS/ (accessed 16 November 2023).

Caucasus Barometer (2020), 'RELGNEW: Which Religion or Denomination, if Any, Do You Consider Yourself Belong To?', *Caucasus Barometer*. Available online:https://www.caucasusbarometer.org/en/cb2020ge/RELGNEW/ (accessed 16 November 2023).

Chichua, N. (2022), '"ap'at'urai: sakartvelos roli evrop'is energomomaragebistvis upro mnishvnelovani gakhda'", *Netgazeti*, 20 April. Available online: https://netgazeti.ge/news/606424/ (accessed 16 November 2023).

Civil.ge (2021), 'Alt-Right Inaugurates Anti-Liberal, Russia-Friendly Party', 20 October. Available online: https://civil.ge/archives/456863 (accessed 16 November 2023).

Clark, M. (2020), 'Russian Hybrid Warfare', *Institute for the Study of War*, September. Available online: https://www.jstor.org/stable/resrep26547.1 (accessed 16 November 2023).

CRRC (2013), 'Survey on the May 17th Events in Tbilisi', *CRRC*, 26 August. Available online: http://www.crrccenters.org/2088/Survey-on-the-May-17th-Events-in-Tbilisi (accessed 16 November 2023).

Crowther, G. A. (2021), 'NATO and Hybrid Warfare Seeking a Concept to Define the Challenge from Russia', in Mikael Weissmann, Niklas Nilsson, Björn Palmertz and Per Thunholm (eds), *Hybrid Warfare*, ch. 2, p. 31, London: I.B. Tauris.

Curanović, A. (2012), *The Religious Factor in Russia's Foreign Policy: Keeping God on Our Side*, London: Routledge.

German, T., and K. Kakachia (2022), 'Achieving Security as a Small State', in T. German, S. Jones and K. Kakachia (eds), *Georgias Foreign Policy in 21 Century: Challenges for a Small State*, London: I. B. Tauris.

Ghvineria, S. (2021), 'shidasakhelmts'ipoebrivi sisust'eebis rusul iaraghad ktsevis hibriduli st'rat'egia sakartvelosa da uk'rainis magalitze', in Tinatin Khidasheli (ed.), *hibriduli omebis anat'omia*, Tbilisi: Palitra L Publising, 235.

Hollis, D. (2011), 'Cyberwar Case Study: Georgia 2008', *Small Wars Journal* (6 January): 2. Available online: https://smallwarsjournal.com/jrnl/art/cyber war-case-study-georgia-2008.

iFact.ge (2022), 'vis da rat'om sjera sakartvelosa da rusetis k'etilmezoblobis?', *iFact. ge*, 21 July. Available online: https://www.ifact.ge/kultura3/?fbclid=IwAR3E5IIUP XAh8hdnKNwJRMXcRkwD-pT0FnVqlCLn9gnLzWiBSxaNoOEJgug (accessed 16 November 2023).

The International Republican Institute – Georgia (2022), 'Public Opinion Survey Residents of Georgia March 2022', *The International Republican Institute – Georgia*, March. Available online: https://www.iri.org/wp-content/uploads/2022/04/IRI-Poll-Presentation-Georgia-March2022_Final.pdf (accessed 16 November 2023).

International Society for Fair Elections and Democracy (2021), 'Activities of the 'Conservative Movement/Alt Info" in the Regions of Georgia', *International Society for Fair Elections and Democracy*, 11 July. Available online: https://isfed.ge/geo/blogi/220711014334test (accessed 16 November 2023).

Kakabadze, S., and A. Makarychev (2018), 'A Tale of Two Orthodoxies: Europe in Religious Discourses of Russia and Georgia', *Ethnopolitics*, 17 (5): 485–502.

Kakachia, K., S. Minesashvili and L. Kakhishvili (2018), 'Change and Continuity in the Foreign Policies of Small States: Elite Perceptions and Georgia's Foreign Policy towards Russia', *Europe-Asia Studies*, 70 (5): 814–31.

Kakachia, K. (2018), 'How the West Should Respond to Russia's "Borderization" in Georgia'., PONARS Eurasia Policy Memo No. 523, April. Available online: https://www.ponarseurasia.org/how-the-west-should-respond-to-russia-s-borderization-in-georgia/ (accessed 16 November 2023).

Kakachia, K., B. Lebanidze and S. Kandelaki (2022), 'National Resilience Strategy for Georgia: Lessons from NATO, EU and Beyond', Policy Paper No. 33, *Georgian Institute of Politics*, December. Available online: https://gip.ge/publication-post/natio nal-resilience-strategy-for-georgia-lessons-from-nato-eu-and-beyond/ (accessed 16 November 2023).

Kakachia, K., B. Lebanidze and S. Kandelaki (2023), 'De-risking Russia: Pathways to Enhanced Resilience for Georgia' Policy Paper No. 39, Georgian Institute of Politics (2023): 19–21.

Kharadze, N. (2011), 'Parliamentma Tavisuplebis Qartia Miigho', *Radio Liberty*, 31 May. Available online: https://www.radiotavisupleba.ge/a/24210559.html (accessed 16 November 2023).

Kincha, S. (2021), 'Georgia's Trump-Loving Alt-Right Begin Broadcasting on TV', *OC Media*, 11 February. Available online: https://oc-media.org/features/georgias-trump-loving-alt-right-begin-broadcasting-on-tv/ (accessed 16 November 2023).

Kuprashvili, N. (2021), 'Characteristics of the Information Domains of the Georgian Information Environment', in N. Bolkvadze et al. (eds), *Georgia's Information Environment through the Lens of Russia's Influence*, Riga: NATO Strategic Communications Centre of Excellence.

Kviris Palitra (2014), 'ras mogvit'ans ant'idisk'riminatsiuli k'anoni', *Kviris Palitra*, 5 May. Available online: https://kvirispalitra.ge/article/21570-ras-mogvitans-antidiskrimi naciuli-kanoni/.

Larsen, J. (2017), 'Deterring Russia's Borderization of Georgia', GIP Commentary Issue #18, *Georgian Institute of Politics*, September. Available online: http://gip.ge/wp-cont ent/uploads/2017/09/Commentary18.pdf (accessed 16 November 2023).

Legislative Herald of Georgia (2021), 'sakartvelos k'iberusaprtkhoebis 2021 – 2024 ts'lebis erovnuli st'rat'egiisa da misi samokmedo gegmis damt'k'itsebis shesakheb', *Legislative Herald of Georgia*, 30 September. Available online: https://matsne.gov.ge/ka/document/view/5263611?publication=0 (accessed 16 November 2023).

Lomsadze, G. (2017), 'Missing the USSR, Even in Georgia', *Eurasianet*, 7 November. Available online: https://eurasianet.org/missing-the-ussr-even-in-georgia (accessed 16 November 2023).

Maisuradze, G. (2011), *chak'et'ili sazogadoeba da misi darajebi*, Tbilisi: Bakur Sulakauri Publishing.

Malvenishvili. M., and N. Balarjishvili (2020), 'Cybersecurity Reform in Georgia: Existing Challenges, International Practice and Recommendations', *Institute for Development of Freedom of Information*. Available online: https://idfi.ge/en/cyber_security_reform_in_georgia_existing_challenges_international_practice_and_recommendations (accessed 16 November 2023).

Mshvidobadze, K. (2013), 'The Global Cyber Domain and New Challenges', Expert Opinion, *Georgian Foundation for Strategic and International Studies*. Available online: https://gfsis.org.ge/files/library/opinion-papers/11-expert-opinion-eng.pdf (accessed 16 November 2023).

Mshvidobadze, K. (2015), 'Georgia Cyber Barometer Report', *Georgian Foundation for Strategic and International Studies*. Available online: https://gfsis.org.ge/publications/view/2423 (accessed 16 November 2023).

Mshvidobadze, K. (2019), 'Massive Cyberattacks on Georgia Calls for Defense and Resilience', *Rondeli Foundation*, 1 November. Available online: https://gfsis.org.ge/blog/view/996 (accessed 16 November 2023).

Ministry of Defense of Georgia (2021), 'Strategic Defence Review: 2021–2025', *Ministry of Defense of Georgia*. Available online: https://mod.gov.ge/uploads/upload_new/tavdacvis_strategiuli_mimoxilva.pdf (accessed 16 November 2023).

Morozov, V. (2015), *Russia's Postcolonial Identity: A Subaltern Empire in a Eurocentric World*, London: Palgrave Macmillan, doi: https://doi.org/10.1057/9781137409300.

National Statistics Office of Georgia (2021), 'Poverty and Gini Coefficients', *National Statistics Office of Georgia*. Available online: https://www.geostat.ge/en/modules/categories/192/living-conditions (accessed 16 November 2023).

Nilsson, N. (2018), *Russian Hybrid Tactics in Georgia*. Washington, DC: Central Asia-Caucasus Institute & Silk Road Studies Program. Available online: https://silkroadstudies.org/resources/pdf/SilkRoadPapers/2018_01_Nilsson_Hybrid.pdf.

North Atlantic Treaty Organization (2023), 'Countering Hybrid Threats', *North Atlantic Treaty Organization*, 18 August. Available online: https://www.nato.int/cps/en/natohq/topics_156338.htm (accessed 15 January 2024).

Paul, C., and M. Matthews (2016), 'The Russian "Firehose of Falsehood" Propaganda Model', *Rand Corporation*, 2 (7): 1–10.

Radio Free Europe/Radio Liberty (2022), 'Protesters in Tbilisi Decry Georgian Government's Inadequate Support for Ukraine', *Radio Free Europe/Radio Liberty*, 1 March. Available online: https://www.rferl.org/a/ukraine-invasion-tbilisi-protest-georgia/31731006.html (accessed 16 November 2023).

Reichborn-Kjennerud, E., and P. Cullen (2016), 'What Is Hybrid Warfare?', Policy Brief [1/2016], *Norwegian Institute of International Affairs*. Available online: https://nupi.

brage.unit.no/nupi-xmlui/bitstream/handle/11250/2380867/NUPI_Policy_Brief_1
_Reichborn_Kjennerud_Cullen.pdf (accessed 16 November 2023).

Sandor, F. (2019), 'The Russian Hybrid Warfare Strategy – Neither Russian Nor
Strategy', *Defense & Security Analysis*, 35 (3): 308–25; 311, doi: https://doi.
org/10.1080/14751798.2019.1640424.

Seskuria, N. (2021), 'Russia's "Hybrid Aggression" against Georgia: The Use of Local
and External Tools', *Center for Strategic and International Studies*, 21 September.
Available online: https://www.csis.org/analysis/russias-hybrid-aggression-against-
georgia-use-local-and-external-tools (accessed 16 November 2023).

Sharafutdinova, G. (2014), 'The Pussy Riot Affair and Putin's Démarche from Sovereign
Democracy to Sovereign Morality', *Nationalities Papers* 42 (4): 615–21.

Tabula (2014), 'p'at'riarki p'arlament's: gadadet ant'idisk'riminatsiuli k'anonp'roekt'is
migheba', *Tabula*, 28 April. Available online: https://tabula.ge/ge/news/562797-patria
rki-parlaments-gadadet-antidiskriminatsiuli.

Transparency International Georgia (2020), 'Georgia's Economic Dependence on
Russia: Trends and Threats', *Transparency International Georgia*, 4 May. Available
online: https://transparency.ge/en/blog/georgias-economic-dependence-russia-tre
nds-and-threats (accessed 16 November 2023).

Tsomaia, T., and A. Keshelashvili (2021), 'How to Respond to Information Operations
While Preserving Commitment to Free Speech and the Free Flow of Ideas?', in N.
Bolkvadze et al (eds), *Georgia's Information Environment through the Lens of Russia's
Influence*, Riga: NATO Strategic Communications Centre of Excellence.

Vice News (2022), 'Russians Are Fleeing to the Country Putin Invaded before Ukraine'
[YouTube], *Vice News*, 16 April. Available online: https://www.youtube.com/
watch?v=HO11wuBcLDU (accessed 16 November 2023).

Weissmann, M., N. Nilsson, B. Palmertz, P. Thunholm and H. Häggström (2021),
'Security Challenges in the Grey Zone: Hybrid Threats and Hybrid Warfare',
in M. Weissmann, N. Nilsson, B. Palmertz and P. Thunholm (eds), *Hybrid
Warfare: Security and Asymmetric Conflict in International Relations*, London: I.B.
Tauris.

8

Russia's utilization of unresolved conflicts and proxy regimes

Niklas Nilsson, Johan Engvall and Mikael Weissmann

Introduction

This chapter focuses on five conflicts – Transnistria, South Ossetia, Abkhazia, Nagorno-Karabakh and Donbass – all of which remain unresolved and with the exception of Donbass are remnants of the break-up of the Soviet Union. In the process of the Soviet political and economic system's collapse and the disintegration of the union, new states emerged along with previously latent conflicts. In the late 1980s and early 1990s, the conflicts between newly established central governments and separatist entities provided opportunities for Russia to insert itself as a key actor and thereby retain a degree of control over the new states even as they gained international recognition as sovereign in their own right.

The pattern of post-Soviet Russian support for separatists and its facilitation of the establishment of 'unresolved' conflicts in the new states where opportunities presented themselves is in synch with a historical pattern of Russia's utilization of local conflicts as a vehicle for establishing dependencies and leverage in areas over which it claimed control. Russia's 'divide and rule' policy was expressed in, for example, the conquering of the Caucasus and Central Asia in the nineteenth century with the subjugation and deportation of Caucasian 'tribes' as well as the institutionalization of ethnic Socialist Republics, Autonomous Republics and Oblasts. In short, Russia has a long historical tradition of establishing loyalties and fuelling tensions between ethnic groups.

In the three decades that have passed since the Soviet Union collapsed, the unresolved conflicts in Transnistria, Abkhazia, South Ossetia and Nagorno-Karabakh have remained important components of Russian policy and influence in Moldova, Georgia, Armenia and Azerbaijan, respectively. After the cessation of immediate hostilities in the 1990s and for much of the 2000s, these conflicts were frequently referred to as 'frozen', denoting a perception that the conflicts remained unresolved but were at the same time locked in a controllable status quo. A frozen conflict has been defined as a 'protracted state of affairs in which major hostilities have ended but the enmity between the actors persists and re-escalation remains a permanent threat'.[1] The concept was adopted by scholars and practitioners alike as a label for a range of situations defined neither by war, nor by peace that emerged in the 1990s after the break-up of the Soviet Union and Yugoslavia. In the Yugoslavian context, the label was used to describe the situations in Kosovo and Bosnia and Herzegovina. The same label has sometimes also been used for the Korea conflict, Cyprus and Western Sahara to give but three examples.[2]

Until the years preceding the 2008 Russian-Georgian war, the Russian strategy had been to keep the conflicts contained and at a low level of intensity. For example, Russia largely utilized South Ossetia and Abkhazia as negotiating chips in its relations with Georgia while it recognized Georgia's territorial integrity.[3] The run-up to and outbreak of the Russian-Georgian war, however, represented a new approach. The notion that these conflicts were 'frozen' was falsified as Russia invaded Georgia, ostensibly in support of its proxy regime in South Ossetia and in response to a Georgian attempt at regaining control of the region by force, and declared South Ossetia as well as Abkhazia to constitute independent states.[4] Nagorno-Karabakh, in turn, saw increasingly violent clashes between Azerbaijani and Armenian forces from the mid-2010s, culminating in Azerbaijan's extensive military operation to re-establish control of the region in 2020. These conflicts therefore proved to be far from 'frozen' and the dynamics surrounding them have changed over the years. Yet, they have remained important components of Russian influence in the affected states. Moreover, the war that Russia instigated in Eastern Ukraine in 2014 had the purpose of

---

[1] Kamil Christoph Klosek, Vojtěch Bahenský, Michal Smetana and Jan Ludvík, 'Frozen Conflicts in World Politics: A New Dataset', *Journal of Peace Research* 58, no. 4 (2021): 849.

[2] See, for example, Thomas D. Grant, 'Frozen Conflicts and International Law', *Cornell International Law Journal* 50, no. 3 (2017) Also see the Frozen Conflicts Dataset prepared by Kamil Klosek, Vojtěch Bahenský, Michal Smetana and Jan Ludvík which identified forty-two cases of frozen conflicts in the 1946–2011 period (twenty-five 'traditional' interstate conflicts and seventeen conflicts between a state and a de facto state. https://www.prcprague.cz/fcdataset.

[3] Niklas Nilsson, *Russian Hybrid Tactics in Georgia* (Washinton, DC: Central Asia-Caucasus Institute & Silk Road Studies Program, 2018).

[4] Niklas Nilsson, 'Between Russia's "Hybrid" Strategy and Western Ambiguity: Assessing Georgia's Vulnerabilities', *Journal of Slavic Military Studies* 34, no. 1 (2021): 60–2.

establishing similar entities separated from the Ukrainian state and governed by proxy regimes in the Donetsk and Luhansk People's Republics, in order to create a similar leverage on Ukraine. In other words, fuelling and sustaining unresolved conflicts in the post-Soviet territories has been and remains an important part of Russia's strategy for exercising influence in its neighbourhood.

This chapter provides an overview of these conflicts and Russia's role in them, with a view to demonstrating patterns of Russian warfare and influence. Moldova's Transnistria, Georgia's Abkhazia and South Ossetia, the Azerbaijani-Armenian conflict over Nagorno-Karabakh and Ukraine's Donetsk and Luhansk are described according to a common structure. Each section includes a brief background of the conflict, the relationship between the states in question and Russia, the current status of the conflict, Russia's utilization of the conflict and the means by which the states have sought to devise responses to the predicament of having unresolved conflicts with more or less heavy Russian involvement on their territory.

Unresolved conflicts and Russian influence

Over the years, the unresolved conflicts in the post-Soviet space have provided Russia with means for influencing the politics, societies and strategic outlook of the affected states.

Militarily, Russia has been able to establish a military presence on the ground in the contested territories. This has been pursued in the guise of peacekeepers in Abkhazia, South Ossetia and Transnistria for an extended time period. This practice has since 2020 been applied also in Nagorno-Karabakh in an addition to Russia's already existing military base in Gyumri, Armenia. The military dimension has also been essential in Donbass since 2014.

Aside from the benefit of maintaining a military presence on the ground and a deterrent against adverse military action, these deployments also allow Russia to present a credible military threat to the states in question. Russia's east-west offensive on Ukraine in 2022 came via Donetsk and Luhansk. The small military presence in Transnistria could be expanded if needed, although this is presently unlikely considering the fledgling war effort in Ukraine. Deployments in Georgia, while reduced during 2022, allows Russia to project military power beyond the Caucasus mountain ridge, otherwise forming a formidable physical barrier to operations in the South Caucasus. Despite increasing dissatisfaction on both the Armenian and Azerbaijani sides with the performance of Russian peacekeeping forces in Nagorno-Karabakh, their deployment in 2020 established a Russian military presence also in Azerbaijan, until then the only country discussed in this chapter that did not have Russian forces deployed on its territory.

Russia's option of retaining a military presence in these regions, and to employ military force if needed, has been underpinned by wide-ranging distribution of Russian passports to residents of Abkhazia, South Ossetia, Transnistria, DNR and LNR. Russia referred to the presence of large numbers of Russian citizens in these regions as a motivation for its invasion of Georgia in 2008, seeking to invoke the UN-approved Responsibility to Protect (R2P).[5] Thus, Russia sought to emulate concepts and policies employed by the West in foreign military interventions, aside from R2P also invoking the 'Kosovo precedent' as a motivation for its enhanced relations with Abkhazia and South Ossetia in the lead-up to the war.

Politically, Russia's influence and control over proxy regimes in these territories have constituted continuous means for influencing the governments in Tbilisi and Chisinau, and during 2014–21 also in Kyiv. In Transnistria, South Ossetia, Abkhazia, DNR and LNR, Russia has established and supported proxy regimes while refusing to acknowledge partisanship in the conflicts, thereby seeking a status quo where governments are forced to negotiate directly with separatist entities, but where progress in negotiations is contingent on concessions to Russian demands.

Yet, Russia's ability to exert political influence through the conflicts has waned over time. In Georgia and Moldova, finding final settlements to the unresolved conflicts and reintegration of territory feature far lower among political priorities today than 15–20 years ago. The foreign policy agendas of both countries, where Moldova is focused on integration with the EU and Georgia with the EU and NATO, have become increasingly detached from the issue of resolving the conflicts. In effect, this has diminished Russia's ability to offer solutions to the conflicts in exchange for abstaining from pro-Western policies.

This, however, has not prevented Russia from utilizing the conflicts for political pressure. This is most prevalent in Georgia, where the continuous borderization of the ABL between Georgia and South Ossetia, along with occasional campaigns for referenda on annexation in the region serve to direct Tbilisi's focus to the conflict while simultaneously demonstrating that neither

[5] Emil Suleimanov, Eduard Abrahamiyan and Huseyn Aliyev, 'Unrecognized States as a Means of Coercive Diplomacy? Assessing the Role of Abkhazia and South Ossetia in Russia's Foreign Policy in the South Caucasus', *Southeast European and Black Sea Studies* 18, no. 1 (2017): 10–11.

the Georgian government, nor Georgia's international partners can do much about Russian infringements on Georgian territory.

In Nagorno-Karabakh, Russia was able to mediate a ceasefire and an agreement between Azerbaijan and Armenia in 2020, which included Russian peacekeepers on the ground. It thus seemed that Russia would be able to retain a key role as an arbitrator in the conflict, even after Azerbaijan's decisive victory in the war. However, since then, Azerbaijan has continued to employ force, including incursions into Armenian territory, in order to coerce Armenia into accepting Azerbaijan's interpretation of the agreement. In a September 2023 offensive, Azerbaijan took control over the remaining parts of the region not previously conquered in 2020. Turkey plays an increasingly important role in the region, underpinned by its close relationship with Azerbaijan. Simultaneously, the Armenian leadership has voiced unprecedented criticism of Russia's role in the process and in January 2023 refused to host the Collective Security Treaty Organization (CSTO) exercises and has since threatened to withdraw from the organization altogether. Azerbaijan's final push to take full control over Nagorno-Karabakh fuelled a significant flow of Armenian refugees from the region to Armenia and large protests have since taken place in Yerevan, with protesters apparently attributing equal blame for the defeat to their own government and Russia. After the 2020 war, the EU and United States took on an increasingly visible role in negotiations between the parties. The overall impression, thus, is that Russia's ability to utilize the conflicts for political influence over Azerbaijan, Armenia, Georgia and Moldova is diminishing.

Nagorno-Karabakh

Ending in 1994, the first war over Nagorno-Karabakh and its aftermath has been a key factor defining geopolitics in the South Caucasus for three decades. The conflict started during Soviet times in 1988 with demands from the region's ethnic Armenian population to transfer the Nagorno-Karabakh Autonomous Oblast within Azerbaijan to Armenia. Ethnic cleansing and pogroms against Armenians in Azerbaijan and against Azeris in Armenia and Nagorno-Karabakh followed and escalated into a war between Azerbaijan and Nagorno-Karabakh separatists. While Armenia was heavily engaged on the side of Nagorno-Karabakh, it did not officially recognize its involvement.[6] In the course of the

---

[6] Svante E. Cornell, 'Undeclared War: The Nagorno-Karabakh Conflict Reconsidered', *Journal of South Asian and Middle Eastern Studies* XX, no. 4 (1997): 8–9.

war, Karabakh separatists and Armenian forces took control of the entire region, along with seven adjacent Azerbaijani regions, resulting in mass expulsions of Azeris from Nagorno-Karabakh and the seven surrounding regions occupied during the war, and from Armenia itself. Simultaneously, hundreds of thousands of Armenians had been expelled from Azerbaijan in the course of the conflict.[7] Nagorno-Karabakh thus became an unresolved conflict, internationally recognized as part of Azerbaijan but de facto controlled by Karabakh authorities. The international alignments of the two states, Armenia with Russia and Azerbaijan with Turkey, set parameters for subsequent intraregional relations as well as external involvement in the conflict. Since 1993, Azerbaijan and Turkey uphold embargoes on Armenia intended to isolate the country economically.[8] This has defined the routes for transportation and energy transit in the region. Azerbaijan's westward hydrocarbon exports transit Georgia to Turkey bypassing Armenia altogether. In turn, Armenia became highly dependent on Russia and, to a lesser extent, Iran.

Negotiations under the auspices of the OSCE Minsk group, established in 1992 and including Russia, the United States and France as co-chairs, made little headway towards resolving the conflict, which nevertheless remained relatively calm for two decades.[9] In the meantime, Armenia supported local authorities in establishing strong defensive positions in Nagorno-Karabakh, expecting that the region would over time gain acceptance and recognition as an independent state. Azerbaijan, in turn, utilized its growing income from oil and gas exports to build military capabilities far exceeding those of Armenia. In 2011, Azerbaijan's defence spending surpassed Armenia's entire national budget.[10]

In April 2016, Azerbaijani and Armenian forces fought a brief but intense four-day war along the contact line. This was the first fighting of this scale since the end of immediate hostilities in 1994.[11] The second Nagorno-Karabakh war was fought between 27 September and 9 November 2020. Azerbaijan launched

---

[7] Estimates of the total number of refugees vary. One 1995 report to the CoE mentions 850,000 Azeri refugees in Azerbaijan and 350,000 Armenian refugees in Armenia. Council of Europe, 'Report on the Humanitarian Situation of the Refugees and Displaced Persons in Armenia and Azerbaijan', https://assembly.coe.int/nw/xml/XRef/X2H-Xref-ViewHTML.asp?FileID=6823&lang=EN.

[8] Svante E. Cornell, 'Turkey and the Conflict in Nagorno-Karabakh: A Delicate Balance', *Middle Eastern Studies* 34, no. 1 (1998): 51.

[9] Robert M. Cutler, 'The Minsk Group Is Meaningless', *Foreign Policy*, 23 July 2021, https://foreignpolicy.com/2021/07/23/armenia-azerbaijan-nagorno-karabakh-osce-minsk-group-meaningless/.

[10] Tracey German, 'Nagorno-Karabakh: Security Situation', *Trans European Policy Studies Association*, https://www.europarl.europa.eu/meetdocs/2009_2014/documents/sede/dv/sede200612expertspresentations_/sede200612expertspresentations_en.pdf.

[11] 'Nagorno-Karabakh Violence: Worst Clashes in Decades Kill Dozens', *BBC*, 3 April 2016, https://www.bbc.com/news/world-europe-35949991.

an offensive along the line of contact on 27 September, making headway especially along the southern, flatter terrain and capturing the city of Shusha on 8 November. Russia brokered a ceasefire that was signed by the Azerbaijani, Armenian and Russian sides on 9 November. The ceasefire agreement granted Azerbaijan control of most of Nagorno-Karabakh and the return of adjacent regions, while provisioning the reopening of transport links including that between Azerbaijan and its Nakhchivan province, and the deployment of 2,000 Russian peacekeepers to Nagorno-Karabakh.[12]

Although Russia has not been directly involved in the Nagorno-Karabakh conflict, its unresolved status has served as an important means for exerting influence over both Armenia and Azerbaijan, and Russia's approaches to the conflict and its resolution have therefore been an important component of its policy towards the South Caucasus. From the ceasefire in 1994 until the mid-2010s, Russia's interest in Nagorno-Karabakh can be summarized as keeping the conflict at a controllable level of instability, not allowing new hostilities to break out while simultaneously avoiding a lasting solution. The status quo cemented the dependence of both Armenia and Azerbaijan on the positions taken by Russia on the conflict, since Russia remained the key arbiter of negotiations between the parties and an essential external party to an eventual solution. The strategy is manifested by the fact that between 2011 and 2020, Russia was the largest arms supplier to both Armenia and Azerbaijan.[13]

Armenia has remained deeply dependent on Russia, politically, economically and militarily. It is a member of the Russia-led military and economic blocs, the CSTO and the Eurasian Economic Union. Azerbaijan, on the other hand, has been able to retain relatively positive relations with Russia while also establishing several other vectors in its foreign policy, having forged a strong partnership with Turkey as well as becoming an important supplier of energy for Europe, providing oil and gas from sources and transit corridors not controlled by Russia. Azerbaijan entered a formal alliance with Turkey with the signature of the Shusha Declaration on 15 June 2021.[14]

---

[12] Edward J. Erickson, 'The 44-Day War in Nagorno-Karabakh: Turkish Drone Success or Operational Art?', *Military Review*, August 2021, https://www.armyupress.army.mil/Portals/7/military-review/img/Online-Exclusive/2021/erickson/Erickson-the-44-day-war.pdf.

[13] Pieter D. Wezeman, Alexandra Kuimova, and Jordan Smith, 'Arms Transfers to Conflict Zones: The Case of Nagorno-Karabakh', *Stockholm International Peace Research Institute*, https://www.sipri.org/commentary/topical-backgrounder/2021/arms-transfers-conflict-zones-case-nagorno-karabakh.

[14] Fuad Shahbazov, 'Shusha Declaration Cements Azerbaijani-Turkish Alliance', *Eurasia Daily Monitor*, 23 June 2021, 100, https://jamestown.org/program/shusha-declaration-cements-azerbaijani-turkish-alliance/.

Russia's strategy of retaining the status quo in Nagorno-Karabakh ultimately became untenable as the military balance shifted drastically in Azerbaijan's favour. Moreover, Armenia's Velvet Revolution in 2018, resulting in the ascent to power of Nikol Pashinyan, ended the country's political dominance of leaders originating in Nagorno-Karabakh since 1998 under Robert Kocharyan and Serzh Sargsyan. While Kocharyan and Sargsyan were both considered loyal partners to Russia, Moscow was deeply skeptical of Pashinyan and the circumstances under which he came to power, as well as his agenda for domestic reform regarding democratization and anti-corruption. The Velvet Revolution did not have geopolitical overtones and Pashinyan's government carefully avoided foreign policy initiatives that would antagonize Russia. Yet Pashinyan also had a track record of statements critical of Russia's role in Armenian politics while in opposition and was consequently viewed with suspicion in Moscow as unreliable and as a likely promoter of Western interests in the country.[15]

During the Second Karabakh War, Russia refused repeated requests from Yerevan to intervene on Armenia's behalf, pointing to the fact that the war played out on Azerbaijani territory, not in Armenia.[16] Russia apparently saw few advantages with openly taking sides in the war, which also provided an opportunity to undermine Pashinyan's standing in Armenia. The ceasefire agreement negotiated by Moscow also initially seemed to enable Russia to consolidate its continued role in the conflict and thus its leverage over the involved parties, not least through the deployment of Russian forces. However, Russia's role as a broker in the conflict increasingly came under challenge, with repeated violations of the ceasefire and clashes along the Azerbaijani-Armenian border, including Azerbaijani incursions into Armenia.[17] Azerbaijan also blocked the Lachin corridor, forming the lifeline between Armenia and the Stepanakert region of Nagorno-Karabakh, which remained under the control of Karabakh authorities. For months, the blockade drastically reduced supplies of commodities and medicine to residents of the region.[18]

[15] Richard Giragosian, 'Paradox of Power: Russia, Armenia, and Europe after the Velvet Revolution', *European Council on Foreign Relations*, https://ecfr.eu/publication/russia_armenia_and_europe_after_the_velvet_revolution/.

[16] Avet Demourian, 'Armenia Asks Moscow for Help Amid Nagorno-Karabakh Fighting', *Associated Press*, 31 October 2020, https://apnews.com/article/nikol-pashinian-moscow-azerbaijan-russia-vladimir-putin-cd2ed7be23043a1bd3170f951eaa399e.

[17] Laurence Broers, 'Is Azerbaijan Planning a Long-Term Presence in Armenia?', *Chatham House*, https://www.chathamhouse.org/2022/09/azerbaijan-planning-long-term-presence-armenia.

[18] Gabriel Gavin, 'Azerbaijan Pledges to Reopen Lachin Corridor to Nagorno-Karabakh', *Politico*, 9 September 2023, https://www.politico.eu/article/azerbaijan-agrees-to-reopen-lachin-corridor-to-nagorno-karabakh/.

From their different positions, the Azerbaijani and Armenian sides have increasingly vocally questioned the presence and performance of Russian peacekeepers, as well as Russia's role as a broker in the conflict.[19] Russia's full-scale invasion of Ukraine and the series of strategic and military debacles that have followed is thus reverberating in the South Caucasus – Russia is losing the clout it previously possessed through its key role in the Karabakh conflict, and both Armenia and Azerbaijan have increasingly ignored Russia's dictates when pursuing their interests. This includes Azerbaijan's increasingly aggressive attempts since 2020 to pressure Armenia into accepting an implementation of the peace agreement on Azerbaijani terms, particularly regarding the establishment of a Zangezur corridor connecting Azerbaijan and Nakhchivan. The Armenian leadership, on its part, declined to sign a joint CSTO declaration after the organization's summit in Yerevan in November 2022, refused to host joint exercises in January 2023 and has openly suggested its potential withdrawal from the organization. The country has also taken steps towards normalizing relations with Turkey, although this process remains fragile and uncertain.[20]

In sum, the second Karabakh war undermined Russia's standing and influence in both Armenia and Azerbaijan. For Armenia, Russia's refusal to assist the country during the war raised serious questions regarding Russia's value as an ally and security guarantor. Thus, the strategic rationale for Armenia's reliance on Russia has increasingly come under question. The loss of Nagorno-Karabakh has removed a significant Russian leverage on Armenia and although the country remains vulnerable to the militarily stronger Azerbaijan, there is little reason to expect Russian assistance if needed. However, notwithstanding the political and public disillusionment with Russia in Armenia, the country nevertheless remains deeply dependent on its ostensible northern ally, not least due to Russian ownership of large parts of Armenia's critical infrastructure and dependency on Russia for energy and other crucial imports.[21] It is therefore difficult to envision a political break with Russia without very substantial external support. Moreover, the anti-government protests in Armenia awards Russia with additional leverage to discourage Armenian overtures to the West,[22]

[19] Joshua Kucera, 'Russian Peacekeepers in Karabakh under Harsh Spotlight', *Eurasianet*, 15 December 2022, https://eurasianet.org/russian-peacekeepers-in-karabakh-under-harsh-spotlight.

[20] Aslı Aydıntaşbaş and Richard Giragosian, 'Acts of Normality: The Potential for Turkey-Armenia Rapprochement', *European Council on Foreign Relations*, https://ecfr.eu/publication/acts-of-normality-the-potential-for-turkey-armenia-rapprochement/.

[21] Giragosian, 'Paradox of Power'.

[22] Guy Faulconbridge, 'Russia Tells Armenian PM: You Are Making a Big Mistake by Flirting with West', *Reuters*, 25 September 2023, accessed 12 October 2023, https://www.reuters.com/world/eur ope/russia-tells-armenian-pm-you-are-making-big-mistake-by-flirting-with-west-2023-09-25/.

and it remains an open question how long the Pashinyan government can remain in power. Azerbaijan for its part has shown increasing disregard for Russia in its push for a final agreement on Nagorno-Karabakh and its criticism of the Russian military presence in the region. Azerbaijan's reestablished control over the entirety of Nagorno-Karabakh and the increased position of its principal ally Turkey in the region considerably reduces the need for taking Russian interests into account.

Russia's full invasion of Ukraine and its demonstrated inability to project power in that theatre is clearly a factor in this regard, emboldening both Armenia and Azerbaijan to pursue their own post-war agendas at the expense of Russian interests.

Abkhazia and South Ossetia

Abkhazia and South Ossetia were both autonomies in the USSR, within the Georgian Soviet Socialist Republic. Abkhazia had the higher status of an autonomous republic while South Ossetia was an autonomous oblast. The deterioration of the central power in the USSR from the late 1980s until 1991 was paralleled with the rise of an ethnically nationalist independence movement in Georgia, similarly to many other successor states, along with a drive among minority-dominated autonomies to in turn establish independence from Georgia. In the years 1991–4, three partly overlapping civil wars played out in Georgia. In 1991–2 and 1992–4, respectively, secessionist wars in South Ossetia and Abkhazia ended with these regions establishing de facto independence from Tbilisi. In 1991–3, supporters of the country's first president Zviad Gamsakhurdia (who was ousted in a military coup during New Year 1991–2) fought forces commanded first by the military council succeeding him and later the government of President Eduard Shevardnadze. As a result of the fighting, South Ossetia and Abkhazia established de facto independence, lacking any international recognition until the Russian-Georgian war in 2008, from the Georgian central government. These areas, along with the region of Adjara which had also enjoyed the status of an Autonomous Republic within Georgia, thus constituted internationally unrecognized separatist entities with their own government structures, albeit with tacit Russian support and with an increasingly heavy political, economic and military dependence on Russia.

Although the background to their separation from Georgia is similar, the two regions display considerable differences. Abkhazia's population has been estimated to be 244,000.[23] During and after the civil war, 250,000 ethnic Georgians fled Abkhazia and the majority still live in Georgia as internally displaced persons. Although Abkhazia depends heavily on Russian economic subsidies, the region has an economic base primarily in the form of agriculture. Moreover, the Abkhaz de facto leadership has, throughout shifts in government, to the extent possible resisted overt Russian control over the region and has insisted that Abkhazia should constitute an independent state of its own.[24]

In contrast, South Ossetia officially states its population to be 56,000 although the actual number is likely 35–45,000.[25] The majority of the population is concentrated at the de facto capital Tskhinvali. South Ossetia has no economic base of its own and relies almost completely on Russian subsidies for salaries, pensions and state functions. Rather than expressing any strong desire for independence, South Ossetia's de facto leaderships have repeatedly voiced a preference for joining North Ossetia, and thus the Russian Federation, and have on several occasions proposed to put this issue to a referendum, most recently in spring 2022.[26]

Russia has played a key role in supporting and sustaining the two regions. It militarily supported their separation from Georgia in the 1990s and subsequently took control over negotiation formats and peacekeeping forces, allowing Russia to establish a military presence in the two regions. While Russia long officially recognized Georgia's territorial integrity, it recognized the two regions as independent states after the 2008 war between Russia and Georgia. It failed to gain international backing for this decision even from some of its closest allies, and the two regions are today recognized only by Venezuela, Nicaragua, Syria and Nauru, aside from Russia.

Although the differences between Abkhazia and South Ossetia outlined above are significant in terms of how the respective de facto leaderships of these regions define their political outlook and interests, these differences matter less in the larger picture of Russian strategy and regional policies. Both are highly dependent on Russia and their room for independent manoeuvre is very limited in the case of Abkhazia and virtually non-existent in the case of South Ossetia.

---

[23] BBC, 'Abkhazia Profile', 28 August 2023, https://www.bbc.com/news/world-europe-18175030.

[24] Emil Avdaliani, 'Fears of Russian Influence Haunt Abkhazia', *Modern Diplomacy*, 5 November 2021, https://moderndiplomacy.eu/2021/11/05/fears-of-russian-influence-haunt-abkhazia/.

[25] A. B. Sebentsov, M. S. Karpenko, A. A. Gritsenko and N. L. Turov, 'Economic Development as a Challenge for "De Facto States": Post-Conflict Dynamics and Perspectives in South Ossetia', *Regional Research of Russia* 12, no. 3 (2022), https://link.springer.com/article/10.1134/S2079970522700277.

[26] Associated Press, 'Georgia's Breakaway South Ossetia Region Sets July Referendum to Join Russia', *Euronews*, 15 May 2022, https://www.euronews.com/2022/05/14/georgia-s-breakaway-south-osse tia-region-sets-july-referendum-to-join-russia.

Russia signed an Alliance and Integration Treaty with South Ossetia in 2015, formally subordinating the region's military and security forces to Russian command, integrating its economy with Russia and effectively abolishing the border with Russia. Abkhazia signed a treaty with Russia on Alliance and Strategic Partnership in 2014, including provisions for setting up a joint military force and integrating Abkhazia's economy with Russia's.[27]

Although both treaties denote a significant level of integration with Russia, Abkhazia has resisted key issues such as the possibility for Russians to obtain Abkhaz citizenship – which would in effect allow Russians to purchase and own land in Abkhazia. Another important difference is the status and control over the respective regions' military and security forces, where Abkhazia has retained its own military whereas South Ossetia's have been subordinated to Russian command and merged with the Russian military presence in South Ossetia. In consequence, a large number of South Ossetian personnel were dispatched to Ukraine in 2022, where they suffered heavy casualties in the first months of the war. Abkhazia has been able to resist a similar utilization of Abkhaz forces.[28]

The two regions remain the principal point of conflict between Russia and Georgia. Whereas Russia insists that the two regions are independent states, and that their future relationship to Georgia must build on a recognition of this fact, Georgia along with an overwhelming majority of the international community considers them to be under Russian occupation.

The regions have over the last three decades played a paramount role in Russia's relations with, and strategy towards, Georgia. Until 2008, the regions functioned largely as negotiation chips. Their unrecognized status along with their dependency on Russia and Russia's control over the conflict resolution processes allowed Russia to 'freeze' the conflicts, keeping them unresolved and their reintegration with Georgia a possibility, thus constituting a key asset regarding Russian influence in Georgia. The role of this asset became increasingly important as Georgia under Eduard Shevardnadze and later Mikheil Saakashvili formulated a clear policy of departing from Russia's orbit, seeking integration

[27] Luke Harding, 'Georgia Angered by Russia-Abkhazia Military Agreement', *The Guardian*, 25 November 2014, https://www.theguardian.com/world/2014/nov/25/georgia-russia-abkhazia-milit ary-agreement-putin; Sinikukka Saari, 'The New Alliance and Integration Treaty between Russia and South Ossetia: When Does Integration Turn into Annexation?', *The Finnish Institute of Foreign Affairs*, https://www.files.ethz.ch/isn/189653/comment9.pdf; Elizaveta Egorova and Ivan Babin, 'Eurasian Economic Union and the Difficulties of Integration: The Case of South Ossetia and Abkhazia', *Connections* 14, no. 2 (2015): 90–7.

[28] Sufian Zhemukhov, 'Abkhazia and South Ossetia: Second-Order Effects of the Russia-Ukraine War', *PONARS Eurasia*, https://www.ponarseurasia.org/abkhazia-and-south-ossetia-second-order-effe cts-of-the-russia-ukraine-war/.

with the Western security community and membership in NATO and the EU. The unresolved status of Abkhazia and South Ossetia became particularly useful in counteracting Georgia's bid for NATO membership, since the existence of unresolved conflicts on the territory of prospective new members was an important argument against NATO enlargement in the case of Georgia.

In the years preceding the 2008 war, Russia utilized its presence and influence in Abkhazia and South Ossetia to prepare the ground for a military intervention in Georgia. Large numbers of inhabitants in the two regions were granted Russian citizenship and passports, thus enabling Russia to motivate its presence there and the decision to invade Georgia with the need to protect Russian citizens.[29] Russia reinforced its military presence in the regions by bringing in heavy military equipment under the guise of 'peacekeeping' contingents and, in the months preceding the war, repaired the railway through Abkhazia for military logistics. Russia denied its involvement in military provocations in the run-up to the war, in Abkhazia's Kodori Gorge and in Tsitelubani close to South Ossetia, while formalizing diplomatic links with the two regions and thus taking steps towards treating them as independent states. This raised alarm in Georgia of their imminent annexation by Russia in response to Kosovo's independence. After a tense July, involving artillery exchanges and bombings, Georgian forces entered South Ossetia on the night of 8 August and motivated this as a response to sustained artillery shelling by South Ossetian units of Georgian villages in South Ossetia and an influx of additional Russian troops to the region. Russia subsequently launched an invasion of Georgia through South Ossetia as well as Abkhazia, a war lasting for five days and leaving Russia in control of the two regions and surrounding areas.[30]

After the 2008 war and Russia's recognition of Abkhazia and South Ossetia as independent states, the leverage associated with their unresolved status became largely obsolete. Yet Russia has continued to utilize its control over the regions as a means for influencing Georgia. The sizeable military forces based in Abkhazia and South Ossetia constitute a credible conventional threat south of the Caucasus mountains. The administrative boundary line (ABL) around South Ossetia is frequently subject to 'borderization' – physical reinforcement and moving further into Georgian territory, while referenda on unification

[29] Emil Suleimanov, Eduard Abrahamiyan and Huseyn Aliyev, 'Unrecognized States as a Means of Coercive Diplomacy? Assessing the Role of Abkhazia and South Ossetia in Russia's Foreign Policy in the South Caucasus', *Southeast European and Black Sea Studies* 18, no. 1 (2017): 8–10.
[30] Heidi Tagliavini, *Independent International Fact-Finding Mission on the Conflict in Georgia: Volume II* (2009).

with North Ossetia, and thereby annexation by Russia, are from time to time promoted in South Ossetia.

The reintegration of Abkhazia and South Ossetia with Georgia was a central item on Tbilisi's political agenda from the de facto independence of the two regions; however, it was not until after the Rose Revolution in 2003 and the ascent of a new Georgian government under Saakashvili that Georgia as a state began to acquire the functions and resources to challenge the de facto governments in these regions and, by extension, Russia's control over them. Georgia's strategy towards the two regions has changed over the years, from offering significant autonomy within Georgia and economic incentives to statements threatening the option of forcible unification (although this was strongly discouraged by Georgia's Western partners). After 2008, Georgia in practice awarded much lower priority to national reunification, adopting a strategy of 'strategic patience'.[31] The Georgian Dream government coming to power after the 2012 parliamentary elections attached an even lower priority to reunification, instead prioritizing the normalization of particularly economic aspects of relations with Russia. Although Georgia continues to consider the regions as occupied territories, the status quo established in 2008 remains.

Overall, Georgia's strategy for establishing and safeguarding its autonomy and independence in relation to Russia has been to build a strong relationship with the West, and especially with the United States. Among the states gaining independence after 1991, Georgia has been unique in its uncompromising Western foreign policy direction and its renouncement of Russian influence. This approach has been consistent across three consecutive governments and has been manifested in a political drive to gain membership in NATO and the EU, as well as a strong commitment to political and economic reform aiming to meet the requirements for membership in these organizations. However, this commitment has periodically come under question and has been paired with excessive government control over political and economic life, infringements on media freedom and civil society, and resistance to reforming the country's politicized judiciary.[32] This was the case during particularly Saakashvili's second term as president as well as under the current Georgian Dream government. Due

---

[31] Niklas Nilsson, *Beacon of Liberty: Role Conceptions, Crises and Stability in Georgia's Foreign Policy* (Uppsala: Acta Universitatis Upsaliensis, 2015).

[32] Vano Chkhikvadze, 'Candidate Status – Georgia at the Crossroads', *Stockholm Centre for Eastern European Studies*, https://sceeus.se/en/publications/candidate-status-georgia-at-the-crossro ads/; Niklas Nilsson, 'Georgia's Rose Revolution: The Break with the Past,' in *The Guns of August 2008: Russia's War in Georgia*, ed. Svante E. Cornell and S. Frederick Starr (New York: M.E. Sharpe, 2009): 95–8.

to these shortcomings, the EU declined Georgia's application for membership candidate status in June 2022, while the status was granted to Ukraine and Moldova. Georgia was instead granted candidate status in December 2023. In March 2023, the government's intention to introduce a law forcing foreign-funded NGOs to register as foreign agents sparked a domestic political crisis and drew heavy criticism form Georgia's international partners.[33]

Moreover, despite its international political outlook, Georgia has sought to retain a low profile in the ongoing confrontation between Russia and the West. The country has not joined international sanctions against Russia although the political opposition argues for a much stronger policy of solidarity with Ukraine after the 2022 invasion, and there are ultimately few signs that Georgia will adopt a radically different approach towards either the conflicts or Russia in the near future.

Transnistria

Transnistria is an unrecognized Moldavian breakaway region sandwiched between the Moldovan-Ukrainian border and the Nistru River. It comprises little more than 10 per cent of Moldova's territory and its approximately 470,000 inhabitants amount to around 13 per cent of the population. The Transnistrian local authorities proclaimed their independence already during Soviet times in 1990. After Moldova became an independent state, a short civil war erupted in early 1992. In July 1992, a ceasefire agreement was concluded in Moscow, ending the bloodshed, while establishing Transnistria as a de facto independent entity with a Russian military presence on Moldova's internationally recognized territory.

Transnistria used to be a region (oblast) in the Moldovan Soviet Socialist Republic but with no special autonomous status. There was, however, an economic specialization; while the rest of Moldova was agrarian, Transnistria was highly industrialized and more prosperous. The conflict did not stand out due to ethnic animosities or other affective ties that feature predominantly in other unresolved post-Soviet territorial conflicts. Transnistria consists of three roughly equal ethnic groups – Moldovans, Russians and Ukrainians. The conflict has also been notable for the relatively low priority attached to the conflict both

---

[33] Paul Kirby, 'Georgia Drops "Foreign Agents" Law after Protests', *BBC*, 9 March 2023, https://www.bbc.com/news/world-europe-64899041.

politically and among the people. Over time, certain periodical pushes towards a settlement have been offset by strong interests preferring the status quo above any solution that would force the parties to make any concessions. A solution to the conflict is further complicated by the fact that the interests and identities of the two sides have become increasingly detached from one another over the past decades. As a result, no tangible progress has been made on conflict resolution.[34]

Without question Russia has played a lead role in both defining the conflict and in how the conflict resolution process has developed. From the outset, Moscow actively supported the de facto secession of Transnistria from Moldova. Then, when a brittle peace was achieved, Russia moved decisively to gain a controlling position in the peacekeeping and negotiation formats for the conflict. Moscow used its influence as a mediator and peacekeeper to consolidate its leverage over the two parties rather than to facilitate a solution to the conflict. Thus, Russia is both a player in the conflict and the ultimate arbiter.[35]

The combination of chronic political instability and severe economic hardships in Moldova has meant that consecutive Moldovan governments have been rather passive in its efforts to reintegrate Transnistria. In the programs of the major Moldovan political parties, there is scant mentioning of Transnistria, even though the conflict negatively affects the country's economic performance and security. A corresponding lack of attention is found among the population.

Moscow's major concrete contribution to the conflict settlement process was the Kozak memorandum developed by President Putin's close ally Dmitry Kozak in 2003. The Kozak memorandum proposed to integrate Transnistria into an asymmetric federal Moldovan state. According to the plan, Russian troops would remain in Transnistria for a twenty-year-long transitional period. The Moldovan government rejected the proposal at the last minute after facing strong protests in the capital Chisinau.[36] More than a decade later, Kozak, who

---

[34] Victoria Rosa, *The Transnistrian Conflict: 30 Years Searching for a Settlement*, SCEEUS Reports on Human Rights and Security in Eastern Europe, no. 4, October 2021, https://www.ui.se/globalass ets/ui.se-eng/publications/sceeus/the-transnistrian-conflict.pdf. https://www.ui.se/globalassets/ui. se-eng/publications/sceeus/the-transnistrian-conflict.pdf.

[35] Negotiations have been pursued within the so-called 5+2 framework, which bring together Moldova and Transnistria with mediators Russia, Ukraine and the OSCE, and the two observers, the EU and the United States. These negotiations are divided into three separate 'baskets': socio-economic, humanitarian and political. The approach has mainly focused on the former two baskets while the political basket concerning the ultimate issue of Transnistria's future political status has been avoided. The intention behind this logic was to eventually build the trust between the two parties that was deemed necessary to move to political discussions. Overall, however, little progress has occurred.

[36] Cristian Urse, 'Transnistria: Prospects for a Solution', *George C. Marshall European Center for Security Studies*, https://www.marshallcenter.org/en/publications/occasional-papers/transnistria-prospects-solution.

has remained the main Russian official for dealing with Russia's near abroad, outlined a similar plan for the Donbas region in Ukraine.

As in the other unresolved conflicts on the former Soviet territories, the original causes of the confrontation at the time of the break-up of the Soviet Union no longer remain as relevant for understanding the contemporary dynamics of the conflict as was once the case. The two sides have developed into two distinct political and economic systems, and the gap between them has widened over time. Over the past three decades, the unrecognized Transnistrian political entity has confronted severe economic and social hardships but has nonetheless made progress in establishing many of the attributes of recognized states.[37] Russian economic and political support as well as Moscow's security guarantees have helped Transnistria withstand pressure to rejoin Moldova with relative ease. The political leadership in the breakaway region has built a Transnistrian identity based on the common belonging to the territory of Transnistria.

Over the past decades, Moscow has financed, directly and indirectly, more than 70 per cent of the Transnistrian budget. When Transnistria in the early 2000s decided to launch a privatization process to bring much-needed money into state coffers, several of the major industries fell into the hands of Russian companies. The major economic asset is the Moldova Steel Work in Rybnitsa, which accounts for more than half of Transnistria's industrial output and is under the control of Russian capital and kept profitable through Russia's subsidization of gas prices. Today, Transnistria's total energy debt to Russia is estimated at more than US$7 billion.[38] This debt is officially due to be paid by Chisinau, but the Moldovan authorities reject this on the ground that they have no control over Transnistria's gas imports from Russia.

Thus, the Transnistrian economic model does not rest on a self-sustainable domestic base but depends on Russian support to stay alive. Besides Russian gas subsidies and pension payments, this also includes cash remittances from expatriate workers in Russia. Thus, Russia dominates the Transnistrian economy to the extent that any conflict settlement would ensure a big Russian influence also over Moldova.

In addition to the so-called peacekeepers, Russia maintains an operational military group in Transnistria of approximately 1,500 soldiers in violation of

[37] Helge Blakkisrud and Pål Kolstø, 'From Secessionist Conflict toward a Functioning State: Processes of State- and Nation-Building in Transnistria', *Post-Soviet Affairs* 27, no. 2 (2011): 178–210.
[38] Kataryna Wolczuk, 'Here We Go Again: Russia's Energy "Diplomacy" in Moldova', *Chatham House*, https://www.chathamhouse.org/2021/12/here-we-go-again-russias-energy-diplomacy-moldova.

both the Moldovan Constitution and international law. Transnistria's own armed forces and security structures are under firm Russian control. After the full-scale invasion of Ukraine, this military presence is becoming increasingly dangerous. Russian Foreign Minister Sergei Lavrov has warned Moldova that 'any actions that will endanger the security of our soldiers [in Transnistria] will be interpreted, in accordance with international law, as an attack on the Russian Federation'.[39]

Besides the military presence in Transnistria, it is estimated that more than 200,000 people in Transnistria hold Russian passports. The figure increased sharply after Russia's annexation of Crimea in 2014. By handing out Russian passports, Moscow claims that it is entitled to protect Russian citizens in Transnistria against the Moldovan government.

Overall, Moldova finds itself in a highly vulnerable situation as Russia has a multitude of tools to use for putting pressure on Moldova. Although Russia's preoccupation with Ukraine since at least 2014 has sheltered Moldova to some extent from a more concerted and effective policy focus, the full-scale Russian invasion of Ukraine on 24 February 2022, however, created shockwaves with profound effects on the Russia-Moldova relationship.[40] It led the current, strongly pro-European government in Moldova to quickly apply for EU membership, and in June 2022, Brussels granted Moldova, together with Ukraine, candidate status to the EU. Nonetheless, the Moldovan government is in a vulnerable position, and Moldovan politics is known for its highly volatile nature.

The political leadership must balance the ambition to integrate into the EU with the country's traditional dependence on Russia, not least for trade and its energy supplies, which are crucial for the country's economic and social stability. Over the years, Russia has repeatedly applied measures to damage the Moldovan economy, including banning imports of wine and fruits and shutting off gas supplies. These dependencies also help explain why the Moldovan government hesitated to join Westerns sanctions against the Russian economy.

The government is supported by a fragile majority in Parliament and challenged by political forces funded by Russia. In February 2023, the Moldovan government officially accused Russia of planning to instigate a coup in the country with the help of foreign provocateurs and opposition politicians bankrolled by

---

[39] Iulian Ernst, 'Moldova Summons Russian Diplomat over Lavrov Threat', *bne IntelliNews*, 2 September 2022, https://bne.eu/moldova-summons-russian-diplomat-over-lavrov-threat-255317/.

[40] See Johan Engvall, Ismail Khan and Kristina Melin, 'Post-Soviet No More – the Transformative Impact of War on Russia's Neighbors', *The SAIS Review of International Affairs*, 18 September 2023, https://saisreview.sais.jhu.edu/post-soviet-no-more-the-transformative-impact-of-war-on-russias-neighbors/.

Moscow.[41] Several anti-government demonstrations have been organized by pro-Russian opposition forces inside and outside the country since Russia's full-scale invasion of Ukraine, leaving domestic stability at peril. According to Georgia's president Maia Sandu, Russia's aim is to prevent Moldova from joining the EU and using the country for its war effort in Ukraine.[42] Thus, rather than being a deep-rooted intra-state conflict, the Transnistrian conflict has become the subject of great power politics with the West against Russia. Transnistria has become a major pawn in Russia's quest to thwart Moldova's ambition to build an independent state that seeks European integration.

The information sphere in Moldova, on both sides of the riverbank, is particularly vulnerable to Russian propaganda. Through its influence over Moldovan news and information, Moscow has successfully engineered a narrative that Chisinau suppresses the Russian language, seeks to reunify Moldova with Romania and wants to sever all ties with Russia in favour of European integration. Moscow's message is further transmitted through various political parties, civic organizations and oligarchic interests in Moldova with close links to the Kremlin.

In short, Transnistria is a bargaining chip for Russia vis-à-vis both the Moldovan government and Western states. Unlike Abkhazia and South Ossetia in Georgia, Moscow has not declared Transnistria an independent state, despite the ambition of Transnistrian authorities to be recognized as such. Therefore, Moscow has seen the current status quo as a way to keep its leverage over Moldova. In contrast, if Russia would either recognize Transnistria as an independent state or annex Transnistria and incorporate it into Russia, this would lead Moscow to lose significant leverage over Moldovan politics.

Ukraine's Donbass: The Donetsk and Luhansk People's Republics

The war in Eastern Ukraine since 2014, and the establishment of two separatist entities in Ukraine's Donbas region, the Donetsk and Luhansk Peoples' Republics (DNR and LNR), had clear precedents in Moldova's Transnistria

---

[41] Tim Lister, 'Secret Document Reveals Russia's 10-Year Plan to Destabilize Moldova', *CNN*, 18 March 2023, https://edition.cnn.com/2023/03/16/europe/russia-moldova-secret-document-intl- cmd/index.html.

[42] President of Moldova, 'Address by President Maia Sandu at the 3rd Edition of Moldova Support Platform, Paris', https://www.presedinte.md/eng/discursuri/address-by-president-maia- sandu-at-the-3rd-edition-of-moldova-support-platform-paris.

and Georgia's Abkhazia and South Ossetia before 2008, as well as in Russia's approaches to the Nagorno-Karabakh conflict. Yet contrary to the unresolved conflicts that emerged during the breakdown of the USSR, Russia's drive to establish separatist entities within Ukraine did not build on the existence of a local ethnified conflict. Instead, Russia deployed a combination of different means, ranging from the threat and eventual use of conventional force, covert military operations, the use of local separatist proxies, political subversion and extensive informational operations to foment a local conflict in which Russia could deny direct involvement.

The establishment of DNR and LNR also stands aside from the quick seizure and annexation of Crimea in early 2014. DNR and LNR represented a Russian strategy of instigating unresolved conflicts within Ukraine intended to serve as leverage with the aim to force the country's federalization and work as an effective veto on Ukraine's Western alignment. However, this strategy proved unsuccessful and became obsolete with Russia's recognition of DNR and LNR as independent states on 21 February 2022 and the subsequent full-scale invasion of Ukraine three days later. Russia proclaimed to have annexed Donetsk and Luhansk, as well as Kherson and Zaporizhzhia, on 30 September 2022.[43] Nevertheless, Russia's actions in Ukraine since 2014, as well as the precedent for these actions in the other conflicts addressed in this chapter, are indicative of the importance and potential that Russia has attributed to the strategic utility of proxy conflicts in its near abroad. This section therefore outlines Russia's attempt to impose the concept of unresolved conflicts on separatist territories governed by proxy regimes on Ukraine in 2014, and Ukraine's response to this. [44]

In early 2014, Russia initiated a campaign to establish 'Novorossiya', or 'New Russia', with the aim of creating a confederation of 'people's republics' encompassing large parts of Southern and Eastern Ukraine. This construct was fuelled by a narrative that portrayed an imminent threat to Russians and Russian-speakers in Ukraine posed by the rise of a 'fascist junta' in Kyiv, promoted through state- and social media as well as agents of influence.[45] Information

---

[43] Reuters, 'Russia's Federation Council Ratifies Annexation of Four Ukrainian Regions', 4 October 2022, https://www.reuters.com/world/europe/russias-federation-council-ratifies-annexation-four-ukrainian-regions-2022-10-04/.

[44] An earlier version of this section is published in Niklas Nilsson, 'De-Hybridization and Conflict Narration', in *Hybrid Warfare: Security and Asymmetric Conflict in International Relations / Edited by Mikael Weissmann, Niklas Nilsson, Per Thunholm, Björn Palmertz*, ed. Mikael Weissmann et al. (London: I.B. Tauris, 2021), 214-231.

[45] Margarita Jaitner, 'Russian Information Warfare: Lessons from Ukraine', in *Cyber War in Perspective: Russian Aggression against Ukraine*, ed. Kenneth Geers (Tallinn: NATO Cooperative Cyber Defence Center of Excellence, 2015).

campaigns remained a crucial component of Russia's operations in Crimea and Donbas, aiming to promote the legitimacy of Novorossiya as well as seeking to undermine Ukraine's military and war efforts. Russian propaganda has portrayed Ukraine's armed forces as weak and incompetent, aiming to demoralize troops and society, and to create a sense of futility about resistance. Moreover, Russia has attempted to isolate Ukraine by presenting it as strategically isolated and as utilized by the EU and NATO, which are depicted as having provoked Russia into the conflict while at the same time lacking any sincere interest in Ukraine per se.[46]

The Novorossiya project failed to gain much traction outside of Donetsk and Luhansk and was countered with a successful mobilization of Ukrainians who opposed it. However, separatist groups and pro-Russian activists, spearheaded by Russian special forces, established control over several cities, including Donetsk, Luhansk, Kramatorsk, Slovyansk and Krasny Liman, proclaiming the establishment of the Donetsk People's Republic (DNR) and Luhansk People's Republic (LNR).[47]

Ukraine responded to these separatist movements by launching an anti-terrorist operation (ATO) with the support of volunteer units.[48] Initially, Russia sought to achieve its goals in Eastern Ukraine without overtly intervening in the conflict. Russia limited its involvement to special forces units and security contractors operating under false identities,[49] also supporting the separatist forces politically and financially by providing them with instructors and equipment, in an involvement that escalated over time.[50]

During April and May 2014, Ukrainian forces exerted sufficient pressure on the separatist militias to force Russia to make a more substantive intervention. From June, Russia continuously provided the separatists with manpower and heavy equipment, for example, armour and anti-aircraft systems. Despite this support, Ukrainian forces continued to advance throughout the summer, and by August threatened to drive a wedge between the two separatist territories. Faced

---

[46] Vladimir Sazonov, Kristiina Müür, and Holger Mölder, eds, *Russian Information Campaign Against the Ukrainian State and Defence Forces* (Tartu: NATO Strategic Communications Centre of Excellence, 2016).

[47] Michael Kofman, Katya Migacheva, Brian Nichiporuk, Andrew Radin, Olesya Tkacheva, and Jenny Oberholtzer, *Lessons from Russia's Operations in Crimea and Eastern Ukraine*, Research report (Santa Monica, CA: Rand Corporation, 2017).

[48] Margerete Klein, 'Ukraine's Volunteer Battalions – Advantages and Challenges,' RUFS Briefing no. 27 (Swedish Defence Research Agency, 2015).

[49] James Miller, Pierre Vaux, Catherine A. Fitzpatrick, and Michel Weiss, *An Invasion by Another Name: The Kremlin's Dirty War in Ukraine* (Institute of Modern Russia; The Interpreter, 2015).

[50] Mark Galeotti, *Armies of Russia's War in Ukraine* (Oxford and New York: Osprey Publishing, 2019).

with the prospect of defeat, Russia sent in conventional mechanized troops organized in battalion tactical groups and supported by heavy artillery, rolling back the Ukrainian advances and defeating the Ukrainian forces at Ilovaisk.[51] Following the signing of the Minsk Protocol in September 2014, Russia began a more concerted effort to train and equip the separatists and undertook a new offensive in January 2015. Following the defeat of Ukrainian forces at Debaltseve, on 12 February Ukraine agreed to implement the Minsk II agreement, which included an OSCE-observed unconditional ceasefire from 15 February.

Ukraine's decision to respond with conventional military force to Russia's covert infiltration of Donbas drew on the experiences attained during the invasion of Crimea. This response proved crucial in reshaping both domestic and international perceptions of the conflict by highlighting Russia's culpability for the aggression and refuting Moscow's characterization of the conflict as a local insurgency.

Aside from Ukraine's ability to reform and expand its military during the ongoing conflict, a key objective of Ukraine's approach was to expose Russia's involvement in the conflict. From Ukraine's perspective, it was crucially important to demonstrate that the conflict was indeed an interstate war, triggered by Russia's subversion of Ukrainians and subsequent invasion of Ukraine. Domestically, an understanding of the conflict as a civil war waged by Kyiv against its citizens would have had detrimental consequences and could potentially have pitted Ukrainian citizens against each other far beyond Donetsk and Luhansk – which was indeed what Russia sought to achieve in the spring of 2014. Moreover, the international support for Ukraine's territorial integrity hinged on its victimhood to Russian aggression. This not only raised sympathies for Ukraine but also obliged the international community to devise a response, through the sanctions regime imposed against Russia in 2014.

In response to Russia's comprehensive information operations, Ukraine restricted Russian information channels on its territory. This included social media platforms and major Russian state-controlled television channels used as instruments of Russian state propaganda.[52] Ukraine and its reforming military also made a considerable effort to promote its own, competing narrative, ranging from the highly localized setting of the conflict zones around DNR and LNR, via national political mobilization in Ukraine, to the international

---

[51]   Kofman et al., 'Lessons from Russia's Operations in Crimea and Eastern Ukraine'.

[52]   Alec Luhn, 'Ukraine Blocks Popular Social Networks as Part of Sanctions on Russia,' *The Guardian*, 16 May 2017. https://www.theguardian.com/world/2017/may/16/ukraine-blocks-popular-russian-websites-kremlin-role-war.

political arena.[53] The general message of Ukraine's information campaign was, and remains, addressed to both the Ukrainian public and international partners. Domestically, it signalled that the country was neither defenceless nor abandoned and that it was indeed possible to resist and repel Russian aggression. To partners in the West, Ukraine's message was, and remains, that the country is capable of safeguarding its territorial integrity and that efforts to support it are not wasted. Thus, Ukraine laid the foundations for its highly successful strategic communication following Russia's full-scale invasion of the country in February 2022.

Russia's invasion of Ukraine and the future of unresolved conflicts

Russia's full-scale invasion of Ukraine in February 2022 has stood many of the prevailing assumptions regarding Russian strategy and influence in its neighbourhood on their head. It has commonly been assumed that Russian attempts to regain control over neighbouring states through large-scale use of force would present high risks, large costs and limited gains. Accordingly, such attempts would be irrational and therefore unlikely. Yet the full-scale invasion of Ukraine happened and has led to a substantial re-evaluation of Russia's priorities, propensity for risk and capabilities. The consequences of the war for Russia and its continued influence in its neighbourhood remain uncertain. The same goes for Russia's continued role in the unresolved conflicts examined in this chapter and the future role of these conflicts in Russian strategy.

Russia's demonstrated inability to attain its military objectives in Ukraine and the economic losses it has sustained from the war effort and as an effect of sanctions puts into question its ability to continue exercising control over and supporting the separatist territories in the future. The fact that Russia's political and military attention is focused almost exclusively on Ukraine has been duly noted in the states affected by unresolved territorial conflicts. This is most visible, although not limited to, the case of Nagorno-Karabakh.

Another aspect is the economic costs imposed on Russia in sustaining the de facto regimes. As the war in Ukraine and the sanctions imposed on Russia strains the federal budget, it might see itself forced to deprioritize funding for particularly Abkhazia and South Ossetia. Russia has already signalled that

---

[53] Nilsson, 'De-Hybridization and Conflict Narration: Ukraine's Defence Against Russian Hybrid.

funding for Abkhazia and South Ossetia will decrease.[54] However, the picture varies among the conflicts – gas transit through Transnistria and the region's electricity production and sales to Moldova provides net income for Russia.

Of course, the future importance of the unresolved conflicts in Russia's relations to Moldova, Armenia, Azerbaijan and Georgia is closely connected with ongoing developments in its overall relations with these states. Due to its engagement in Ukraine, Russia's capacity to project military, political and economic power elsewhere has diminished, with direct implications for its future ability to exert influence on neighbouring states.

However, the changing geopolitical context in Eastern Europe and the South Caucasus, as well as in Central Asia, also affects the longer-term foreign and domestic political outlook for the five states in focus in this chapter. These have embarked on processes of reorienting their foreign policies to either depart from Russia's orbit (Georgia, Moldova and Ukraine) or forge strong relationships with other important regional powers in order to balance Russia (Azerbaijan). Even Armenia, which remains highly dependent on Russia, is increasingly seeking international options to Russia and its memberships in the Eurasian Economic Union (EEU) and CSTO.

Moreover, domestic political processes in all five states have delimited the significance of unresolved conflicts as vulnerabilities and means for indirect influence. In Ukraine, the DNR and LNR never acquired the de facto status quo common to the other conflicts and have been the focus of an interstate war between Ukraine and Russia since 2014. In Moldova and Georgia, policies of strategic patience in relation to the conflicts coupled with a focus on integration processes with the EU and NATO and domestic reform have reduced the significance and priority given to the conflicts. Ukraine and Moldova were granted EU candidate status in June 2022, and Georgia in December 2023. In Azerbaijan, the decision to re-establish control over Nagorno-Karabakh by force effectively diminished Russia's role as an arbiter in this conflict. Finally, Armenia has undergone its own peaceful political revolution and domestic reform process, and the extent to which it will remain dependent on Russia in the future is to a large extent contingent on how it will process the trauma of losing Karabakh, the perceived need for protection against continued Azerbaijani aggression and its continued relationship with Turkey. Yet Armenia's ability to redirect its foreign

---

[54] Civil Georgia, 'Moscow Says Abkhazia, S. Ossetia Shall Be Less Dependent on Russia', 10 March 2022, https://civil.ge/archives/478378.

outlook would also require very substantial Western support, given its deep structural dependency on Russia.

The war in Ukraine has also further enhanced the geopolitical importance of the region for Europe and the United States, as well as for China. The urgency in ending European dependence on Russian gas has increased the importance of Azerbaijani hydrocarbons and the established Southern Gas Corridor, running from Azerbaijan via Georgia to Turkey for further transport to the European market. The redrawn energy map has also contributed to revitalizing discussions on enhanced trans-Caspian energy transit, in order to make the vast hydrocarbon resources of Kazakhstan and Turkmenistan available to European consumers. Moreover, the South Caucasus, along with Central Asia, is emerging as an increasingly important conduit for transportation between Europe and China, bypassing Russia. Thus, Russia's proven unreliability as an energy exporter and trade partner is increasingly placing the South Caucasus in the geopolitical spotlight, potentially warranting previously unseen degrees of political attention and economic resources from the West.

Russia will in all likelihood be struggling to curtail these trends and the opportunities they offer to the five states in focus. Nevertheless, as the trajectory of the war has become a serious threat to Russia's imperial ambitions and its ability to exercise influence in its neighbourhood, as well as to the Russian regime itself, it is also conceivable that the separatist territories and continued Russian control over them will become even more important in Russian strategy than has previously been the case. This is all the more so since the attack on Ukraine and its consequences has seriously undermined Russia's other means for exercising influence in Tbilisi, Baku, Yerevan and Chisinau.

Bibliography

Associated Press (2022), 'Georgia's Breakaway South Ossetia Region Sets July Referendum to Join Russia', *Euronews*, 15 May. Available online: https://www.euron ews.com/2022/05/14/georgia-s-breakaway-south-ossetia-region-sets-july-referen dum-to-join-russia (accessed 12 October 2023).

Avdaliani, E. (2021), 'Fears of Russian Influence Haunt Abkhazia', *Modern Diplomacy*, 5 November. Available online: https://moderndiplomacy.eu/2021/11/05/fears-of-russ ian-influence-haunt-abkhazia/ (accessed 12 October 2023).

Aydıntaşbaş, A., and R. Giragosian (2022), 'Acts of Normality: The Potential for Turkey-Armenia Rapprochement', *European Council on Foreign Relations*. Available online: https://ecfr.eu/publication/acts-of-normality-the-potential-for-turkey-arme nia-rapprochement/ (accessed 16 November 2023).

BBC (2016), 'Nagorno-Karabakh Violence: Worst Clashes in Decades Kill Dozens', *BBC*, 3 April. Available online: https://www.bbc.com/news/world-europe-35949991 (accessed 16 November 2023).

BBC (2023), 'Abkhazia Profile', *BBC*, 28 August. Available online: https://www.bbc.com/ news/world-europe-18175030 (accessed 12 October 2023).

Blakkisrud, H., and P. Kolsto (2011), 'From Secessionist Conflict toward a Functioning State: Processes of State- and Nation-Building in Transnistria', *Post-Soviet Affairs*, 27 (2): 178–210.

Broers, L. (2022), 'Is Azerbaijan Planning a Long-Term Presence in Armenia?', *Chatham House*. Available online: https://www.chathamhouse.org/2022/09/azerbaijan-plann ing-long-term-presence-armenia (accessed 16 November 2023).

Chkhikvadze, V. 'Candidate Status – Georgia at the Crossroads', *Stockholm Centre for Eastern European Studies*. Available online: https://sceeus.se/en/publications/candid ate-status-georgia-at-the-crossroads/ (accessed 12 October 2023).

Civil Georgia (2022), 'Moscow Says Abkhazia, S. Ossetia Shall Be Less Dependent on Russia', 10 March. Available online: https://civil.ge/archives/478378 (accessed 12 October 2023).

Council of Europe (1995), *Report on the Humanitarian Situation of the Refugees and Displaced Persons in Armenia and Azerbaijan*. Available online: https://assembly.coe. int/nw/xml/XRef/X2H-Xref-ViewHTML.asp?FileID=6823&lang=EN (accessed 16 November 2023).

Cornell, S. E. (1997), 'Undeclared War: The Nagorno-Karabakh Conflict Reconsidered', *Journal of South Asian and Middle Eastern Studies*, 20 (4): 1–24.

Cornell, S. E. (1998), 'Turkey and the Conflict in Nagorno-Karabakh: A Delicate Balance', *Middle Eastern Studies*, 34 (1): 51–72.

Cutler, R. M. (2021), 'The Minsk Group Is Meaningless', *Foreign Policy*, 23 July. Available online: https://foreignpolicy.com/2021/07/23/armenia-azerbaijan-nagorno-karab akh-osce-minsk-group-meaningless/ (accessed 16 November 2023).

Demourian, A. (2020), 'Armenia Asks Moscow for Help Amid Nagorno-Karabakh Fighting', *Associated Press*, 31 October. Available online: https://apnews.com/article/ nikol-pashinian-moscow-azerbaijan-russia-vladimir-putin-cd2ed7be23043a1bd 3170f951eaa399e (accessed 16 November 2023).

Erickson, E. J. (2021), 'The 44-Day War in Nagorno-Karabakh: Turkish Drone Success or Operational Art?', *Military Review*, August. Available online: https://www.arm yupress.army.mil/Portals/7/military-review/img/Online-Exclusive/2021/erickson/ Erickson-the-44-day-war.pdf (accessed 16 November 2023).

Egorova, E., and I. Babin (2015), 'Eurasian Economic Union and the Difficulties of Integration: The Case of South Ossetia and Abkhazia', *Connections*, 14 (2): 90–7.

Engvall, J., I. Khan and K. Melin (2023), 'Post-Soviet No More – the Transformative Impact of War on Russia's Neighbors', *SAIS Review of International Affairs*,

18 September. Available online: https://saisreview.sais.jhu.edu/post-sov iet-no-more-the-transformative-impact-of-war-on-russias-neighbors/ (accessed 12 October 2023).

Ernst, I. (2022), 'Moldova Summons Russian Diplomat over Lavrov Threat', *bne IntelliNews*, 2 September. Available online: https://bne.eu/moldova-summons-russ ian-diplomat-over-lavrov-threat-255317/ (accessed 12 October 2023).

Faulconbridge, G. (2023), 'Russia Tells Armenian PM: You Are Making a Big Mistake by Flirting with West', *Reuters*, 25 September. Available online: https://www.reuters. com/world/europe/russia-tells-armenian-pm-you-are-making-big-mistake-by-flirt ing-with-west-2023-09-25/ (accessed 12 October 2023).

Galeotti, M. (2019), *Armies of Russia's War in Ukraine*, Oxford: Osprey.

Gavin, G. (2023), 'Azerbaijan Pledges to Reopen Lachin Corridor to Nagorno-Karabakh', *Politico*, 9 September. Available online: https://www.politico.eu/article/ azerbaijan-agrees-to-reopen-lachin-corridor-to-nagorno-karabakh/ (accessed 16 November 2023).

German, T. (2012), 'Nagorno-Karabakh: Security Situation', *Trans European Policy Studies Association*. Available online: https://www.europarl.europa.eu/meetd ocs/2009_2014/documents/sede/dv/sede200612expertspresentations_/sede200612 expertspresentations_en.pdf (accessed 16 November 2023).

Giragosian, R. (2019), 'Paradox of Power: Russia, Armenia, and Europe after the Velvet Revolution', *European Council on Foreign Relations*. Available online: https://ecfr.eu/ publication/russia_armenia_and_europe_after_the_velvet_revolution/ (accessed 16 November 2023).

Grant, T. D. (2017), 'Frozen Conflicts and International Law', *Cornell International Law Journal*, 50 (3): 362–413.

Harding, L. (2014), 'Georgia Angered by Russia-Abkhazia Military Agreement', *The Guardian*, 25 November. Available online: https://www.theguardian.com/ world/2014/nov/25/georgia-russia-abkhazia-military-agreement-putin (accessed 12 October 2023).

Jaitner, M. (2015), 'Russian Information Warfare: Lessons from Ukraine', in K. Geers (ed.), *Cyber War in Perspective: Russian Aggression against Ukraine*, 87–94, Tallinn: NATO Cooperative Cyber Defence Center of Excellence.

Kirby, P. (2023), 'Georgia Drops "Foreign Agents" Law after Protests', *BBC*, 9 March. Available online: https://www.bbc.com/news/world-europe-64899041 (accessed 12 October 2023).

Klein, M. (2015), 'Ukraine's Volunteer Battalions – Advantages and Challenges', RUFS Briefing no. 27, Swedish Defence Research Agency. Available online: https://www. foi.se/rest-api/report/FOI%20MEMO%205312 (accessed 15 January 2023).

Klosek, K. C., V. Bahenský, M. Smetana and J. Ludvík (2021), 'Frozen Conflicts in World Politics: A New Dataset', *Journal of Peace Research*, 58 (4): 849–58.

Kofman, M. et al. (2017), *Lessons from Russia's Operations in Crimea and Eastern Ukraine*, Research report, Santa Monica, CA: Rand Corporation.

Kucera, J. (2022), 'Russian Peacekeepers in Karabakh under Harsh Spotlight', *Eurasianet*, 15 Decembe. Available online: https://eurasianet.org/russian-peacekeep ers-in-karabakh-under-harsh-spotlight (accessed 16 November 2023).

Lister, T. (2023), 'Secret Document Reveals Russia's 10-Year Plan to Destabilize Moldova', *CNN*, 18 March. Available online: https://edition.cnn.com/2023/03/16/ europe/russia-moldova-secret-document-intl-cmd/index.html (accessed 12 October 2023).

Luhn, A. (2017), 'Ukraine Blocks Popular Social Networks as Part of Sanctions on Russia', *The Guardian*, 16 May. Available online: https://www.theguardian.com/ world/2017/may/16/ukraine-blocks-popular-russian-websites-kremlin-role-war (accessed 15 January 2024).

Miller, J., P. Vaux, C. A. Fitzpatrick and M. Weiss (2015), *An Invasion by Another Name: The Kremlin's Dirty War in Ukraine*, Institute of Modern Russia; The Interpreter. Available online: https://www.imrussia.org/media/pdf/An_Invasion_by_ Any_Other_Name.pdf (accessed 15 January 2024).

Nilsson, N. (2009), 'Georgia's Rose Revolution: The Break with the Past', in S. E. Cornell and S. F. Starr (eds), *The Guns of August 2008: Russia's War in Georgia*, 85–103, New York: M.E. Sharpe.

Nilsson, N. (2015), *Beacon of Liberty: Role Conceptions, Crises and Stability in Georgia's Foreign Policy*, Uppsala: Acta Universitatis Upsaliensis.

Nilsson, N. (2018), *Russian Hybrid Tactics in Georgia*, Washinton, DC: Central Asia-Caucasus Institute & Silk Road Studies Program.

Nilsson, N. (2021), 'Between Russia's "Hybrid" Strategy and Western Ambiguity: Assessing Georgia's Vulnerabilities', *Journal of Slavic Military Studies*, 34 (1): 50–68.

Nilsson, N. (2021), 'De-Hybridization and Conflict Narration: Ukraine's Defence against Russian Hybrid Warfare', in M. Weissmann , N. Nilsson, B. Palmertz and P. Thunholm (eds), *Hybrid Warfare: Security and Asymmetric Conflict in International Relations*, 214–31, London: I.B. Tauris.

President of Moldova (2022), 'Address by President Maia Sandu at the 3rd Edition of Moldova Support Platform, Paris', 21 November. Available online: https://www.pre sedinte.md/eng/discursuri/address-by-president-maia-sandu-at-the-3rd-edition-of-moldova-support-platform-paris (accessed 12 October 2023).

Reuters (2022), 'Russia's Federation Council Ratifies Annexation of Four Ukrainian Regions', 4 October. Available online: https://www.reuters.com/world/europe/russ ias-federation-council-ratifies-annexation-four-ukrainian-regions-2022-10-04/ (accessed 12 October 2023).

Rosa, V. (2021), *The Transnistrian Conflict: 30 Years Searching for a Settlement*, SCEEUS Reports on Human Rights and Security in Eastern Europe, no. 4, October. Available online: https://www.ui.se/globalassets/ui.se-eng/publications/sceeus/the-transnistr ian-conflict.pdf (accessed 12 October 2023).

Saari, S. (2015), 'The New Alliance and Integration Treaty between Russia and South Ossetia: When Does Integration Turn into Annexation?', *Finnish Institute of Foreign Affairs*. Available online: https://www.files.ethz.ch/isn/189653/comment9.pdf (accessed 12 October 2023).

Sazonov, V., K. Müür and H. Mölder, eds (2016), *Russian Information Campaign against the Ukrainian State and Defence Forces*, Tartu: NATO Strategic Communications Centre of Excellence.

Sebentsov, A. B., M. S. Karpenko, A. A. Gritsenko and N. L. Turov, 'Economic Development as a Challenge for "De Facto States": Post-Conflict Dynamics and Perspectives in South Ossetia', *Regional Research of Russia*, 12 (3). Available online: https://link.springer.com/article/10.1134/S2079970522700277 (accessed 12 October 2023).

Shahbazov, F. (2021), 'Shusha Declaration Cements Azerbaijani-Turkish Alliance', *Eurasia Daily Monitor*, 23 June, 18 (100). Available online: https://jamestown.org/program/shusha-declaration-cements-azerbaijani-turkish-alliance/ (accessed 12 October 2022).

Suleimanov, E, E. Abrahamiyan and H. Aliyev (2017), 'Unrecognized States as a Means of Coercive Diplomacy? Assessing the Role of Abkhazia and South Ossetia in Russia's Foreign Policy in the South Caucasus', *Southeast European and Black Sea Studies*, 18 (1): 73–86.

Tagliavini, H. (2009), *Independent International Fact-Finding Mission on the Conflict in Georgia: Volume II*. Available online: https://www.mpil.de/files/pdf4/IIFFMCG_Volume_II1.pdf (accessed 12 January 2024).

Urse, C. (2007), 'Transnistria: Prospects for a Solution', *George C. Marshall European Center for Security Studies*. Available online: https://www.marshallcenter.org/en/publications/occasional-papers/transnistria-prospects-solution (accessed 12 October 2023).

Wezeman, P. D., A. Kuimova and J. Smith (2021), 'Arms Transfers to Conflict Zones: The Case of Nagorno-Karabakh', *Stockholm International Peace Research Institute*. Available online: https://www.sipri.org/commentary/topical-backgrounder/2021/arms-transfers-conflict-zones-case-nagorno-karabakh (accessed 16 November 2023).

Wolczuk, K. (2021), 'Here We Go Again: Russia's Energy "Diplomacy" in Moldova', *Chatham House*. Available online: https://www.chathamhouse.org/2021/12/here-we-go-again-russias-energy-diplomacy-moldova (accessed 12 October 2023).

Zhemukhov, S. (2022), 'Abkhazia and South Ossetia: Second-Order Effects of the Russia-Ukraine War', *PONARS Eurasia*. Available online: https://www.ponarseurasia.org/abkhazia-and-south-ossetia-second-order-effects-of-the-russia-ukraine-war/ (accessed 12 October 2023).

9

A diverse picture of Russian warfare and influence

Niklas Nilsson and Mikael Weissmann

Introduction

This volume has provided case studies of Russian warfare and influence in states at the intersection of the East and the West. Russian strategies for influence have been analysed in the cases of Ukraine, Belarus, the Baltic states, Serbia, Kosovo and Georgia, as well as in relation to Russia's role in and utilization of the unresolved conflicts over Transnistria, Abkhazia, South Ossetia, Nagorno-Karabakh and Ukraine's Donbass. A unifying theme of these studies has been to examine Russia's targeting and exploitation of specific existing vulnerabilities, which are country- and context-specific, but also exhibit common features in a broader sense. Importantly, the chapters have also examined how the states in question have devised strategies of their own to counteract, counterbalance or exploit Russian influence depending on national interests and priorities in foreign and domestic policies. This volume thus demonstrates the importance of accounting for the context-specific patterns of government and elite interests, vulnerabilities and capabilities in any assessment of external influence and its impact. Moreover, this underscores the importance of applying a dynamic and time-sensitive perspective on the interplay between hybrid threats and efforts to counter them, as pointed out in the introduction to this volume.[1]

This chapter outlines the findings and implications of the case studies. It concludes with a perspective, which must remain speculative at this point in time, on how the war in Ukraine and its future trajectory may affect Russia's

---

[1] See Introduction, this volume; Weissmann et al., *Hybrid Warfare*.

continued capacity for exercising external influence in states located at the intersection of the East and West.

Russian warfare and influence in states at the intersection of the East and the West

This section provides a summary of the respective findings of the case studies, with a focus on Russia's means for exercising influence; the specific vulnerabilities targeted in the state in question and how the state has sought to address its exposure to external influence.

In the chapter on Ukraine, Hanna Shelest outlines the full spectrum of means that Russia has employed to exercise power, influence and control over the country. These have ranged from the utilization of historical and cultural ties, via concerted information operations, coercive diplomacy, utilization of economic pressure and energy trade, subversion and offensive cyberattacks, to full-scale employment of conventional military force and threats of nuclear escalation.

Shelest argues that Ukraine's experience of Russian warfare and influence is unique in its comprehensiveness and as a case study of the interplay over time between kinetic and non-kinetic means in Russia's toolbox. While the threat of, and eventual use of, military force has been a constant feature of Russia's approaches to Ukraine, its role has varied over time, between constituting a reinforcing component of other, softer and deniable means for establishing control over Ukraine's society and political system, to full-scale employment and main effort. However, the priority given to different means employed has been a question of focus and priority rather than significant shifts in overall strategy. Shelest observes that Ukraine has come a long way in developing its capacity to withstand Russia's means for exerting influence in the country since 2014, especially through significant investment into its military capabilities.

Over the longer term, Ukraine needs to continue constructing a strategic national resilience system capable of withstanding the full range of coercive means that Russia is employing or may potentially employ against the country. This includes proactively offsetting information operations, withstanding economic shocks, limiting energy dependence and increasing cybersecurity. Shelest also highlights the importance of identifying and understanding existing vulnerabilities, including perceived strengths of democratic processes and Russia's potential utilization of these. Moreover, Shelest particularly points to media ownership, investments in strategic industries and sponsorship of political parties and groups as areas in need of special attention. Russia is playing a long game in Ukraine, seeking to establish a wide set of levers that can be activated and utilized as opportunities arise.

Belarus stands out among the cases examined in this volume as the country most unambiguously dependent on Russia and with the fewest international options and alternatives. Belarus' persistently authoritarian political system and treatment of its domestic opposition, and its support for Russia's full-scale invasion of Ukraine, have motivated the West to impose a range of sanctions on the country, reinforcing its reliance on Russia. Yet Grigory Ioffe points out that the basic foundation for Belarus' dependence on Russia, and hence vulnerability to Russian influence, runs much deeper than the country's political set-up or its domestic and foreign policies.

A large number of Belarusians have yet to develop a distinct national identity that detaches them from Russia, which also firmly remains the centre of Belarus' socio-cultural and information space. In effect, there is little incentive among the country's ruling elite or a large part of the population to take meaningful actions to alter the current state of Russia–Belarus relations, for example, by restructuring the Belarusian economy that currently predominantly processes raw materials and semi-finished products from Russia. Thus, Ioffe argues that Russia does not need to employ any aggressive strategy of 'hybrid warfare' vis-à-vis Belarus. The country's vulnerabilities in the relationship with Russia are much more profound than in other cases, and Russia needs only to sustain these by exploiting existing historical, cultural and social ties, combined with offering favourable economic conditions that affect a sufficient share of Belarus' population. In this light, Ioffe argues that the sanctions imposed on Belarus are counterproductive in the sense that they reinforce Belarus' vulnerabilities vis-à-vis Russia, diminish its scope for developing balancing relationships in foreign policy and trade, and thus drive Belarus deeper into Russia's fold.

In the chapter on the Baltic states, Jānis Bērziņš outlines how Russia pursues the strategic objective of 'finlandization', through non-kinetic means due to the deterrent granted by NATO membership and the developed defensive capabilities of these states. Bērziņš outlines a series of means that Russia has employed towards the Baltic states since the early 1990s, divided into political, economic and social, diplomatic and informational, and energy. Yet, due to the firm political and economic integration of the Baltic states with the West, the impact of Russia's approaches has been very limited. Since Russia has been unable to present itself as an attractive alternative, its focus has over time shifted from promoting pro-Russian sentiment to attempts to undermine the image and perception of the West in the Baltic States. Thus, Bērziņš argues that the main targets of Russian influence operations are the idiosyncrasies of the Neoliberal Western model of political and economic governance, and that political elites in these states need to identify and address vulnerabilities in this system in order to further reduce the scope for Russian influence.

Vuk Vuksanovic shows how Serbia performs a delicate balancing act between Russia and the West, in a manner that has allowed Serbia's political leadership to leverage the country's relations with competing external actors for foreign and domestic political gains. In what Vuksanovic describes as an opportunistic partnership, Russia utilizes Serbia to retain a foothold in the Balkans and as a bargaining chip with the West, while the Serbian leadership uses its ties with Russia as leverage against the West regarding key issues like Kosovo and as a deterrent from overt criticism of illiberal trends in Serbian domestic politics. As Serbia's main economic and security partnerships have over time increasingly pivoted towards the West, Russia's means for influence in Serbia have become reduced to three specific instruments: energy, the unresolved dispute over Kosovo and Russia's popularity among a significant share of the population. These instruments are potential sources of Serbian vulnerability that Russia can utilize if Belgrade were to undergo a radical shift away from Russia. Yet both fundamental changes in Serbian foreign policy and Russia's employment of coercive measures against the country are unlikely as long as Belgrade and Moscow perceive their relationship as mutually beneficial.

Dorthe Bach Nyemann outlines Russia's double-pronged approach to Kosovo, based on hard diplomacy and soft coercion. As Russia's overall role and influence in the Balkans has diminished in the past decade, Serbia's importance has grown and with it the significance of Kosovo's future. Russian diplomacy regarding Kosovo primarily aims to preserve the status quo regarding the region's international status, and to continually promote the need for Kosovo to remain part of Serbia. A more pragmatic approach on the part of Belgrade regarding this issue would reduce Serbia's dependence on Russia.

However, keeping the Serbian government in line with Russian interests also incentivizes Russia to focus on the broader situation for Serbia in the Balkans and to use other, softer and more indirect approaches. These approaches are tailored to the Serb communities throughout the Balkans, not just Kosovo. The narrative is broader than the unification of Serbia and Kosovo, focusing instead on the concept of a 'Serbian World', a concept that offers opportunities to push Serbia towards Russian objectives. In promoting a Serbian World to different subgroups in the Serb community, Russia can instrumentalize its experiences in establishing a Russian World in the post-Soviet space. Serbia copied the Russian concept to some extent, although the Serbian world is not an official Serbian policy. The Serbian World combines the preservation of the cultural heritage of Serbs inside and outside the Serbian territory with the ambition that Belgrade should make decisions on issues of vital importance concerning Serbs and protect them wherever they live.

After Russia's full-scale invasion of Ukraine, Serbia may try to keep its close relations with Russia and continue its policies on Kosovo despite the changing international environment. Yet geopolitical changes at a much larger scale are affecting the dynamics in the Balkans. The EU, NATO and the United States are investing significantly to pressure Serbia and Kosovo to finalize the road to normalization.

In the chapter on Georgia, Kornely Kakachia and Shota Kakabadze examine the most protracted conflictual relationship with Russia among the case studies of this volume. Since its independence, Georgia has experienced Russian interference in its domestic conflicts – the war of 2008 and continued occupation of Georgian territory, economic coercion and political subversion. The authors point to Russian hybrid activities in Georgia that take place in several domains: ideological and informational, cyber and, through proxy forces in South Ossetia and Abkhazia. Kakachia and Kakabadze also examine specific vulnerabilities that Georgian society is facing and the state's capacities to mitigate these challenges. Indeed, the case of Georgia offers lessons with a wider applicability, as the country has partly served as a laboratory for approaches that Russia has later employed elsewhere.

The authors argue that partnership with NATO and the EU must be a fundamental pillar of Georgia's resilience against hybrid threats and Russian subversive activities. Yet resilience will also very much depend on Georgia's own ability to devise proactive policies aimed at establishing security guarantees as well as on close cooperation between state, private and civil society stakeholders, in order to avoid becoming Russia's next target after Ukraine.

Finally, Niklas Nilsson, Johan Engvall and Mikael Weissmann examine Russia's influence in neighbouring states through the utilization of unresolved conflicts as means for bargaining and coercion. The conflicts in question are Nagorno-Karabakh, Abkhazia, South Ossetia, Transnistria, and the Donetsk and Luhansk 'People's Republics' in Ukraine's Donbass. The chapter examines patterns common to these conflicts, as Russia has over time utilized the establishment and support of proxy regimes in Georgia, Moldova and Ukraine, while its role in Nagorno-Karabakh has been less direct, to apply both political and military pressure on the states involved.

However, as regional dynamics are changing, Russia's long-term strategy to utilize unresolved conflicts as political leverage on neighbouring states is providing diminishing returns. The attempt to coerce Ukraine into foreign and domestic political concessions via proxy regimes in DNR and LNR became obsolete with the full-scale invasion of 2022. In Georgia and Moldova, resolving the conflicts has attained a decidedly lower political priority over the last decade. Azerbaijan's decisive victory in the 2020 war with Armenia over Nagorno-Karabakh, and subsequent push in September 2023 to take control over region in its entirety, has undermined Russia's ability to exert influence over both states. Russia's inability to achieve a quick military victory in Ukraine, and its commitment of military and economic resources to the war, will likely further reduce its ability to sustain its proxy regimes in Georgia and Moldova. However, as the trajectory of the war has become a serious challenge to Russia's imperial designs on neighbouring states, its control over Abkhazia, South Ossetia and Transnistria may become even more important in Russia's perspective.

Beyond Russia's war in Ukraine

The eventual outcome of the war in Ukraine will be decisive to Russia's future ability to exert influence in states in its surroundings, as well as its motivation to do so and the available means that it can deploy for this purpose. At the finalization of this manuscript in January 2024, the eventual trajectory of the war very much remains an open question. Russian offensives in early 2023 and Ukraine's later offensive in the summer and fall resulted in limited territorial gains and the two sides are currently fighting a war of attrition along for the most part static frontlines. Developments this year and 2025 will to a large extent depend on the ability of both sides to regain offensive capabilities by recruiting and training soldiers and military units as well as replenishing crucial military equipment. Whereas Russia has put its economy and industrial base on a war footing aiming to outspend and outlast its opponent, the continuation of Ukraine's proven ability to withstand Russia's aggression and regain the initiative and advantage depends in large part on the resolve of its Western partners. The year 2024 is thus set to be a pivotal year in terms of whether the transatlantic community proves able to commit the defence spending and increases in defence production required to provide Ukraine with the sufficient training and military capabilities to prevail in the war. This objective is both clearly realistic and a by far a less dangerous option to the Euro-Atlantic community than a scenario involving a Russian victory in Ukraine, as pointed out in a recent report.[2]

While the war has resulted in a significant degradation of Russia's military capability and thereby limited its options for armed aggression elsewhere, an eventual Russian victory in Ukraine would likely embolden Russia to utilize its full spectrum of resources, including its military, to further expand its external influence.

Regardless of the eventual outcome of Russia's war in Ukraine, the countries subjected to case studies in this volume, as well as other states sharing the same geography, are likely to face an increasingly revisionist, aggressive and potentially desperate Russia in the years to come. While this state of affairs will not be principally different from the years preceding Russia's full-scale invasion of Ukraine, the trajectory of the war poses a threat to the Russian regime and its imperial ambitions that is potentially existential in nature.

The Kremlin's ability to deploy military resources to reinforce its influence abroad, or to prevent losing more influence than the war in Ukraine has already incurred, as well as seeking to break the unity of NATO and the EU over the support for Ukraine, is limited as long as the bulk of these resources are tied up in Ukraine. This incentivizes the Kremlin to put an even heavier emphasis on pursuing these objectives via non-kinetic, covert and deniable methods than has previously been the case.

Yet at the same time, the weakening of Russia which is a consequence of the war also reduces its ability to translate these means into actual political outcomes, particularly since it will be struggling to back them up with significant military and economic resources. The shifting balance of power emerging in Eurasia is increasingly creating inroads for other, more or less contending actors to boost their relations with and increase their influence in states where Russia would like to claim imperial superiority.[3] Aside from the United States, NATO and the EU, this is true for China, Turkey and Iran, as well as India. Non-EU and NATO members of Eastern Europe, the states of the South Caucasus, as well as the Central Asian states increasingly find themselves at geopolitical fault

2 Republic of Estonia, Ministry of Defence, *Setting Transatlantic Defence up for Success: A Military Strategy for Ukraine's Victory and Russia's Defeat*, December 2023. https://kaitseministeerium.ee/sites/default/files/kaitseministeerium_2023veeb_17.12.pdf.

3 Johan Engvall, Ismail Khan and Kristina Melin, 'Post-Soviet No More – the Transformative Impact of War on Russia's Neighbors', *The SAIS Review of International Affairs*, 18 September 2023. https://saisreview.sais.jhu.edu/post-soviet-no-more-the-transformative-impact-of-war-on-russias-neighbors/.

lines, attracting interest from external powers. Two concrete manifestations of this geopolitical shift is the reinvigorated interest in the perspective of trans-Caspian hydrocarbon imports to Europe and an increased potential for the Middle Corridor for Eurasian trade as an alternative to the Northern Corridor transiting Russia.[4] In this context, the states located in Russia's proximity are facing a significant geopolitical shift that holds significant dangers along with options and opportunities.

The war in Ukraine and the confrontation between Russia and the West signifies an era where conventional military force has regained prominence, as a tool of state power as well as a necessary deterrent. However, it is also an era where the necessity of taking a holistic perspective on hybrid threats and resilience, and the interplay between them, has become blatantly clear. While taking different expressions, the states studied in this volume all have extensive experience of being subjected to and responding to a range of Russian tools for exerting influence and control. This volume has sought to document and analyse these experiences in order to build on them, in order to support the effort of building strategies and systems for counteracting malign external influence.

Bibliography

Çolakoğlu, S. (2023), 'The Middle Corridor and the Russia-Ukraine War: the Rise of New Regional Collaboration in Eurasia?', *Central Asia-Caucasus Analyst*, 31 January. Available online: https://www.cacianalyst.org/publications/analytical-articles/item/13744-the-middle-corridor-and-the-russia-ukraine-war-the-rise-of-new-regional-collaboration-in-eurasia?.html (accessed 15 January 2024).

Engvall, J., I. Khan and K. Melin (2023), 'Post-Soviet No More – the Transformative Impact of War on Russia's Neighbors', *SAIS Review of International Affairs*, 18 September. Available online: https://saisreview.sais.jhu.edu/post-soviet-no-more-the-transformative-impact-of-war-on-russias-neighbors/ (accessed 15 January 2024).

Republic of Estonia, Ministry of Defence (2023), *Setting Transatlantic Defence up for Success: A Military Strategy for Ukraine's Victory and Russia's Defeat*, December. Available online: https://kaitseministeerium.ee/sites/default/files/kaitseministeerium_2023veeb_17.12.pdf (accessed 15 January 2024).

---

[4] Selçuk Çolakoğlu, 'The Middle Corridor and the Russia-Ukraine War: The Rise of New Regional Collaboration in Eurasia?', *Central Asia-Caucasus Analyst*, 31 January 2023. https://www.cacianalyst.org/publications/analytical-articles/item/13744-the-middle-corridor-and-the-russia-ukraine-war-the-rise-of-new-regional-collaboration-in-eurasia?.html.

Index